Southern Manna

Recipes Rich in Southern Tradition

First United Methodist Church
Waycross, Georgia

ISBN 0-941162-22-2

Additional copies may be obtained from

Dot Gibson Publications
P. O. Box 935
Waycross, GA 31502

Cover art by
Bradley Clark

Printed in the U.S.A.
By

FATHER & SON
PUBLISHING, INC.

4909 N. Monroe Street
Tallahassee, Florida 32303

1972 Sanctuary - Gilmore Street

SOUTHERN MANNA - is a delightful cookbook that offers you delicious and enticing recipes. Some are simple some more elaborate, some from scratch, others with the proverbial mushroom soup but ALL are great and worthy of being added to your list of favorites.

Methodists and especially Southern Methodists seem to put meeting and eating together. No matter if it is a business meeting, or a social one, there is always the call "who will bring 8 dozen cookies, who will bring a salad, what type casserole are you bringing and so on." For this reason, you can always count on a Methodist cookbook having great recipes.

There was a cute joke about this -

There were 3 women who arrived in heaven together. St. Peter asked them why they thought they should be admitted to heaven. The first lady, a good Baptist, reaching in her pocketbook pulled out a worn Bible and said, "See how worn this is, how much I have used it?" St. Peter agreed and said go on in.

The second lady, a good Catholic, dug around in her pocketbook and pulled out a worn Rosary and said, "See how worn it is? You can see how I have used it." St. Peter agreed and said go on in.

The third lady was a good Methodist and she dug around in her pocketbook and said, "Wait a minute, I know I have a casserole in here somewhere."

This book is loaded with mouth watering recipes perfect for the family or for special company from delicious appetizers to delectable desserts and of course - Great Casseroles.

COOKBOOK COMMITTEE

Lylbum Booker

Mary Ann East

Genie Fesperman

Jane Gillis

Kathy Hackel

Jean Hancock

Nancy Lee

Martha Mason

Margaret Park

Landy Rimes

Happie Stewart

Susan Sweat

Bunny Winge

IN DEDICATION TO
Bunny Winge

Leader, teacher, musician, and friend
who had the dream and energy to see
<u>Southern Manna</u> a reality.
Thank you for your selfless gift.

Table of Contents

Menus

and

Entertaining

Menus and Entertaining

Southern Sideboard

Confederate Caviar page 41

Chicken and Dumplings page 239

Fried Green Tomatoes page 172

Turnip Greens page 173

Creamed Fried Corn page 152

Clara's Biscuits page 116

Southern Pecan Pie page 291

Preacher's Coming to Dinner

Crab Soup page 99

Standing Rib Roast with Yorkshire Pudding page 226 & 227

Patrician Potatoes page 161

Mushroom Casserole page 157

Penny Carrots page 150

Broccoli - Mandarin Orange Salad page 71

Angel Biscuits page 115

Cloister Lemon Meringue Pie page 288

Women of the Church Tea

Easter Celebration

Sister's Leg of Lamb page 230

or

Baked Ham with Raisin Sauce page 86

Asparagus Casserole II page 144

Pineapple Soufflé page 356

Shredded Yams page 171

Frozen Fruit Salad page 77

Bunny Rolls page 130

Strawberry Cake page 324

Thanksgiving Feast

Grandmother's Roast Turkey page 249

Cornbread Dressing with Giblet Gravy page 250

Sweet Potato Snowballs page 171

Broccoli Casserole page 147

Scalloped Oysters page 192

Cranberry Orange Salad page 62

Holiday Relish page 364

Basic Yeast Rolls page 131

Fruit Cake page 306

Pumpkin Cheesecake page 327

Christmas Bazaar Luncheon

First Methodist Chicken Casserole page 241

Green Beans India page 148

Strawberry Pretzel Salad page 61

Carolyn's Quick and Easy Rolls page 132

Cream Cheese Pound Cake with Caramel Glaze page 297

Italian Cream Cake page 314

Lemon Cheese Cake page 309 & 310

Southern Chocolate Pound Cake page 301

ENTERTAINING

Hospitality comes from the heart. It is the giving of oneself, the opening of one's home to friends or near strangers that creates a warm and welcome spirit. The most simple extra touch tells guests that they are special and welcome. Remember: Above all, always be yourself.

Good Parties do not JUST happen. A successful party is the result of careful planning. Plan in advance the guest list, the menu, the food preparation and presentation, the table setting, the flowers and/or table decorations. It has been said that a good hostess is like a duck in the middle of a pond - cool and calm on the surface and paddling madly underneath. Southern hospitality is noted for its charm, grace and ability to always make guests feel completely at ease.

TABLE APPOINTMENTS

LINENS -

TABLECLOTH: For a seated meal, the tablecloth should overhang approximately 12 inches. For a buffet or tea table, an overhang of approximately 18 inches is in good proportion.

NAPKINS: These are placed, neatly folded, at the left side of the place setting. In a formal setting, the napkin can be placed on the service plate. Remember: 20 to 22 inch napkins for dinner and 12 inch napkins for luncheon are appropriate. Napkins, silver, and china should be placed about one inch from the edge of the table. (Rule of thumb - the first joint of the thumb is a readily available measure for one inch.)

GLASSWARE: Goblets are placed directly above the knife and spoon.

CHINA: Bread and butter plates go above the forks on the left, with the butter spreader placed horizontally across the plate, cutting edge facing the guest. In formal settings, bread and butter plates are omitted. If salad is to be served with the main course, the salad plate is placed to the left of the forks.

CENTERPIECE: Be creative and let the centerpiece be the topic of conversation.

FLOWERS: If using flowers, a good rule for the height of the arrangement is to place the elbow on the table, hold the hand straight up and measure from the elbow through to the finger tips. That is the maximum height for the centerpiece.

CANDLES: If candles are used, they should be high enough so that the flame is above the level of the eyes of the guest. Do not use candles on the table unless they are lighted. Candle light is not suitable for luncheons. Remember: Talk over flowers, under candles. (Votive candles are the exception.)

TABLE SETTING: A table may be set with the finest porcelain, crystal, and silver, or it may be set with earthenware on a checked cotton tablecloth. Mix or match whatever you have. Use your antique treasures or your flea market trivia.

FLATWARE: Place knives, (sharp edges toward plate) and spoons at the right of the plate. Forks are place to the left. All are placed in order of their use. Oyster forks are placed on the right side of the spoons. Seldom does one have all the silverware pieces as shown below. However, it is helpful to know all the correct placement and usage, if ever needed.

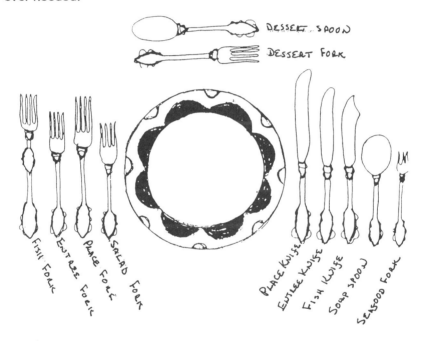

REMEMBER: The table is set so that one uses the silver from the outside in.

BUFFET

One of the easiest ways to entertain is with a buffet. A buffet dinner can provide a delightful fun filled evening, allowing the host or hostess to entertain in a relaxed style. It also lets one entertain a larger number of people than can be comfortably seated at a standard dining room table. The table setting may range from formal elegance to casual informality, depending on the occasion. However, a buffet is always acknowledged as an informal type of service. Plan to use the dining room table for the buffet. Place dinner plates, silver and napkins nearest the end where the guests will approach the table. Silver may be arranged in a row, or wrapped in the napkin. The food should be conveniently arranged in a logical sequence. A dessert tray may be included or the dessert may be placed on the buffet table after the guests have finished with the first course and the dishes have been removed. A buffet style meal can be used to entertain at brunch, lunch, or for dinner.

Appetizers

and

Beverages

Appetizers and Beverages

ARTICHOKE DIP

1 (14 ounce) can artichoke
   hearts, drained and
   chopped
1 cup fresh grated Parmesan
   cheese
1 clove garlic, minced
1/2 cup Hellmann's mayonnaise

1 teaspoon Dijon mustard,
   optional
1/2 cup yogurt, optional
Dash or two of Tabasco,
   optional
Crackers

Combine artichoke hearts, Parmesan cheese, garlic, mayonnaise, yogurt, Tabasco and Dijon mustard. Place in shallow casserole dish. Bake at 325° until bubbly, about 25 minutes. Serve hot with crackers.

VARIATION: Substitute 1 1/2 to 2 cups Vidalia onions for artichokes and 1 cup Hellmann's mayonnaise for 1/2 cup mayonnaise and 1/2 cup yogurt. Omit garlic, Tabasco and Dijon mustard. Serve with Triscuit crackers.

Jane Crawley

MEXICAN DIP
7 Layer Dip

3 mashed avocados
2 teaspoons lemon juice
1 package Lawry's taco
   seasoning mix
3 tablespoons mayonnaise
1 (10 1/2 ounce) container
   bean dip

1 cup shredded Cheddar cheese
1 cup shredded Jack cheese
3 chopped green onions
3 tomatoes, peeled and diced
1 can sliced black olives
Doritos

Mash 3 avocados and add 2 teaspoons of lemon juice. Set aside. Mix 1 package taco mix with 3 tablespoons mayonnaise. Layer in dish beginning with bean dip, then top with avocados, taco mix, Cheddar cheese, Jack cheese, green onions, tomatoes and black olives. Serve with Doritos or your own choice.

Martha Mason

21

HOT CHEESY-SALZA DIP

1 (10 ounce) can Ro-tel diced
    tomatoes and green
    chilies

1 (16 ounce) Velveeta
    cheese, shredded
Tostito bite-size tortilla chips

Combine tomatoes and cheese in top of double boiler until cheese has melted. Stir well. Serve hot with Tostito bite-size tortilla chips. Delicious!

Anne Fesperman

TROPICAL DIP FOR FRUIT

1 (7 ounce) jar marshmallow
    creme
1 (8 ounce) package softened
    Philadelphia cream cheese

1 (8½ ounce) can crushed
    pineapple, well drained

Combine marshmallow creme and cream cheese. Whip with the electric beater until smooth. Then, add the pineapple. Keep refrigerated until ready to use. Use with strawberries, pineapple sticks, apple or pear wedges. Delicious!

Mary Ann East

PICO DE GALLO

2 ripe tomatoes, seeded and
    finely chopped
1 medium red onion, chopped
2 green onions or scallions,
    chopped, including green
5 tablespoons vegetable oil
Juice of 1 lemon
4 fresh green chilies, seeded
    and finely chopped

1 to 2 tablespoons fresh
    chopped cilantro
4 tablespoons tomato juice
Salt
Freshly ground pepper
Jalapeño, chopped to taste,
    optional

Mix the tomatoes, onions, oil, lemon juice, chilies and cilantro in large bowl. Add tomato juice, salt and pepper as needed. Do not use food processor - too mushy. Cover and refrigerate. Will keep up to 5 days. Makes 2 cups.

Kathy Hackel

ADRIENNE'S DELIGHT

1 stick (1/4 cup) butter or
  margarine
1 (8 ounce) package cream
  cheese
1/2 cup sour cream
1/2 cup sugar
1 envelope plain gelatin

1/4 cup cold water
Zest of 3 lemons
1/2 cup white raisins
1 cup slivered almonds,
  toasted
Ginger snaps

Cream together butter, cream cheese, and sour cream. Gradually add sugar and beat constantly. Soften gelatin in cold water, then heat over low flame to dissolve. Add dissolved gelatin to butter mixture. Add lemon zest, raisins, and almonds. Blend well. Pour into a 1-quart fluted mold and refrigerate until set. Serve with ginger snaps.

Coy Gaston

BOURSIN

8 ounce package cream
  cheese, softened
1/4 cup sweet butter,
  softened
1/3 cup sour cream
1 small clove garlic, minced

1 tablespoon chives,
  chopped
1 tablespoon parsley,
  chopped
Salt and white pepper, to
  taste

Blend softened cream cheese and butter with sour cream. Add garlic, chives, parsley, salt and pepper and mix well. Put in small mold and chill for at least 12 hours. Serve with crackers, seedless grapes and sliced Granny Smith apples.

Caroline Herzig

CREAM CHEESE SPREAD

1 cup mayonnaise
1 (8 ounce) package cream
   cheese
1/2 teaspoon lemon juice

Chopped green onion tops,
   to taste
Crackers

Combine mayonnaise, cream cheese, lemon juice, and green onion until smooth. Serve with crackers.

Claire Smith

MISS BESSIE'S CREAM CHEESE, PICKLE AND BACON PARTY SANDWICH

8 ounce package cream
   cheese, room
   temperature
1 tablespoon mayonnaise to
   thin for spreading

1 large dill pickle, chopped
3 slices crisp bacon,
   crumbled
1 loaf of bread
Paprika, for garnish

Combine cream cheese, mayonnaise, pickle and bacon. Spread on small circles of cut bread - about the size of a half-dollar. (You can cut four circles from a slice of giant sandwich bread.) Sprinkle finished sandwiches with paprika.

NOTE: Miss Bessie was a school teacher who could do anything from cooking to grafting camellias. She catered for weddings and parties in the 1950's and shared several recipe favorites through the years.

Miss Bessie Maynard

DILL PICKLE-CREAM CHEESE PARTY SANDWICHES

1 (8 ounce) package cream
   cheese
2 to 3 tablespoons milk or
   mayonnaise

Loaf bread, trimmed
Dill pickles, whole

Soften cream cheese to spreading consistency using milk or mayonnaise. Spread cream cheese on bread. Using 1½ slices per pickle, roll bread around pickle. Chill. When ready to serve, cut into small, round slices.

NOTE: For convenience, several wrapped pickles can be placed end-to-end, placed on wax paper to make one long roll. Refrigerate on tray until ready to cut and serve.

Genie Fesperman

BAKED GARLIC WITH ROSEMARY

6 heads elephant garlic
3 tablespoons butter
¼ cup olive oil
2 chicken bouillon cubes,
   dissolved in 12 ounces
   of water or chicken broth

¼ cup dry white wine
2 teaspoons chopped
   rosemary
Pepper
Extra rosemary, for garnish

Cut ½ inch off each garlic head. Remove loose paper outer skin. Place in non-aluminum dish. Top garlic with butter and oil. Add dissolved bouillon cubes and wine. Sprinkle with chopped rosemary and pepper. Bake at 375° for about one hour or until tender, basting about four times. When ready to serve, remove cooked rosemary and replace with fresh for garnish. Serve on baggette with brie or bleu cheese.

Georgianne McGee

LEMON NUT SANDWICH FILLING

3 tablespoons lemon juice
1 teaspoon grated lemon
   rind
1/2 cup sugar

4 egg yolks, slightly beaten
1 tablespoon butter
1/3 cup chopped pecans

Combine lemon juice and rind, sugar, egg yolks, and butter. Cook in double boiler, stirring constantly, until thick. Cool and stir in pecans. Makes 1 cup. Cut bread into rounds if open-faced sandwiches are desired.

Mary Cox

CREAMY PIMIENTO CHEESE SPREAD

1 (8 ounce) package cream
   cheese, softened
2 cups (8 ounces) shredded
   sharp Cheddar cheese,
   softened
1/4 cup plus 2 tablespoons
   mayonnaise

1/8 teaspoon garlic powder
   (use less if you do not
   like garlic)
1 (4 ounce) jar diced
   pimiento, drained

Combine cheeses in a large mixing bowl; beat at medium speed of electric mixer until light and fluffy. Add mayonnaise and garlic powder; mix well. Stir in pimiento. For best consistency serve at room temperature. To store, cover and refrigerate.

NOTE: I use a food processor to mix this recipe. For a festive party sandwich, use one loaf of unsliced white and one loaf of unsliced wheat bread. Trim crusts and slice lengthwise into 3 sections. Spread one white layer with cheese spread, top with one wheat layer, repeat. Cut crosswise into slices.

Jewell Kopp

VEGETABLE SANDWICHES

1 (8 ounce) package cream
 cheese, softened
$2/3$ cup carrot, shredded fine
$2/3$ cup celery, chopped fine
$1/3$ cup cucumber, shredded
 fine and drained on paper
 towel

$1/3$ cup green pepper, diced
$1/3$ cup onion, chopped fine
2 tablespoons mayonnaise
1 tablespoon lemon juice

Prepare one day in advance of serving time. Combine cream cheese, carrot, celery, cucumber, green pepper, onion, mayonnaise, and lemon juice. Spread on thin white or wheat bread. Cut into finger sandwiches or roll jelly-roll style and cut into thin slices.

Lisa Fesperman

BRIE WITH BROWN SUGAR

1 whole brie round   **Slivered almonds, toasted**
Brown sugar

Heat brie. Top with brown sugar and slivered almonds. Heat until sugar melts. Delicious with thin crackers.

Genie Fesperman

CHEESE BLINTZ

1½ loaves sandwich bread

FILLING:
2 egg yolks   **½ cup sugar**
2 (8 ounce) packages cream   **Melted butter**
   cheese   **Cinnamon and sugar**

DIP:
1 pint sour cream

Trim crust from bread and roll thin as paper (put between waxed paper to roll). Beat egg yolks, cream cheese and sugar until creamy. Spread over bread. Roll up and brush with melted butter. Roll in cinnamon and sugar. Cut in half and place on cookie sheet. Bake at 350° for 10 or 15 minutes. Serve with sour cream for dip.

Lylburn Booker

CHEESE BALL

2 (8 ounce) packages cream
   cheese
1 (4 ounce) package blue
   cheese
1 tablespoon plus sour
   cream

1 to 2 teaspoons
   Worcestershire sauce
2 teaspoons garlic salt
2 teaspoons celery salt
Ground nuts
Crackers

Mix cream cheese and blue cheese, thinning with sour cream as needed. Add Worcestershire, garlic and celery salt. Roll into a ball, chilling overnight. Roll in ground nuts to serve.

Geneie Fesperman

CHEESE STRAWS

2 cups sifted plain flour
1 teaspoon salt
1/2 teaspoon red pepper
1 (10 ounce) package extra
   sharp Kraft Cracker
   Barrel cheese, grated

1 stick butter, softened
Pecan halves, optional

Combine flour, salt and pepper. Combine cheese and butter. Cut cheese mixture into flour mixture to make thin dough. Put dough in cookie gun, and spread on ungreased cookie sheet. Cook at 350° for 8 to 10 minutes or until edges begin to look darker. Cut straws desired size and place on paper towels to cool. Or, roll into 3 rolls about 7 inches long and size of silver dollar. Chill and slice thin. Top with pecan half, before baking, if desired. Makes 3 dozen.

Lois Groszmann

CHEESE BITS

2 cups grated sharp cheese
2 sticks margarine
2 cups self-rising flour

2 cups Rice Krispies
Dash cayenne pepper,
optional

Blend cheese and margarine. Work in flour. Add Rice Krispies. Form in 1 inch balls and press slightly. Bake 8 to 10 minutes at 375°.

Cindy Coppage

CREAM CHEESE CHEESEBALL

2 (8 ounce) packages cream
cheese, softened
1 (0.7 ounce) package
Hidden Valley ranch
dressing mix

2 tablespoons hot sauce (or
to taste)
Parsley or nuts

Mix cream cheese and dressing mix thoroughly. Form into a ball. Cover with parsley or nuts to finish. Refrigerate until hardened.

Cindy Hitt

"MISS BESSIE'S" GARLIC CHEESE LOG

2 or 3 big cloves of garlic
1 (8 ounce) package cream
cheese, softened
1 pound sharp Cheddar
cheese, grated

1 (2 ounce) jar chopped
pimiento
1/2 cup finely chopped nuts
Paprika

Combine cream cheese and Cheddar cheese together, blending well. Add pimientos, garlic and nuts. Roll into log. Sprinkle lots of paprika on wax paper. Roll log in paprika. Wrap in Saran Wrap and store in refrigerator. Serve with crackers.

Acey Winge

CLAM DIP

2 (6 ounce) cans minced
  clams
1 (8 ounce) package cream
  cheese, softened

1 tablespoon onion, chopped
Juice of 1 lemon
Potato chips

Drain clams, saving liquid. Mix clams, cream cheese, onion, and lemon juice. Add enough clam liquid to make moist enough to serve with chips. Chill for 2 to 3 hours before serving. Serve with potato chips or your favorite cracker. This is a very popular recipe of a successful Denver, Colorado hostess. Enjoy!

Cynthia Raynor

CATHY MCGEE'S HOT CRAB DIP

1 (8 ounce) package cream
  cheese, softened
2 teaspoons milk
Dash of pepper
1/2 teaspoon horseradish

2 tablespoons onion, grated
1/4 teaspoon salt
6 1/2 ounces flaked crab
1/3 cup slivered almonds

Combine cream cheese, milk, pepper, horseradish, onion, salt, and crab. Top with almonds and bake at 375° for 15 minutes. Serve hot with your favorite cracker.

Cathy McGee

CRABMEAT MOLD

1 (8 ounce) package cream
cheese, softened
1 (10³/₄ ounce) can tomato
soup
1 cup mayonnaise
1 cup onion, chopped fine
1 cup bell pepper, chopped
fine

1 cup celery, chopped fine
2 (6 ounce) cans crab meat
(or 12 to 14 ounces
frozen)
1½ packages unflavored
gelatin, softened in ¼
cup water
Butter flavored crackers

Mix cream cheese, soup, and mayonnaise over low heat in saucepan whisking until smooth. Add vegetables and picked crab meat, blending well. Add gelatin softened in warm water and mix well. Pour into 5 to 5½ cup oiled copper mold. Refrigerate overnight and turn out onto serving tray. Serve with crackers.

Coy Gaston

CRAB ST. THOMAS
Excellent Dip

1 stick margarine
1 cup chopped onions
1 (8 ounce) package cream
cheese
½ teaspoon salt
¼ teaspoon pepper

¼ teaspoon cayenne
pepper
¼ teaspoon Tabasco
1 pound crab meat, fresh or
canned

Place margarine in a 2 quart casserole dish. Microwave on high until melted (1 minute). Add onions and sauté on high for 3 minutes. Add cream cheese, salt, pepper, cayenne, and Tabasco; mix well. Fold in crab meat. Microwave on high 1 to 3 minutes, just until heated through. Serve with crackers.

Dot Gibson

SALMON PATÉ

1 (14.75 ounce) can salmon,
   drained
2 tablespoons onion,
   chopped fine
2 tablespoons mayonnaise

1/2 cup butter, melted
1 tablespoon lemon juice
1 teaspoon dill weed
Town House Club crackers

Mix salmon, onion, mayonnaise, butter, lemon juice and dill weed. Place in mold and chill. Serve with Town House crackers or your favorite cracker.

Genie Fesperman

BROILED SCALLOPS

1 pound bacon

1 pound scallops, preferably
   deep sea

Cut bacon strips in half. Wrap 1/2 bacon slice around each scallop. Secure with a toothpick. Broil, in broiler pan lined with foil for easy clean-up, until bacon is brown and crisp. Serve hot.

Jane Gillis

GOURMET SHRIMP

2 pounds fresh or frozen
   shrimp (thawed)
4 tablespoons butter or
   margarine

1/4 cup chopped parsley
1 clove minced garlic
3/4 teaspoon salt

Wash shrimp in strainer under cold, running water. Remove shell and vein. Place in bowl and chill until ready to cook. Just before serving, melt butter in medium-sized frying pan. Add shrimp, parsley, garlic, salt and sauté, stirring often for 2 to 4 minutes, or until shrimp are firm and pink. Time carefully; overcooking makes shrimp tough. May be served on toothpicks.

Carol Harley

PICKLED SHRIMP

5 pounds shrimp, boiled and
   peeled
2 large onions, sliced
1 (3 ounce) bottle capers and
   liquid
1 teaspoon powdered sugar

1 teaspoon mustard
Dash paprika
2 cups vinegar
2 tablespoons lemon juice
Dash cayenne

Layer shrimp and onions in a deep flat dish or large mouth gift jars. Combine capers, powdered sugar, mustard, paprika, vinegar, lemon juice, and cayenne; pour over shrimp and onions. Cover, place in refrigerator for 24 hours before serving (stir several times).

Dot Gibson

TUNA FISH DIP

1 (6 ounce) can tuna, drained
2 cups sour cream
2 (0.7 ounce) envelopes
   Good Seasons Italian
   dressing

Mix tuna, sour cream and dressing mix. Serve with crackers or celery sticks.

Pauline Hopkins

ASPARAGUS ROLL-UPS

12 slices white bread (thin)
8 slices crisp bacon,
  crumbled
1 (8 ounce) package cream
  cheese

12 asparagus spears
  (canned)
Melted butter

Trim crusts from bread and roll very thin with a rolling pin. Blend bacon and cream cheese and spread on the bread slices. Lay a cold asparagus spear on each slice and roll up. Place with seams down on an ungreased baking sheet. Cover and refrigerate. When ready to serve, brush with melted butter and broil until lightly brown. Serve immediately.

Lucy Mason

MARY KATHRYN'S CARAMEL CORN

2 cups brown sugar
1/2 cup Karo syrup
2 sticks (1 cup) butter
1 pinch cream of tartar

1 pinch salt
1/2 teaspoon soda
6 quarts popped corn

Combine sugar, Karo, butter, cream of tartar and salt in saucepan. Bring to a boil, let boil 5 minutes (do not scorch). Add 1/2 teaspoon soda and stir until mixture foams. Pour over corn (I divide corn into 2 large jelly roll pans - it's easier to work with). Stir to mix well. Place in 200° oven for 1 hour or until mixture is dry. Stir occasionally - it is extra good if you add pecans, peanuts or a jar of mixed nuts to the popped corn. Take up and store in airtight containers.

Bonnie Storey

HAM AND CHEESE PARTY ROLLS

1 (8 ounce) package party or dinner rolls
1 (10 ounce) package Danish ham
1 (8 ounce) package Swiss cheese
1 stick margarine, melted
1 tablespoon poppy seed
1 tablespoon prepared mustard or Grey Poupon
1 tablespoon minced onion
1 tablespoon Worcestershire sauce

Cut cheese and ham to fit rolls. Set aside. Combine margarine, poppy seed, mustard, onion, and Worcestershire. Pour over top of rolls. Cover and bake at 350° for 25 minutes. Freezes well. Serves 20.

Claire Smith

HERBED TOASTIES

1 loaf Pepperidge Farm thin sliced white bread
2 sticks butter or margarine
1 teaspoon dried tarragon
Dash garlic salt
1 (4 ounce) can grated Parmesan cheese
Cream cheese, optional

Trim crusts from bread and cut each slice into 4 squares. Put on two sheet pans. Melt butter, add tarragon and garlic salt. Brush heavily on squares. Sprinkle Parmesan on top. Bake at 250° for 1 hour or at 200° for 2 hours. Can add a dab of cream cheese on top before serving. (To freeze, put cooked toasties on cookie sheets, then in freezer bags. Warm to serve.)

Caroline S. Herzig

CHEESY OLIVE APPETIZERS

1 cup shredded Swiss
   cheese
6 slices bacon, cooked and
   crumbled
1/4 cup chopped
   pimiento-stuffed olives
1/4 cup mayonnaise

2 tablespoons chopped
   onion
20 slices party rye bread
Additional sliced
   pimiento-stuffed olives,
   for garnish

Combine Swiss cheese, bacon, chopped olives, mayonnaise, and onion. Mix until well blended. Spread about 1 tablespoon cheese mixture on each slice of bread. Top each with an olive slice. Broil 2 minutes or until the cheese melts; serve hot. Yield: 20 appetizers.

Coralyn Gaston

SEASONED OYSTERETTE SNACKS

1/2 cup vegetable oil
1/2 teaspoon garlic salt
1 tablespoon dill weed
1 (0.7 ounce) package
   Hidden Valley ranch
   dressing

1 pound box oysterette
   crackers

Mix oil, garlic, salt, dill weed, Hidden Valley Ranch dressing together. Pour over oysterette crackers. Gently shake oysterettes. Place in airtight container. Preparation time: 15 minutes.

NOTE: These are so good, you may want to double the recipe.

Martha Mason

PEPPER FEET

1/3 cup catsup
2 tablespoons olive oil
1 to 2 tablespoons cider
   vinegar

1 to 2 tablespoons cracked
   black pepper
4 quail, halved

Combine catsup, olive oil, cider vinegar, and cracked pepper. Pour over quail and allow to marinate 30 minutes. Grill, 2 to 3 minutes per side over hot coals or until done. Yield: 8 appetizer servings. If quail is unavailable, try chicken wings or drumettes.

NOTE: I serve this as an appetizer or side dish at Thanksgiving, Christmas, or whenever my father visits.

Susan Sweat

SAUSAGE PINWHEELS

2 cups plain flour
3 to 4 tablespoons Crisco
1 teaspoon salt
1/3 cup corn meal
2 tablespoons baking
   powder

1/3 cup milk (or less)
1 pound hot or medium
   sausage, uncooked

Combine and cut in flour, Crisco, salt, corn meal, and baking powder. Add enough milk to form dough. Roll dough 1/2-inch thick and top with sausage. Roll up jelly-roll style. Cut slices 1/2-inch thick. Bake at 400° for 20 minutes.

NOTE: Let sausage come to room temperature so it will spread easily over pastry.

Lisa Fesperman

SESAME SEED WAFERS

3/4 cup sesame seeds
3/4 cup vegetable oil
2 cups firmly packed brown
    sugar
1 egg

1 cup all-purpose flour
1/2 teaspoon baking powder
1/4 teaspoon salt
1 teaspoon vanilla extract

Brown sesame seeds in a heavy skillet, stirring frequently until light brown; set aside. Combine oil, brown sugar and egg in a large bowl; beat well until light and fluffy. Add flour, baking powder and salt; mix well. Stir in vanilla extract and sesame seeds. Drop dough by half teaspoonful onto greased cookie sheets. Bake at 325° about 10 minutes or until golden. Remove from oven; let stand about 1 minute before removing from pan. Cool. Store in covered container.

Missouri Talley

WHITE TRASH

1 (12 ounce) box Golden
    Graham cereal
1 (12 ounce) box raisins
3 cups roasted peanuts (24
    ounce jar)
2 cups peanut butter

1 (12 ounce) package
    semi-sweet chocolate
    morsels
1 stick margarine
1 (16 ounce) box
    confectioners' sugar

Mix cereal, raisins and peanuts in large container. Over low heat, melt peanut butter, chocolate morsels and butter, stirring well. Let cool and pour over cereal mixture and mix well. After cooling, place mixture in large paper bag. Pour in box of confectioners' sugar and shake until mixture is coated. Keep in airtight container. Great snack for a crowd, especially teenagers. Yield: Enough for a crowd.

NOTE: This makes a large amount and it is easier to handle if you divide it into two batches when you do the shaking.

Ida Rodocker

PETAL-PERFECT BLOOMING ONIONS
Georgia Times-Union featured this recipe that is offered in Australian-style outback steak houses.

Large onions, Spanish, red
  or Vidalia
Vegetable or canola oil
Salt, pepper, Cajun spices
  (to taste)

3 eggs
1/2 cup milk
Flour to dredge onions

Cut a 1/4 inch slice off the stem end of a large onion. Cut vertically through the onion skin on one side and peel the onion, leaving the root end intact. Cut the onion straight across 3/4 of the way through to the root end. Turn the onion and again cut straight across 3/4 of the way through to make 4 quarters. Repeat process, cutting across the onion until there are 8 even sections. Carefully cut each of the 8 sections in half, still keeping the root end intact. Onion should have 16 even sections that can separate into individual petals. Place onion upside down in a bowl of ice water. Place bowl in the refrigerator for at least 24 hours. This helps petals separate. Remove onion from water and drain on towel. In a large bowl, whisk together 3 eggs and 1/2 cup milk. Dip onion in egg mixture, pouring some mixture over the onion to coat inner petals. In another large bowl, combine 2 cups flour with salt and pepper, Cajun spice, or spice mixture of your choice. Dip onion in to flour and sprinkle extra flour over the petals. Repeat. Carefully drop onion, upside down, into vegetable, or canola oil heated to 350°. There should be enough oil to submerge one onion at a time. When onion begins to brown, turn it over. Cooking time: 6 to 8 minutes. Drain onion on paper towel and serve immediately.

Lylburn Booker

EASY CHICKEN WINGS

1 (5 ounce) bottle soy sauce
1 box brown sugar

Bag of chicken wings

Mix together the soy sauce and brown sugar. In a baking pan or dish, make one single layer of chicken wings. Pour the sauce over the chicken, cover and bake at 300° for 3 hours.

Claire Smith

CONFEDERATE CAVIAR

3 (15 ounce) cans
  black-eyed peas, drained
1/4 cup chopped green onions
1/4 cup chopped green bell
  pepper

2 tablespoons diced
  pimiento
1 jalapeño pepper, seeded
  and micned

Combine black-eyed peas, green onions, green pepper, pimiento, and jalapeño pepper in a large bowl, stirring well. Set aside.

VINAIGRETTE:
3/4 cup vegetable oil
1/4 cup red wine vinegar
1/8 teaspoon garlic powder
1/8 teaspoon salt

1/8 teaspoon black pepper
4 dashes Tabasco
Tortilla chips

Whisk together the vegetable oil, vinegar, garlic powder, salt, pepper, and Tabasco. Pour over peas; toss gently. Cover and marinate in refrigerator overnight. Serve with tortilla chips.

NOTE: Black-eyed peas have been a basic ingredients in Southern households since long before the War Between the States. This tasty appetizer gives them a new respect.

Cookbook Committee

BLACK BEAN RELISH FROM ABIGAIL'S

1 teaspoon chopped garlic
2 tablespoons applie cider
  vinegar
1 teaspoon sugar
1/2 teaspoon ground cumin
Salt and pepper, to taste

2/3 cup chopped green onion
1/2 cup chopped red and
  green bell pepper
1 whole fresh tomato, diced
1 (16 ounce) can black
  beans, drained and rinsed

In a food processor or blender, blend the garlic, vinegar, sugar, cumin, salt and pepper. Combine onion, pepper, tomato and black beans. Pour marinade over and refrigerate several hours or overnight before serving. Will keep in the refrigerator for several days.

Linda Nazworth

CAJUN PECANS

Scant 3 tablespoons
   margarine or butter
1/2 teaspoon salt

Scant 3/4 teaspoon ground
   red pepper (cayenne)
2 cups pecan halves

Melt butter or margarine on high (about 1 minute) in microwave-safe baking dish big enough for pecans to be spread out in one layer. Stir in salt, red pepper, and nuts. Cook 7 minutes on high. Stir every two minutes. (My microwave is 700 watts and this time works for me. You might have to adjust for your oven.)

Fran Spear Lormand

SPICED PECANS

1 egg white
1 teaspoon cold water
1 cup sugar

1 tablespoon pumpkin pie
   spice
4 cups pecans

Combine egg white and water, beat slightly. Pour in pecans to wet thoroughly. Use a clear plastic bag or a brown paper bag and pour in sugar and spice to mix. Pour wet pecans into bag and mix or shake well. Pour in a single layer onto a greased 11x16 inch cookie sheet. Bake at 300° for 20 to 25 minutes. Let cool before removing from cookie sheet.

Marie McDonald

GINGER NUTS
I make this recipe during the Christmas holidays.

1 cup of sugar
1/2 cup of water

2 1/2 teaspoons ginger
2 cups of nuts

Cook sugar and water until it spins a thread. Stir in ginger carefully. Then add the nuts. Quickly pour out on wax paper. Break apart before cooling. Yields: 2 cups nuts.

Marguerite Oldenbuttel

CRYSTALLIZED PECANS

1 quart whole pecans
1 cup sugar
1/2 teaspoon cinnamon
1/2 teaspoon salt

1/4 teaspoon cream of tartar
5 tablespoons water
2 teaspoons vanilla

Toast pecans in 350° oven for 10 to 12 minutes. Set aside. Boil sugar, cinnamon, salt, cream of tartar, and water on medium heat until soft ball is formed in cold water (stir constantly). This should take approximately 10 minutes. Add the vanilla and nuts, stir until sugary. Pour onto waxed paper and separate nuts with two forks.

NOTE: 6 tablespoons of evaporated milk may be substituted for water and cream of tartar.

Hazel Shipes

SUGAR PEANUTS

**2 cups raw peanuts (do not   1 cup sugar
    remove husk)   1/2 cup water**

Combine water and sugar together in a saucepan. Bring to a boil. and add peanuts. Cook over medium heat until all the water is gone. Sugar will stick to peanuts. Place peanuts on cookie sheet and bake at 325° for 20 to 30 minutes, stirring occasionally.

Hiram Peeler

TOASTED PECANS

**4 cups pecans   3 teaspoons salt
1/4 cup margarine or butter,
    melted**

Spread pecans on cookie sheet. Put in 325° oven for 10 minutes. Then pour melted margarine over pecans and sprinkle with salt. Mix well. Return to 250° oven and bake for 20 to 25 minutes. Store cooled nuts in airtight container.

Pauline Hopkins

FAMILY EGGNOG

12 eggs, separated
12 tablespoons powdered
sugar

10 tablespoons flavoring
1/2 pint whipping cream
Nutmeg, optional

Beat egg whites to a dry froth. Beat sugar into whites. Beat yolks until lemon-colored and then add flavoring. Drizzle mixture into egg white/sugar mixture. Whip cream separately and then cut in to the above mixture. Enjoy. Optional: sprinkle each serving with nutmeg.

NOTE: My family has been perfecting this recipe for over forty years.

McGregor Lott

COFFEE PUNCH

2 cups sugar
1 gallon hot strong coffee (3
teaspoons per cup water)
1 pint coffee cream (half and
half)

2 quarts milk
3 quarts vanilla ice cream

Stir sugar into hot coffee and refrigerate until well chilled. When ready to serve, combine coffee with coffee cream, milk, and ice cream. Cut into small chunks (do not skimp on ice cream). Serve in silver punch bowl. Very popular beverage for morning coffee in my hometown.

Mary Ann East

FOUR SEASONS CELEBRATION PUNCH

GOLDEN GLOW:

6 ounce can frozen
lemonade concentrate,
thawed
6 ounce can frozen orange
juice concentrate, thawed
6 ounce can frozen tangerine
juice concentrate, thawed

2 cups water
2 (28 ounce) bottles ginger
ale, chilled
Ice cubes or ice mold

This is just right for fall parties, Halloween and Thanksgiving. In a large pitcher, or punch bowl, combine concentrates and water. Just before serving, add ginger ale and ice; stir to blend. Garnish as desired. Makes 25 (4 ounce) servings.

GORGEOUS GREEN: This is so festive to serve at Christmastime, St. Pat's Day, or spring parties. Substitute 2 (6 ounce) cans frozen limeade concentrate, thawed, for orange and tangerine concentrates.

PASSION PURPLE: This is a favorite for children's birthday parties, spring and Easter. Substitute 2 (6 ounce) cans frozen grape juice concentrate, thawed, for orange and tangerine concentrates.

ROSY RED: This is a brilliant color so appropriate for Christmas, Valentine's Day, or 4th of July. Substitute 2 (6 ounce) cans frozen cranberry juice concentrate, thawed, for orange and tangerine concentrates.

Kathy Hackel

FRUIT PUNCH

1 (3 ounce) package gelatin,
  any flavor
1 cup boiling water
1 cup sugar
1 (12 ounce) can frozen orange
  juice concentrate, mixed
  according to directions

1 (6 ounce) can frozen lemonade
  concentrate, mixed according
  to directions
1 (46 ounce) can of pineapple
  juice, unsweetened
4 bananas, mashed
2 quarts of chilled ginger ale

Dissolve gelatin in boiling water. Add sugar, stir until dissolved. Add reconstituted orange juice, reconstituted lemonade, pineapple juice and bananas. Add ginger ale when ready to serve. This punch can be frozen. If frozen, it needs to be stirred at least 2 times before it completely freezes. Take punch out of freezer at least 3 hours before serving time. Add ginger ale when ready to serve.

Ruth Reese

GEORGE'S RED PUNCH

1 (46 ounce) can Hawaiian
  Punch (original red)
1 (12 ounce) can apricot
  nectar

8 ounces frozen concentrate
  orange juice
1 (2 liter) bottle ginger ale

Mix together Hawaiian Punch, apricot nectar and frozen orange juice using a wire wisk, until orange juice is dissolved and well mixed in. Add ginger ale just before serving. When using ice ring, add about 1 liter ginger ale after ring has melted some. Make ice ring from the above mixture WITHOUT ginger ale. If more sweetness is desired, dissolve some sugar in the juice. For less sweetness, add some soda water to taste. Ice ring can also be crushed.

Hildegard Amspacher

LEMONADE PUNCH
If you don't have a punch bowl, a large glass salad bowl, crock, or other large container may be substituted.

3 (2 quart size) packages
    unsweetened lemonade
    mix
3 cups sugar
2 quarts water

1 (46 ounce) can
    unsweetened pineapple
    juice
2 (28 ounce) bottles ginger
    ale

Mix together lemonade mix, sugar and water and pineapple juice. Add ginger ale when ready to serve. Serve over ice cubes and garnish with fresh fruit slices. Makes 35 to 50 servings.

Margaret Park

ORANGE PUNCH

1 (3 ounce) box orange
    flavored gelatin
2 cups hot water
1³/₄ cups sugar
1 (6 ounce) can frozen
    lemonade concentrate

2 cups cool water
1 (46 ounce) can
    unsweetened pineapple
    juice
2 quarts ginger ale, chilled

Dissolve gelatin in hot water. Add sugar, lemonade, cool water, and pineapple juice, stirring until thoroughly mixed. Freeze solid. Take out of freezer 1¹/₂ hours before serving. Add ginger ale when ready to serve. Makes 35 to 40 punch servings.

Dorothy Cross

TEA PUNCH WITH ICE RING

3 cups sugar
1 quart hot strong tea (6 tea
   bags to 1 quart)
1 (#2) can pineapple juice

2 cups orange juice
1 cup lemon juice
1 stick cinnamon

Dissolve sugar in hot tea. Add pineapple, orange, and lemon juices and cinnamon. Serve over ice. Perfect for our sultry summers.

ICE RING:
7 cups of tap water
Various fresh fruits (create
   ring with one fruit or all),
   such as strawberries,
   melon balls, orange, mint
   leaves, raspberries,
   lemon, lime, star fish

The day before serving punch, boil 7 cups of water for 1 minute; let cool at room temperature (this eliminates cloudiness). Pour 3 cups of the water into a 6 cup ring mold. Freeze. Set remaining water aside. Arrange fruit on top of ice. Use strawberries, raspberries, melon balls, slices of orange, lemon or lime, sliced kiwi or sliced star fish and mint leaves (tips with several leaves). Fill the mold with remaining water to within 1/3 inch of top. Freeze. To unmold, let stand at room temperature a few minutes until loosened. To store, remove mold and put in a large plastic zip-lock. Freeze. Good for a 2 gallon bowl of punch.

Mary Ann East

HOT CHOCOLATE MIX
Great for youngsters - no mess.

1 (2 pound) box Nestles Quik
1 (8 quart) box powdered
   milk
1 (8 to 10 ounce) jar
   powdered coffee cream

1 pound box powdered
   sugar

In large bowl, combine Quik, powdered milk, coffee cream, and powdered sugar. Store in tightly covered container. Place 4 or 5 teaspoonfuls in cup and add boiling water. This is great for every age - no milk to heat - no mess. This makes enough for your family and some extra for a gift.

Dot Gibson

SPICED TEA

1 gallon boiling water
1 or 2 sticks cinnamon
1 teaspoon whole cloves
1 teaspoon whole allspice

3 family size tea bags
3 cups (or less) sugar
2 cups orange juice
1 cup lemon juice

Pour boiling water over spices and tea. Let steep 15 minutes. Remove tea bags and spices. Add sugar and juices. This tea is better after it is cooled and reheated.

Patsy Blalock

PERCOLATOR PUNCH
A hot spiced drink.

3 cups apple juice or apple
   cider
2¹/₂ cups pineapple juice
2 cups cranberry juice
¹/₂ cup light brown sugar

¹/₄ teaspoon salt
2 sticks cinnamon
1 teaspoon whole cloves
¹/₂ teaspoon whole allspice

In coffee percolator mix juices, brown sugar and salt. In basket, place cinnamon, cloves and allspice. Plug in coffee pot and run through cycle. Serves 10.

Genie Fesperman

RUSSIAN TEA

2 cups Tang
¹/₂ cup of Lipton
   decaffeinated ice tea
   mix, sugar-free with
   natural lemon flavor

2 teaspoons ground
   cinnamon
1 teaspoon ground cloves

Combine Tang, tea mix, cinnamon, and cloves. Put 2 teaspoons of mixture to 1 cup hot water. Store in airtight container.

Virginia Lott

NOTES

Salads, Soups and Dressings

Salads, Soups and Dressings

ASHEVILLE LUNCHEON SALAD

1 (10³/4 ounce) can
   condensed tomato soup
1¹/2 tablespoons (1¹/2
   envelopes) unflavored
   gelatin
1/2 cup cold water
2 (3 ounce) packages cream
   cheese

1 cup mayonnaise
1 cup chopped celery
2 tablespoons chopped
   green pepper
1 teaspoon minced onion, if
   desired
1/2 cup broken California
   walnuts or pecans

Heat tomato soup. Soften gelatin in cold water, then add to hot soup, stirring until dissolved. Cool. Thoroughly combine cream cheese, mayonnaise, celery, green pepper, onion, and nuts. Add to gelatin mixture. Pour into mold; chill until firm. Makes 8 to 10 servings.

NOTE: In individual, bell-shaped molds, it is our traditional Christmas salad.

Eddie Mae Spear

BLUEBERRY SALAD

2 (3 ounce) packages grape
   or raspberry flavored
   gelatin
2 cups boiling water

1 (20 ounce) can blueberry
   pie filling
1 (20 ounce) can crushed
   pineapple, drained

Dissolve gelatin in boiling water. Add pie filling and pineapple. Pour into 9x13 inch pan. Refrigerate until set.

TOPPING:
1 (8 ounce) package cream
   cheese, softened
1/2 pint sour cream

1/2 cup sugar
1/2 cup chopped pecans

Mix cream cheese, sour cream, and sugar until smooth. Spread over firm gelatin. Sprinkle pecans on top.

Sharon Moseley

ASPARAGUS SALAD

2 envelopes unflavored
   gelatin
1/2 cup cold water
3/4 cup sugar
1 cup water
1/2 cup vinegar
1 teaspoon salt
1/4 cup sliced olives

1 cup celery, chopped
1 tablespoon onion, grated
1 (2 ounce) jar pimiento
1/2 cup slivered almonds or
   1/2 cup water chestnuts
2 (15 ounce) cans asparagus
   spears (use the can of
   choice, long or regular)

Soak gelatin in cold water. Mix sugar, 1 cup water, vinegar, and salt in pan and bring to boil. Combine gelatin and sugar mixture and pour in 9x13 inch dish. Stir in olives, celery, onion, pimento, almonds or chestnuts. Lay asparagus spears on top of mixture, alternating the tips. Chill until set. Cut into squares. Serves 12.

SAUCE:
1/2 cup mayonnaise
1 teaspoon prepared mustard

1 teaspoon lemon juice

Combine mayonnaise, mustard and lemon juice. Top salad squares with sauce. Sauce is optional.

Mary Winn Pruet

CONGEALED FRUIT SALAD

1 (8 ounce) can crushed
   pineapple
1 (16 ounce) can fruit cocktail
1 (6 ounce) package lime
   flavored gelatin

1 (5 ounce) can evaporated
   milk
1/2 (10 ounce) jar salad cherries
1/2 cup or more chopped
   nuts

Drain juice from pineapple and fruit cocktail, heating in saucepan. Add lime gelatin and dissolve. Cool and add evaporated milk, pineapple, fruit cocktail, cherries, and nuts. Stir well and pour into 71/2x71/2x2 inch pan. Refrigerate until firm. Serve on lettuce. Makes 8 servings.

Nelle Pinson

CARDINAL SALAD
A favorite from the Green Frog Restaurant - great for Christmas or summer luncheons.

1 (3 ounce) package lemon
    flavored gelatin
1 cup boiling water
3/4 cup beet juice
3 tablespoons vinegar
1/2 teaspoon salt

2 teaspoons grated onion or
    onion juice
1 tablespoon horseradish
3/4 cup celery, diced
1 cup cooked canned beets,
    diced

Dissolve gelatin in boiling water. Add beet juice, vinegar, salt, onion or onion juice and horseradish. Chill until partially set. Fold in celery and beets. Pour into mold or individual molds. Chill until firm.

MAYONNAISE DRESSING:
1 cup mayonnaise   Sour cream or yogurt

Unmold salad on crisp lettuce and serve with mayonnaise, thinned with sour cream or plain yogurt.

Jeanette Darden

CONGEALED PINEAPPLE SALAD

2 envelopes plain gelatin
1 cup cold water
1 (20 ounce) can crushed
    pineapple
3/4 cup sugar
1 (8 ounce) package cream
    cheese (can use fat-free),
    softened

1 cup sour cream (can use
    fat-free)
1 cup chopped pecans
Cherries, optional

Soak gelatin in cold water to soften. In saucepan, drain juice from pineapple and add sugar to juice. Bring to a boil, add gelatin mixture. Pour into dish. Chill until slightly thickened. Fold in softened cream cheese, sour cream, pineapple, and nuts. May add cherries to gelatin or use as a garnish.

Shannon Stewart

CHRISTMAS RIBBON RING

CRANBERRY LAYER:

1 (3 ounce) package
   strawberry gelatin
1 (16 ounce) can whole
   cranberry sauce

1¼ cups boiling water

Dissolve strawberry gelatin in 1¼ cups boiling water. Add cranberry sauce, mixing well. Chill until partially set. Pour into 8 cup ring mold. Chill until almost firm; top with cheese layer.

CHEESE LAYER:

1 (3 ounce) package lemon
   flavored gelatin
1 (8 ounce) package cream
   cheese, softened
1 (9 ounce) can crushed
   pineapple, undrained

1¼ cups boiling water
¼ cup salted pecans,
   chopped

Dissolve lemon gelatin in 1¼ cups boiling water, add softened cheese, beating smooth with electric beater. Add pineapple (with syrup); chill until partially set. Stir in pecans, then pour over cranberry layer in mold. Chill until almost firm. Top with grapefruit layer.

GRAPEFRUIT LAYER:

1 (3 ounce) package lime
   flavored gelatin
2 tablespoons sugar

1 (16 ounce) can grapefruit
   sections, undrained
1 cup boiling water

Dissolve lime gelatin and sugar in 1 cup boiling water. Add grapefruit (with juice). Chill until partially set. Pour over cheese layer. Chill overnight. Unmold on bed of lettuce. Serve with mayonnaise. Serves 10 to 12.

NOTE: This is a festive, delectable salad!

Christine Shields

CONGEALED SPINACH SALAD

1 envelope unflavored
  gelatin
1/4 cup cold water
2 (6 ounce) packages lemon
  flavored gelatin
2 cups boiling water
2 (10 ounce) packages
  frozen chopped spinach
  (cooked, drained, and
  cooled)

1 cup chopped celery
4 tablespoons chopped
  onion
1/2 cup mayonnaise
2 tablespoons vinegar
2 cups small curd cottage
  cheese
Dash of Tabasco

Soften unflavored gelatin in cold water. Dissolve lemon gelatin in boiling water, and add softened gelatin to dissolve. Add spinach, celery, onion, mayonnaise, vinegar, cottage cheese, and Tabasco. Pour into Pyrex dish and chill until set. Cut into squares and serve on lettuce.

Hazel Shipes

CONGEALED SUNSET SALAD

1 (20 ounce) can crushed
  pineapple (in heavy
  syrup)
1/2 cup sugar
2 envelopes unflavored
  gelatin
1/2 cup cold water
2 cups grated mild Cheddar
  cheese

1 (7 ounce) jar pimiento
  (chopped and drained)
1 cup mayonnaise
1 cup chopped nuts
  (optional)
1/2 cup chopped cherries
  (optional)

Boil pineapple and sugar 3 minutes. Remove from heat. To this mixture, add the gelatin which has been softened in 1/2 cup cold water and stir until dissolved. Add cheese. (Mixture should be warm enough to melt cheese.) Add pimiento, mayonnaise, nuts and cherries. Pour into 9x13 inch dish and chill before serving.

Joel Hansford

TOMATO ASPIC

3 envelopes unflavored gelatin
5¼ cups tomato juice, divided
1 scant teaspoon salt
1½ teaspoons sugar

1½ teaspoons
  Worcestershire sauce
¾ teaspoon Tabasco
6 tablespoons lemon juice

Sprinkle gelatin on 1½ cups tomato juice to soften. Place over low heat and stir until gelatin is dissolved. Remove from heat and stir in remaining tomato juice, salt, sugar, Worcestershire, Tabasco, and lemon juice. Turn into 8 cup ring mold or individual molds. Chill until firm. Garnish with salad greens and black olives. Serve with dollop of salad dressing.

VARIATIONS: Pour tomato mixture into ring mold to depth of ¼ inch. Chill until partially set and place one of the following in mixture: (1) 1 (14 ounce) can artichoke hearts, drained and halved, (2) slices of avocado, (3) ¾ to 1 pound of shrimp, cut up or (4) cheese balls (to make, mix 2 (3 ounce) packages cream cheese, 3 tablespoons each of finely minced celery, chopped green olives and chopped chives and 1 teaspoon salt; form into balls about the size of a quarter). Chill vegetable layer and when set cover with remaining tomato mixture and chill until firm.

Christine Shields

SODA POP SALAD

1 (6 ounce) package lemon
  flavored gelatin
1 cup boiling water
1 tablespoon sugar
1 teaspoon vanilla
2 (3 ounce) packages cream
  cheese, softened

1 (10 ounce) bottle 7-Up
1 (8 ounce) can crushed
  pineapple, drained
1 cup chopped nuts

Dissolve gelatin in boiling water. Mix together sugar, vanilla, and cream cheese, mashing and stirring until cheese is almost dissolved. Add 7-Up, pineapple, and nuts. Add to gelatin. Pour in a 8x12 inch Pyrex dish. Chill until set.

Margaret Park

STRAWBERRY PRETZEL SALAD

CRUST:

2 cups pretzels, crushed   1½ sticks butter, melted
¼ cup sugar

Mix pretzels, sugar, and melted butter together and press in a 9x13 inch greased pan. Bake at 325° for 8 minutes. Cool.

MIDDLE LAYER:

1 (8 ounce) package cream   1 cup sugar
   cheese, softened   2 cups whipped topping

Cream together softened cream cheese and sugar. Add whipped topping, mixing well. Spread evenly and completely over cooled crust.

TOP LAYER:

2 (10 ounce) packages   1 (6 ounce) package
   frozen strawberries,   strawberry flavored
   thawed   gelatin
2 cups pineapple juice

Heat pineapple juice and dissolve gelatin. Cool and add thawed strawberries. Refrigerate until thick and spread over cream cheese layer. Refrigerate until firm. Cut into desired shape and serve on bed of lettuce.

Patti White

CRANBERRY ORANGE SALAD

1 (3 ounce) package
   raspberry flavored gelatin
1 cup boiling water
1 cup Ocean Spray Cran
   Orange relish

3/4 cup cold water
1 cup drained, crushed
   pineapple
1/4 cup chopped nuts

Dissolve gelatin in 1 cup boiling water. Blend in Cran Orange relish. Add 3/4 cup cold water. Chill until slightly thickened. Fold in pineapple and 1/4 cup nuts. Pour into mold or 9 inch square pan. Chill until firm.

NOTE: This is best made early in the morning, or the day before serving.

Mikell McKee

CUCUMBER CONGEALED SALAD

3/4 cup cucumber, unpeeled
   and drained
1/2 package unflavored
   gelatin
1 (3 ounce) package lime
   flavored gelatin

1 cup cottage cheese or
   sour cream
1 cup mayonnaise
2/3 cup slivered almonds
1 small onion, grated

Drain cucumber and save liquid. Soften gelatin in 1/4 cup cold water. Combine cucumber liquid with boiling water to yield 3/4 cup, and dissolve both gelatins. Combine cottage cheese/sour cream and mayonnaise. Add almonds, onions, and gelatin mixture. Mix and congeal in Pyrex dish. Yields 6 to 8 servings.

Sarah Harrell

GRAPEFRUIT CONGEALED SALAD

3 envelopes unflavored
   gelatin
1/2 cup cold water
1 cup sugar
1 cup boiling water
3 (16 ounce) cans
   grapefruit, drained

1 teaspoon lemon juice
1 cup nuts, chopped
3 (3 ounce) packages cream
   cheese, softened

Soften gelatin in cold water. Dissolve sugar in boiling water. Combine gelatin and sugar mixtures. Add grapefruit and lemon juice. Add nuts to cream cheese. Put 1/2 grapefruit mixture into mold. Refrigerate until firm. Add a layer of cream cheese and nuts. Top with remaining grapefruit mixture. Refrigerate until firm. Unmold on lettuce.

Mary Jane Lott

HAWAIIAN CONGEAL

1 cup crushed pineapple,
   drained
3/4 cup pineapple syrup
3 cups boiling water
6 ounces lime flavored
   gelatin

8 ounces cream cheese,
   softened
1/2 cup pecans
1 (3 ounce) package lime
   gelatin for garnish

Drain pineapple, set aside reserving juice. Heat pineapple juice and water to boiling. Pour over gelatin, stirring to dissolve. Gradually add dissolved gelatin to cream cheese. Chill until thickened. Whip at high speed on mixer 5 minutes, fold in pineapple and pecans. Pour into a 1 1/2 quart mold or individual molds. Chill until firm. Prepare garnish of lime gelatin according to package. Cut into cubes. Unmold salad and surround with lime cubes. Makes a pretty picture as mold is light green surrounded by dark green cubes. Makes 12 (1/2 cup) servings.

Hildergard Amspacher

RED, WHITE, AND BLUE JELLO MOLD

1 package of unflavored gelatin, divided (1¹/₂ teaspoons each)

This will be used in red layer and blue layer.

RED LAYER:

1 (6 ounce) package
   strawberry gelatin

2 (10 ounce) packages frozen
   strawberries, thawed

Soften half package of unflavored gelatin in 1 tablespoon cold water. Dissolve the strawberry gelatin and the unflavored gelatin in 2 cups boiling water. When completely dissolved, add 1 cup cold water, stirring well. Add strawberries and pour into 2 or 3 quart dish or mold. Chill red layer until set, but not too firm. Prepare white layer.

WHITE LAYER:

1 (3 ounce) package lemon
   gelatin
1 (8 ounce) package cream
   cheese, softened

2 tablespoons confectioners
   sugar
¹/₂ cup milk
1 teaspoon vanilla

Dissolve lemon gelatin in 1¹/₂ cups boiling water. Cool. Combine cream cheese, sugar, milk, and vanilla in blender. Add lemon gelatin mixture and stir in blender until completely mixed. Carefully spoon this layer over the red layer. Chill until completely set. Prepare blue layer.

BLUE LAYER:

1 (6 ounce) package
   blackberry gelatin (or
   black cherry gelatin)

1 (21 ounce) can blueberry
   pie filling

Soften half package of unflavored gelatin in 1 tablespoon cold water. Dissolve the blackberry gelatin and unflavored gelatin in 2 cups boiling water. When completely dissolved, add 1 cup cold water, stirring well. Add blueberry pie filling, blending well. Carefully spoon blue layer over white layer. Refrigerate overnight. Cut into squares and top with dollop of mayonnaise, salad dressing, or whipped topping, if desired.

(continued on next page)

NOTE: This colorful layered gelatin mold makes a beautiful presentation on a bed of red tip lettuce. This festive salad is ideal for a patriotic celebration!

Janet Herrin

MY FAVORITE CONGEALED SALAD

1 (3 ounce) package raspberry flavored gelatin
1 (21 ounce) can cherry pie filling
1 (3 ounce) package cream cheese
1 (3 ounce) package lemon flavored gelatin
1/3 cup mayonnaise or salad dressing
1 (8 3/4 ounce) can (1 cup) crushed pineapple, undrained
1/2 cup whipping cream
1 cup miniature marshmallows
2 tablespoons chopped nuts

Dissolve raspberry gelatin in 1 cup boiling water, stir in cherry pie filling. Turn into 9x13x2 inch Pyrex dish. Chill until partially set. Dissolve lemon gelatin in 1 cup boiling water. Beat together cream cheese and mayonnaise. Gradually add to lemon gelatin mixture. Stir in undrained pineapple. Whip 1/2 cup whipping cream; fold into lemon mixture with 1 cup miniature marshmallows. Spread atop cherry layer that has congealed. Top with 2 tablespoons chopped nuts. Chill until set. Makes 12 servings.

Kathy Hackel

PICKLE PEACH SALAD

1 (6 ounce) package lemon
   flavored gelatin
1 cup boiling water
1 cup pickled peach juice
1 (22 ounce) jar pickled peaches,
   seeded and chopped

1 orange
1 (8 ounce) jar maraschino
   cherries, drained
1 cup chopped pecans

Dissolve gelatin in one cup boiling water. Add one cup peach pickle juice. Section orange, removing membranes. Halve cherries. Add peaches, orange sections, cherries, and pecans to cool but shaky gelatin. Spray single or one large mold with vegetable no-stick spray and pour in salad. Refrigerate. Unmold and top with homemade mayonnaise with a sprinkle of cinnamon added.

NOTE: Colorful salad, a nice compliment to ham - particularly good in fall or winter.

Georgianne McGee

PEACH BLISS

1 (8¼ ounce) can crushed
   pineapple
1 (16 ounce) can peaches,
   drained
1 (3 ounce) package peach
   flavored gelatin

1 (4 ounce) frozen whipped
   topping, thawed
1 cup buttermilk
Mayonnaise, optional
Pecans, optional

Heat pineapple and peaches. Stir in peach gelatin to dissolve. Let cool to room temperature. Fold in whipped topping and buttermilk. Pour into 8 inch square dish to congeal. Serve on lettuce leaf topped with mayonnaise. Options: use any kind of fruit and/or line bottom of dish with chopped pecans.

Lucille Murray

ARTICHOKE RICE SALAD

1 (6 ounce) package Uncle
    Ben's chicken vermicelli
    (Rice-A-Roni)
2 (6 ounce) jars artichoke
    hearts

1/4 to 1/3 cup mayonnaise
3/4 teaspoon curry
2 green onions, chopped
1/2 green pepper, chopped
12 stuffed olives, sliced

Cook chicken vermicelli as directed. Cool and set aside. Drain artichokes, reserving liquid from one jar. Slice artichokes in half. Combine artichoke liquid, mayonnaise, curry, cooked chicken vermicelli, artichoke hearts, onions, peppers, and olives. Chill. Can be made two days in advance.

Missouri Talley

BROCCOLI SALAD

4 hard cooked eggs,
    chopped
1 cup sliced mushrooms
1 cup sliced olives
1 large bunch broccoli, cut
    in flowerettes

1/2 cup mayonnaise
1/2 cup sour cream (or plain
    yogurt)
2 teaspoons lemon juice
1 teaspoon sugar
Salt and pepper, to taste

Mix eggs, mushrooms, olives, broccoli, mayonnaise, sour cream (or yogurt), lemon juice, sugar, salt and pepper. Serve and enjoy.

Cheryl Monroe

CALIFORNIA SALAD WITH TARRAGON DRESSING

1/2 cup mayonnaise
1/4 cup vegetable oil
1 tablespoon lemon juice
1 tablespoon tarragon
   vinegar
1 1/2 teaspoons
   Worcestershire sauce
1/2 teaspoon soy sauce
1/4 teaspoon pepper
1 tablespoon crushed tarragon

4 cups mixed salad greens
   (red leaf, Boston, Bibb)
2 cups fresh mushrooms
1 (11 ounce) can mandarin
   oranges, drained
1 medium avocado, peeled
   and coarsely chopped
1/4 cup slivered almonds,
   toasted

Combine mayonnaise, vegetable oil, lemon juice, vinegar, Worcestershire, soy sauce, pepper, and tarragon, whisking well. Store in container and chill several hours before serving. Toss together salad greens, mushrooms, mandarin oranges, avocado, and almonds in a large salad bowl; add dressing, as desired. Makes 6 to 8 servings.

Coralyn Gaston

CELEBRATION SALAD

1 large head Romaine lettuce
1 large tomato
1 medium red onion
1 large ripe avocado

3 ounces blue cheese,
   crumbled
6 slices cooked bacon,
   crumbled

Combine torn lettuce, chopped tomato, chopped onion, sliced avocado, blue cheese, and crumbled bacon.

DRESSING:
3/4 cup vegetable oil
1/4 cup vinegar
1 clove garlic, minced

1 teaspoon salt
4 teaspoons sugar

In separate bowl, blend vegetable oil, vinegar, minced garlic, salt, and sugar. Pour over lettuce mixture and toss.

Ivy Stewart Monroe

CURRY SPINACH SALAD

1 1/2 pounds fresh spinach,
   torn
1/2 cup slivered almonds
3/4 cup chopped dates

1 large banana, peeled and
   chopped
1 Bermuda onion, sliced

Mix together torn spinach, almonds, dates, banana, and sliced onion.

DRESSING:
3/4 cup olive oil
3 1/2 tablespoons wine
   vinegar

1 clove garlic, crushed
1 teaspoon curry powder
1/8 teaspoon white pepper

In separate bowl, combine olive oil, wine vinegar, curry powder, and white pepper. Mix well. Store in refrigerator until ready to use. Add to spinach mixture just before serving and toss.

Lynn Smith

FRESH CORN SALAD
Yield: 12 to 14 servings

3 cups corn, cut from cob
   (about 6 ears)
1 large onion, chopped
2 medium zucchini,
   unpeeled and cubed
1 bunch green onions, sliced
1 sweet red pepper, chopped
1 green pepper, chopped
1/4 cup minced parsley

1 clove garlic, minced
1/4 teaspoon salt
1/8 teaspoon pepper
2 teaspoons sugar
1 teaspoon ground cumin
2 teaspoons Dijon mustard
1/2 teaspoon hot sauce
2/3 cup vegetable oil
1/3 cup white vinegar

Cook corn, covered, in boiling water to cover 8 to 10 minutes; drain and cool. Combine corn, onion, zucchini, green onion, red pepper, green pepper, and parsley. Set aside. Combine garlic, salt, pepper, sugar, cumin, mustard, hot sauce, oil, and vinegar, stirring well. Toss gently with vegetables. Chill 8 hours. Serve with a slotted spoon.

Kathy Hackel

FAVORITE POTATO SALAD

6 medium potatoes
1 cup green onions, chopped
   with tops
1 cup parsley, chopped
1½ cups mayonnaise

1 cup sour cream
1 teaspoon celery seed
1½ teaspoons horseradish
½ teaspoon salt

Peel and cube potatoes. Cook until tender, drain and cool. Mix onions and parsley. Layer on top of potatoes in casserole dish. In separate bowl, mix mayonnaise, sour cream, celery seed, horseradish, and salt. Spread on top of onions and parsley. Cover and refrigerate overnight.

Ellen Council

FRENCH KRAUT

2 quarts coarsely ground
   cabbage
2 medium onions, chopped
1 green and 1 red pepper,
   chopped
1 cup vinegar

¾ cup sugar
1 teaspoon salt
½ teaspoon mustard seed
1 teaspoon celery seed
1 teaspoon turmeric powder

Mix cabbage, onions, red pepper, vinegar, sugar, salt, mustard seed, celery seed, and turmeric and let stand in refrigerator at least 24 hours before serving. Will keep several weeks.

Mary Hood

FRESH BROCCOLI MANDARIN SALAD

1 egg plus one egg yolk
1/2 cup sugar
1 1/2 teaspoons cornstarch
1 teaspoon dry mustard
1/4 cup vinegar
1/4 cup water
3 tablespoons butter, softened
1/2 cup mayonnaise
4 cups fresh broccoli florets
1/2 cup golden raisins

6 slices bacon, cooked and
  crumbled
2 cups sliced fresh
  mushrooms
1/2 cup slivered almonds,
  toasted or cocktail peanuts
1 (11 ounce) can mandarin
  oranges
1/2 red onion, sliced 1/8 inch
  rings

In top of double boiler, whisk together egg, egg yolk, sugar, cornstarch, and mustard. Combine vinegar and water slowly with egg mixture. Place over hot water and cook, stirring constantly until mixture thickens. Remove from heat, stir in butter and mayonnaise. Chill. Toss dressing with broccoli, raisins, bacon, mushrooms, almonds, oranges and onions in serving bowl. Store chilled. Makes 10 to 12 servings.

Mary Hereford

GASPACHO SALAD

2 cucumbers, peeled and
  finely diced
4 tomatoes, seeded and
  diced
2 green peppers, seeded
  and finely slivered
1 onion, finely chopped
8 black olives, pitted
2 cloves garlic

1/4 teaspoon salt
1/4 teaspoon cumin
1/4 cup vinegar
1/2 cup olive oil
1 tablespoon parsley, finely
  chopped
1 tablespoon chives or
  shallots, finely chopped

Layer cucumbers, tomatoes, green peppers, onion, and olives in crystal bowl. In a mixing bowl, crush garlic with salt and cumin. Beat in vinegar, olive oil, parsley, and chives. Pour dressing over vegetables and chill for several hours.

Georgianne McGee

GERMAN POTATO SALAD

2¹/₂ to 3 pounds potatoes
1 medium onion
2 beef bouillon cubes
1¹/₂ cups water
3 tablespoons oil

2 tablespoons vinegar
1 teaspoon salt
1 teaspoon sugar
Dash (¹/₈ teaspoon) pepper

Boil whole potatoes until tender. Peel and slice thin while potatoes are still warm. Chop onion very fine. Dissolve bouillon cubes in water, add onions, and cook until tender, about 3 to 5 minutes. Mix oil, vinegar, salt, sugar, and pepper, pouring over potatoes. Add bouillon/onion mixture (either hot or cold), to potatoes. Mix gently, letting stand for ¹/₂ hour or more. Ideal to carry on a picnic as it contains no mayonnaise. Keeps several days in the refrigerator.

NOTE: Every region in Germany has it's own version of potato salad. This one is from the central south region - from Ulm to Stuttgart to Karlsruhe.

Hildegard Amspacher

SAUERKRAUT SALAD

4 cups sauerkraut, drained
   (use type in glass jars)
1 cup sliced celery
1 cup diced green pepper

1 (7 ounce) jar pimiento
1 cup chopped onions
1 (5 ounce) can water
   chestnuts

Combine sauerkraut, celery, green pepper, pimiento, onion, and chestnuts. Set aside.

DRESSING:
¹/₃ cup water
²/₃ cup vinegar

¹/₃ cup oil
1¹/₂ cups sugar

Heat the water, vinegar, oil, and sugar until sugar dissolves. Pour over vegetables, mixing well. Chill.

Frankie Miles

SLAW FOR 75

6 (16 ounce) packages of
   prepared slaw mix
2 (16 ounce) bottles of
   Hidden Valley slaw
   dressing

4 (20 ounce) cans of crushed
   pineapple, drained
6 tablespoons of sweet
   pickle relish, drained
Salt and pepper, to taste

Mix slaw mix, slaw dressing, pineapple, pickle relish, salt and pepper. Refrigerate one hour before serving. Serves 75 people.

Walt Miller

SPLENDID SALAD WITH RASPBERRY WINE VINEGAR

1/4 cup raspberry wine
   vinegar
2 tablespoons maple syrup
2/3 cup olive oil or vegetable
   oil
Lettuce (red leaf, green leaf,
   Bibb)

Fresh raspberries or
   strawberries
4 ounces crumbled blue
   cheese or feta cheese
1/4 to 1/2 cup walnuts or
   toasted pine nuts

Combine raspberry wine vinegar and maple syrup. Gradually add oil, stirring with wire whisk. Combine lettuce, raspberries, blue cheese and walnuts. Add dressing, as desired. Serves 4 to 6.

Coralyn Gaston

ST. SIMONS BROCCOLI SALAD

1 bunch fresh broccoli (cut
    flowerets to desired size)
4 to 6 ounces fresh
    mushrooms, sliced
10 to 12 stuffed olives, sliced

1 red onion, sliced as much
    as desired
1 (5 ounce) can sliced water
    chestnuts

Combine broccoli, mushrooms, olives, onion, and water chestnuts.

DRESSING:
1/2 cup Miracle Whip salad
    dressing
1/4 cup tarragon vinegar
1/4 cup sugar

2 tablespoons olive juice
    from bottle
Dash paprika

In separate bowl, mix salad dressing, vinegar, sugar, olive juice, and paprika. Pour dressing over broccoli mixture. Chill before serving.

Martha McCrary Hannah

STUFFED VIDALIA ONION SALAD

4 to 6 large vidalia onions,
    peeled
1 (8 ounce) package cream
    cheese
2 tablespoons deviled ham
1 teaspoon dry mustard

1 tablespoon chopped
    pimiento
1/4 teaspoon salt
Few grains pepper
Lettuce leaves

Remove centers of onions with an apple corer, leaving a shell approximately 1 inch in thickness; set aside shells. Beat cream cheese until soft and creamy. Blend in deviled ham, dry mustard, pimiento, salt and pepper. Fill centers of onion with mixture and chill several hours or until cheese centers are firm. To serve, slice onions and place on lettuce leaves. Makes 6 to 8 servings.

Carol Garbutt

WONDER SALAD

1 (16 ounce) can stewed
   tomatoes (mash well or
   use blender)
1 small (3 ounce) package
   strawberry gelatin

2 tablespoons tarragon
   vinegar

Heat tomatoes to a boiling point. Add gelatin; let dissolve. Add vinegar. Place in mold. Serve on lettuce with mayonnaise.

Georgia McDonald

BANANA SPLIT SALAD

1 (8 ounce) package cream
   cheese, softened
1/2 cup sugar
1 (20 ounce) can crushed
   pineapple, drained
1 (10 ounce) package frozen
   sliced strawberries, thawed

2 medium firm bananas,
   chopped
1 (12 ounce) carton frozen
   whipped topping
1 cup nuts
Red food coloring (optional)

Beat cream cheese and sugar. Stir in pineapple, strawberries, and bananas. Fold in the whipped topping, nuts and food coloring if desired. Pour into oiled 13x9x2 inch dish. Cover and freeze until firm, at least 3 hours. Remove from freezer 30 minutes before serving.

Gloria Murray

CREAMY FROZEN SALAD

2 cups dairy sour cream
2 tablespoons lemon juice
3/4 cup sugar
1/8 teaspoon salt

1 (8 1/2 ounce) can crushed
   pineapple
1/4 cup pecans, chopped
1 banana, sliced

Blend sour cream, lemon juice, sugar, and salt. Stir in pineapple, pecans, and banana. Pour into 1 quart mold, or cup cake papers. Freeze. Makes 8 servings (recommended storage time, about 2 weeks).

Eleanor Harrison

FROZEN FRUIT SALAD

1 (17 ounce) can apricots,
   cut in small pieces
1 (20 ounce) can fruit
   cocktail, cut in small pieces
1/2 cup juice from canned
   fruits

1/2 (6 ounce) bottle cherries,
   chopped
1/2 cup Miracle Whip salad
   dressing
1/2 pint whipping cream,
   whipped

Mix apricots, fruit salad, fruit juice, cherries, and salad dressing together.
Fold into whipped cream. Put into freezer the day before serving. Leave
until ready to serve.

Clyde King

MARINATED SALAD

1 (15 ounce) can white
   asparagus spears,
   drained
1 (14 ounce) can artichoke
   hearts, drained and cut in
   half
1 (14 ounce) can hearts of
   palm, drained and cut into
   1/2 inch slices
1 (4 ounce) can sliced
   mushrooms, drained

1/2 cup ripe olives, sliced
1/2 cup pimiento stuffed
   olives, sliced
12 cherry tomatoes, halved
1/2 purple onion, sliced and
   separated into rings
1 (8 ounce) bottle Italian
   salad dressing
Romaine lettuce

Combine asparagus, artichokes, hearts of palm, mushrooms, olives, tomatoes, and onion. Add dressing, stirring gently. Drain salad, and serve on lettuce. If you serve this salad from a buffet, layer the ingredients in a glass bowl or trifle dish for a showy presentation. To make ahead, combine and chill 8 hours. Drain before serving. Yield 6 servings.

Madge Herrin

MARINATED SLICED TOMATOES

4 large tomatoes, peeled and
   sliced
1/4 cup salad oil
1 tablespoon lemon juice

1/2 teaspoon minced garlic
1/2 teaspoon salt
1/2 teaspoon dried oregano
   leaves

Slice tomatoes in thick slices. Arrange slices in shallow Pyrex dish. Combine salad oil, lemon juice, garlic, salt, and oregano. Pour over tomatoes and chill. Let stand for 6 hours or overnight. Good served with chicken salad.

Pauline Hopkins

MARINATED VEGETABLE SALAD

1 (16 ounce) can French
   style green beans
1 (16 ounce) can Lesuer
   peas
1 (12 ounce) can Green
   Giant shoe peg white corn
1 small (2 ounce) jar
   chopped pimiento
1 cup chopped celery

1 cup chopped onion
1/2 cup chopped green
   pepper
1 cup sugar
3/4 cup vinegar
1 cup canola oil
Salt
Pepper

Drain well and mix together the green beans, peas, corn, and chopped pimiento. Add celery, onion, and green pepper. Combine in saucepan; sugar, vinegar, oil, salt, and pepper. Heat until sugar melts. Cool and pour over vegetables. Refrigerate. Keeps 2 to 3 weeks.

Landy Rimes

APPLE SALAD

1/2 cup flour
1 (20 ounce) can crushed
   pineapple (in own juice)
1 cup sugar
3 tablespoons butter or
   margarine

6 medium apples
8 ounces Cool Whip
Cherries, optional
Chopped nuts, optional

Cook flour, pineapple and sugar together until thick. Remove from heat and add butter or margarine. Let cool to room temperature. Peel and chop apples. Add apples to cooked mixture, then Cool Whip. Pour in bowl and decorate with cherries and nuts.

Bonnie Lynn

CURRIED FRUIT SALAD

2 (17 ounce) cans fruit for
   salad
1 (11 ounce) can mandarin
   orange sections
1 medium apple, chopped
1/2 cup raisins
2 teaspoons finely chopped
   onion
2 teaspoons lemon juice

1 1/2 teaspoons curry
   powder
1/4 teaspoon ground
   cinnamon
Lettuce leaves
1/3 cup mayonnaise
1/3 cup dairy sour cream
1/4 cup finely chopped
   peanuts

Drain 1 can of fruit for salad; drain orange sections. Reserve drained liquid for later use. Combine drained and undrained fruits for salad, orange sections, apple, raisins, onion, lemon juice, curry, and cinnamon. Cover and chill for 3 hours. Spoon onto 8 lettuce lined plates. Make a dressing from 2 tablespoons of the reserved syrup from fruit, mayonnaise and sour cream and drizzle over fruit. Sprinkle peanuts over top. Serves 8.

Jane Hart

MILLIONAIRE SALAD

4 eggs
Juice of 2 lemons
2 tablespoons flour
1 cup milk
1 cup Queen Ann white
    cherries

1 cup pineapple tidbits
1 (16 ounce) bag
    marshmallows
2 bananas
1 (12 ounce) tub whipped
    topping

Cook eggs, juice from lemons, flour, and milk until thick. Cool. Add cherries, pineapple, marshmallows, bananas, and whipped topping. Freeze.

Happie Stewart

OVERNIGHT LAYERED FRUIT SALAD

2 cups shredded iceberg
    lettuce
2 navel oranges or 1 (11
    ounce) can mandarin
    oranges, drained (reserve
    juice)

2 Granny Smith apples,
    unpeeled and sliced
2 cups seedless red or
    green grapes, sliced in
    half

Place shredded lettuce in a deep 2 quart glass serving bowl. Peel and section oranges, reserving juice. Combine apple slices and orange juice, toss to coat. Layer apple slices over lettuce, top with orange sections and grapes.

TOPPING:
1/3 cup mayonnaise
1/3 cup sour cream

1 cup mild Cheddar cheese

Combine mayonnaise and sour cream in a small bowl; stir well. Spread this mixture over salad, sealing to edge of bowl. Sprinkle with cheese. Cover and chill at least eight hours. Serves 8 to 10.

Coralyn Gaston

FRENCH DRESSING

1 (10³/₄ ounce) can cream
   of tomato soup
¹/₂ cup vegetable oil
¹/₂ cup vinegar

¹/₃ cup sugar
³/₄ tablespoon
   Worcestershire
¹/₂ teaspoon salt

Mix soup, oil, vinegar, sugar, Worcestershire, and salt in a quart jar. Shake well. Will keep well if refrigerated. Add a bit of bleu cheese, if desired.

NOTE: Always salt and pepper salad before adding dressing.

Marguerite Oldenbuttel

POPPY SEED DRESSING

¹/₂ cup sugar
1 teaspoon dry mustard
1 teaspoon finely grated
   onion
1 teaspoon salt

¹/₃ cup honey
5 tablespoons vinegar,
   divided
1 cup salad oil
Poppy seeds

Combine sugar, mustard, onion, salt, honey, and 2 tablespoons vinegar in small bowl of electric mixer; beat well. Add oil, a small amount at a time, beating constantly. When all oil has been added and mixture is thick, add amount of poppy seed desired and remaining 3 tablespoons vinegar. Store, covered, in a jar in the refrigerator.

Christine Shields

"MOULTRIE" DRESSING

1/2 cup sugar	1 teaspoon dry mustard
1 teaspoon celery seed	1/2 teaspoon onion juice
1 teaspoon salt	1 cup vegetable oil (cold)
1 teaspoon paprika	4 tablespoons vinegar

Mix sugar, celery seed, salt, paprika, and mustard together in a small mixer bowl; stir in onion juice. Alternate 1/4 cup oil with 1 tablespoon vinegar FOUR times, while beating well. (This helps the dressing to thicken.) This is good on fruit salads, and also on ham steak. Just add a little before removing ham from pan. Store in refrigerator.

Anna Mayo

THOUSAND ISLAND DRESSING

1/3 cup of chili sauce	Dash of onion
1 cup of mayonnaise	1 tablespoon of chopped
1 tablespoon chopped dill	olives
pickle	1/3 cup of whipped cream
Sprinkle of parsley	

Mix all ingredients together. Store in refrigerator.

Alberta Mayo

ZESTY DRESSING

1/4 cup sugar
1/4 cup red wine vinegar
1 large clove garlic, crushed
1/2 teaspoon dry mustard

1/4 teaspoon salt
1/4 teaspoon Worcestershire
  sauce
1/3 cup vegetable oil

Put all ingredients except oil into blender. Start blender on next to highest speed. Remove top and slowly add oil. Blend 15 to 30 seconds. Chill until ready to serve. Serves 6. Easy.

Laura Strickland

SPINACH SALAD DRESSING

1/2 cup catsup
1 cup vegetable oil
3/4 cup sugar

1 medium onion, chopped
1/4 cup vinegar
Dash Worcestershire

Mix all ingredients together. Blend well. Store in refrigerator.

Lisa Fesperman

"MISS BESSIE'S" BLEU CHEESE DRESSING

2 cups mayonnaise
1 tall can evaporated milk
2 button garlic
1/2 teaspoon white pepper

1/4 teaspoon salt
6 tablespoons lemon juice
1/2 pound bleu cheese

Pour milk in ice tray and when crystals form, whip until stiff. Slowly fold in mayonnaise. Add lemon juice, salt and pepper. Mince garlic or run through press, and add to mixture. Lastly, add cheese broken into pieces about the size of one's thumb. Put into a jar and refrigerate. Let stand for several hours before using as this time allows flavor to go through dressing. This may be stored in refrigerator until all is used.

Acey Winge

PIQUANTE SAUCE FOR BROCCOLI

½ cup mayonnaise   **Dash Worcestershire sauce**
¼ cup horseradish
2 tablespoons Grey Poupon
   mustard

Blend all ingredients. Serve over steamed broccoli.

Coralyn Gaston

HONEY-MUSTARD SAUCE FOR HAM

3/4 cup mayonnaise
3 tablespoons honey
3 tablespoons prepared
    mustard, spicy-brown

1 tablespoon lemon juice

Combine all ingredients; stir well. Cover and chill for two or three hours. Makes 1 1/4 cups sauce.

Cindy Hitt

BARBEQUE SAUCE

1 cup brown sugar
1 cup lemon juice
1 cup prepared mustard
1 whole onion
1 pint vinegar

1/3 bottle Worcestershire sauce
1 stick margarine
1 teaspoon black pepper
1 teaspoon salt
Dash red pepper (optional)

Mix all ingredients together. Simmer for 1 1/2 hours. Remove onion. Cool. Refrigerate. In covered container, this lasts for weeks.

Betty Hopkins

RAISIN SAUCE FOR HAM

6 to 8 ounces raisins (4 tiny
    boxes)
1 cup brown sugar
15 red cherries
1 (8 ounce) can crushed
    pineapple

3 tablespoons ground
    cinnamon
1/4 teaspoon ground cloves
1 1/4 cups water

Boil raisins in water. Add sugar, cherries, pineapple, cinnamon, and cloves. Stir well. Serve with ham, either hot or cold.

Edmund Pedrick

BEST BAR-B-QUE SAUCE

1/3 cup vinegar
1 cup ketchup
2 tablespoons brown sugar
3 tablespoons
   Worcestershire sauce

1/2 teaspoon red pepper
1/8 teaspoon black pepper

Stir all together in small saucepan. Bring to boil over medium heat. Store in refrigerator any leftovers. Keeps indefinitely. Makes 1 1/2 cups.

NOTE: Excellent with ribs, shredded smoked pork, pork chops.

Sharon Goble

EASY HORSERADISH SAUCE
Serve with rare roast beef.

1 cup sour cream
1/4 cup prepared
   horseradish, drained

1 tablespoon white vinegar
1 teaspoon sugar
1/2 teaspoon salt

Mix sour cream, horseradish, white vinegar, and sugar. Goes wonderfully with roasted prime rib of beef.

Georgianne McGee

MOTHER'S COCKTAIL SAUCE FOR SHRIMP

2/3 cup chili sauce (Del
   Monte brand - can use
   catsup, but it will be
   thinner)
1/4 cup lemon juice

1 1/2 tablespoons prepared
   horseradish
2 teaspoons Worcestershire
   sauce
1/4 teaspoon Tabasco

Mix well. Makes 1 cup.

Mary Ann East

87

CUCUMBER SAUCE

1/2 cup mayonnaise
1/2 cup sour cream
1/3 cup drained, shredded
   cucumber

1 tablespoon fresh lemon
   juice, optional
1 teaspoon chopped fresh
   dill, optional

Mix ingredients. Especially good on salmon (baked or grilled). Keep refrigerated.

Jane Hart

CREOLE SAUCE

4 to 5 slices bacon, cooked
   and crumbled
1 small onion, chopped
1 bell pepper, finely chopped
2 stalks celery, finely
   chopped

2 tomatoes, peeled and
   chopped
1/2 teaspoon salt
1/4 teaspoon pepper
1/2 teaspoon sugar
Dash of Tabasco

Sauté onion, pepper, and celery in bacon drippings. Add tomatoes and heat to just before boiling. This is a marvelous sauce for seafood or meatloaf.

Cookbook Committee

SIMPLE GRAVY

1 1/3 cups water
1 teaspoon cornstarch
1 chicken or beef bouillon
   cube

Dash pepper

In small saucepan, combine water and cornstarch. Add crumbled bouillon cube and pepper; stir to dissolve bouillon cube; bring to boiling. Cook 1 minute. Makes 1 cup gravy.

Jane Hart

GINGER DRESSING

1 cup pineapple or orange
   juice
2 tablespoons cornstarch
1 egg yolk
3/4 cup sugar
Pinch of salt

1 tablespoon butter
Juice of 1 lemon
Powdered ginger, to taste
1 cup cream, whipped (or 8
   ounces Cool Whip)

Heat 3/4 cup juice. Mix remaining 1/4 cup cold juice with cornstarch. Stir cornstarch mixture into hot juice and cook until mixture thickens. Mix sugar and beaten egg yolk together and add to hot mixture. Cook until smooth. Add butter, ginger, and lemon juice. Cool and stir in whipped cream.

NOTE: This Ginger Dressing was served at the old Okefenokee Golf Club. It is delicious over fresh peaches, honeydew melon, catalope or any fruit in season.

Louise Kellam

JAKE'S CARAMEL SAUCE

1 pound light brown sugar
1 teaspoon salt
1 cup half and half

1/4 pound butter
12 marshmallows

Mix all ingredients in a double boiler. Stir until smooth over medium-high heat. Keep in well sealed jar. Warms over well.

NOTE: This recipe is how it was done about a 100 years ago - it doesn't get ANY better than this.

Lynn Sims Ford

HOT FUDGE SAUCE

4 squares unsweetened
   chocolate
2 tablespoons butter or
   margarine
2 cups sugar

1 cup canned evaporated
   milk
1 can Eagle Brand
   condensed milk

In double boiler, melt the chocolate and butter. Add sugar and evaporated milk. Cook until slightly thickened. Add condensed milk and cook over medium-low heat 20 minutes.

NOTE: Wonderful poured warm over pound cake or ice cream. Even better is a spoonful from the refrigerator as is!

Jane Hart

STEAK AND ALE'S HAWAIIAN MARINADE

1 cup pineapple juice
1/4 cup sugar
1/4 cup soy sauce

1/2 teaspoon garlic powder
   or garlic granules
Pineapple rings

Marinate boneless chicken breasts for 12 to 24 hours in sauce. Grill chicken over medium coals on grill. Put pineapple rings on grill to warm; then serve with chicken.

Lisa Fesperman

VEGETABLE MARINADE

3/4 cup red wine vinegar
1/2 cup oil
1 cup sugar

1 tablespoon water
1 teaspoon salt
1 teaspoon pepper

Bring all ingredients to a boil. Let cool. Pour over raw carrots, broccoli, cauliflower, onions. Cover. Refrigerate for four hours.

Cathy McGee

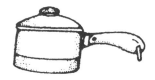

PESTO

2 cups fresh basil leaves,
thoroughly washed and
patted dry
4 good-size garlic cloves,
peeled and chopped
1 cup shelled walnuts or
pine nuts
1 cup best-quality olive oil

1 cup freshly grated
imported Parmesan
cheese
1/4 cup freshly grated
imported Romano cheese
Salt and freshly ground
black pepper, to taste

Combine the basil, garlic and walnuts in the bowl of a food processor -
or halve the recipe and use a blender - and chop. Leave the motor
running and add the olive oil in a slow, steady stream. Shut the motor
off, add the cheeses, a big pinch of salt and a liberal grinding of pepper.
Process briefly to combine, then scrape out into a bowl and cover until
ready to use. Makes 2 cups - enough to sauce 2 pounds of pasta.

PASTA WITH PESTO:
1 pound linguine or thick
narrow noodles such as
fettucine
1 1/2 tablespoons salt
4 quarts water
1/4 cup heavy cream
1 cup Pesto (preceding
recipe)

Freshly ground black
pepper
Freshly grated imported
Parmesan or Romano
cheese (optional)

Bring water to a boil in a large kettle or stockpot. Add the salt and then
add the pasta when the water boils again. Use a wooden fork or spoon
to stir pasta until all strands are under water. Boil rapidly until done to
taste; we like it tender but not mushy. (To test, occasionally lift and bite a
strand.) Stir 2 tablespoons of the hot pasta water and the heavy cream
into the pesto. Drain the pasta in a colander and return it to the hot pan.
Stir in the pesto and toss well to combine. Serve immediately on warm
plates. More freshly ground pepper is welcome, but additional cheese is
not really necessary. Makes 6 to 8 moderate first-course portions, 4
generous main-course portions.

(continued on next page)

PESTO TIPS: *When storing basil pesto and pistou in refrigerator or freezer, add a film of olive oil about 1/8 inch thick to the top to prevent sauce from drying out. Mix it in when ready to use. Always bring chilled pesto mixtures to room temperature before serving. *Before dressing hot pasta with pesto, add 2 to 3 teaspoons of hot water to pesto for better consistency. *Marble mortars and pestles are best for making pesto, but ceramic or porcelain can be used. Wood is fine for crushing dried spices and nuts, but should not be used for pesto. *When using a mortar, never fill to more than half its volume or the ground mixture will overflow. *Use a firm, circular motion with the pestle. For best results, grind ingredients against sides of mortar rather than against the bottom.

Georgianne McGee

BRUNSWICK STEW

**2 pounds pork Boston butt
    roast or pork shoulder
    roast**

Cut off all fat before placing in a pressure cooker. Cover with water and steam until very tender. Place in refrigerator for several hours until fat congeals on top; remove all fat. Return meat to the pressure cooker; steam until the pork can be shredded before adding the following:

**2 large onions, chopped
3 medium size potatoes,
    diced**

**1 (14½ ounce) can tomatoes
Season to taste with salt,
    pepper, hot sauce**

COOK UNTIL TENDER; THEN ADD:

**1 (15 ounce) can English
    peas (with its liquid)**

1 (12 ounce) can cream corn

Simmer on low heat approximately one hour; serve over individual slices of bread. Approximate servings: 25 to 30. Can be kept safely in refrigerator for a week.

Mary Dillard

DADDY'S BRUNSWICK STEW

1 chicken
2 pound beef roast
2 pound pork roast
3 quarts water
2 large onions, ground
1/2 cup Worcestershire sauce
1/2 cup vinegar

2 cups ketchup
1 teaspoon garlic powder
2 teaspoons salt
1 teaspoon black pepper
2 (14 1/2 ounce) cans tomatoes
2 (14 1/2 ounce) cans corn or
    creamed corn

Cook chicken in three quarts water. Reserve stock. Remove bones from chicken and chop into bite-size pieces. Chop beef and pork; brown in skillet. Put all meats in three gallon pot and add: chicken stock, onions, Worcestershire sauce, vinegar, ketchup, garlic powder, and salt. Add pepper, tomatoes and corn. Cook, covered, on low heat for 3 hours or longer, stirring often to prevent sticking.

NOTE: This was my father's recipe, perfected by him and enjoyed by all.

Julie Tomlinson

QUICK AND EASY BRUNSWICK STEW

1 (24 ounce) can of
    Brunswick stew
1 (10 ounce) can of barbecue
    beef or chicken
1 (10 ounce) can of barbecue
    pork
1 (12 ounce) can of whole
    kernel corn
1 (12 ounce) can of cream
    corn
1 (12 ounce) can of tiny
    green peas (optional)

2 (14.5 ounce) cans diced
    tomatoes
1 tablespoon vinegar
1 tablespoon lemon juice
1 tablespoon Worcestershire
    sauce
2 teaspoons seasoned salt
1/2 teaspoon salt
1/2 teaspoon pepper

Blend all ingredients in a large pot. Heat thoroughly - let simmer 20 to 30 minutes. Stir often to prevent sticking. Enjoy!

Cathy McGee

FAMILY SIZE BRUNSWICK STEW

1½ pounds ground chuck
¾ pound pork
1 slice smoked bacon
3 (14½ ounce) cans
   tomatoes
1 pound Irish potatoes, diced
2 medium onions, diced
2 (14½ ounce) cans cut
   okra, drained
2 (12 ounce) cans white
   corn, drained

2 (8 ounce) cans green
   limas, drained
1 clove garlic, diced
Tabasco
1 tablespoon vinegar
1 tablespoon Worcestershire
1 bay leaf
Salt and pepper, to taste

Grind chuck, pork, and bacon together one time. Salt and pepper ground meat and sear with the garlic in hot fat until brown. Stir in tomatoes, potatoes, onions, Tabasco, vinegar, Worcestershire, and bay leaf. Check salt and pepper and season to taste. Blend in okra, corn and limas. Cook in iron pot or a heavy pot that won't stick. Cook on low heat for 1½ to 2 hours. Stew should have a golden look when it is ready to serve. Add water from time to time, if needed. Stir often. DO NOT BURN!

Judge Ben Smith

GEORGIA CHILI

1 pound ground beef
Salt and pepper
1 onion, chopped
3 tablespoons chili powder,
  divided
1 tablespoon shortening

2 cups tomato juice
2 stalks celery, diced
1 green pepper, diced
1 (14 1/2 ounce) can tomatoes
1 (14 1/2 ounce) can kidney
  beans

Season ground beef with salt and pepper. Brown beef and onion, mixed with 1 tablespoon chili powder in the shortening. Add tomato juice, celery, green pepper, and remaining 2 tablespoons of chili powder. Simmer slowly for 45 minutes, or until vegetables are tender. (If mixture cooks down, add more juice.) Add tomatoes and simmer 15 minutes longer; then add kidney beans and simmer a few minutes more.

Eddie Rimes

CHASEN'S CHILI

1 cup pinto beans
5 cups of canned tomatoes
3 cups of chopped green
  pepper
4 cups chopped onions
1 1/2 tablespoons salad oil
2 cloves crushed garlic
1/2 cup butter

2 1/2 pounds of ground chuck
1 pound lean pork, ground
1 small can chili powder
2 tablespoons salt
1 1/2 teaspoons pepper
1 1/2 teaspoons cumin seed
1 1/2 teaspoons Accent

Mix all ingredients in large pot. Simmer, covered for one hour. Cook, uncovered, for thirty minutes. Serves 8 to 10.

Fran Lormand

ADRIATIC SEAFOOD CHOWDER
Harry's Seafood Bar, Venice, Italy

6 to 8 fish filets
2 tablespoons butter
2 stalks celery, chopped
1 medium onion, chopped
1/2 carrot, grated
2 medium potatoes
2 cups water

2 chicken bouillon cubes
1 tablespoon soy sauce
2 cans stewed tomatoes
1/2 teaspoon Jane's Krazy
   Mixed-Up salt
1 pound peeled, deveined
   shrimp

Broil salted fish filets in melted butter until almost done. Check for bones after fish cools. Put fish and any butter or juice from fish into saucepan. Cook onion, potatoes, celery and carrot in water with bouillon cubes, soy sauce and salt and pepper until tender. To this, add one can stewed tomatoes that have been chopped in food processor. Add Jane's Krazy Mixed-Up salt to taste. Last, add shrimp. Simmer until all flavors have blended, about 30 minutes. Serve with fresh fruit salad and saltines.

Genie Fesperman

OYSTER STEW
Feeds 75 people.

3 gallons whole milk
1 1/2 pounds butter (or
   margarine)
1/4 (5 ounce) bottle Lea and
   Perrins Worcestershire
   sauce

1 gallon medium oysters
1 teaspoon Tabasco sauce

Add white pepper to taste. Sauté oysters in frying pan until they curl, then add to heated milk in which the butter has been melted and sauces added. Do not let boil but serve hot with crackers.

Walt Miller

BAYSHORE DINER LOUISIANA SEAFOOD GUMBO

4 tablespoons butter
1/2 onion, diced
1/2 green pepper, diced
1/2 red pepper, diced
4 tablespoons flour
2 tablespoons gumbo filé seasoning
1 tablespoon tomato paste
1 quart fish stock or chicken stock
6 ounces Andouille sausage

6 ounces diced tomatoes, canned
3 tablespoons chili sauce
6 ounces okra
6 ounces shrimp meat
6 ounces cod fish, boneless
2 teaspoons Worcestershire sauce
1 teaspoon Tabasco
1/2 teaspoon cayenne pepper
1/2 teaspoon fennel seeds

Melt butter in a large soup pot. Add onions, green and red pepper and sauté for 3 to 4 minutes. Add flour and gumbo filé; cook for 5 minutes or until a little brown. Add tomato paste and cook for 3 minutes. Add fish stock and bring the whole mixture to a boil. Cook for 10 minutes at low heat. Add Andouille sausage, diced tomatoes, chili sauce, okra, shrimp meat and cod fish. Simmer at low heat for 20 minutes. Add the rest of the seasoning and adjust seasoning with basil, thyme, salt and pepper to taste. Yield: 8 to 10 servings.

NOTE: I searched for a good gumbo recipe from here to New Orleans, but this is as good as I have found and easy enough for me to do. I found it in California!

Jeanette Darden

CRAB SOUP

5 (10 3/4 ounce) cans cream of celery soup
3 (14 ounce) cans evaporates milk

1 pound butter (not margarine)
1 quart half and half (cream)
2 pounds of crab meat

Combine soup, evaporated milk, a pound of butter, half and half, and 2 pounds of crab meat together. Cook for 1 hour on low heat. Use 1 large pot. After cooking, enjoy!

Brett Miller

CRAWFISH BISQUE
Shrimp will work just as well - serves 4.

3 cups cleaned crawfish
1/3 cup cooking oil
3 tablespoons butter
1 cup flour
2 large onions, ground
1 stalk celery, ground
1 large bell pepper, ground
1 clove garlic, ground

41/2 cups water or broth
1 teaspoon salt (taste first, especially if using salty broth)
1/4 teaspoon red pepper
1/2 cup chopped green onion tops
1/2 cup chopped parsley

Make a dark brown roux with butter, oil and flour. (In Southwest Louisiana you don't have to say "brown". Any "roux" is brown.) You do this by stirring flour constantly in hot oil while it browns. When brown, add ground (or very finely chopped) vegetables. Stir well, partly cover and let simmer a few minutes. Add salt and pepper. Gradually add 41/2 cups boiling water. Stir until well combined and thickened. Simmer 15 or 20 minutes. Add crawfish. Simmer another 15 or 20 minutes. (If using shrimp, simmer only 5 or 10 minutes, just until done.) Add onion tops and parsley. Serve in bowls and let everybody spoon in as much plain, steamed, long grain white rice as they want. If you're using uncooked shrimp, use only 31/2 cups water. You can always add more if you need it. This is a thick soup.

NOTE: A real crawfish bisque, contains stuffed crawfish shells, but no self-respecting Georgia Cracker will get mixed up in that.

NOTE: Making a roux is a real pain. There's a fine line between not quite brown enough and scorched. Doing it in the microwave is easier, but still risky. After 34 years I finally found a roux mix that's as good as homemade. It's called Kary's (Dark) Dry Roux. 3 to 4 tablespoons Kary's to 1 cup liquid is just about right. If you're lucky enough to find some Kary's, soften vegetables in oil, then stir in dry roux mix, then liquid, and proceed.

Fran Spear Lormand

GEORGE'S SHRIMP SOUP

1 pound shrimp, peeled and
   headed
1 onion (baseball size)
1 green bell pepper
2 celery stalks
2 tablespoons fresh (or jar)
   minced garlic (do not use
   powder)
4 tablespoons butter
1/2 teaspoon black pepper

1/2 teaspoon cumin
1/2 teaspoon thyme
1 teaspoon Jamaican jerk
   spice
1 tablespoon salt
2 fresh tomatoes (skinned
   and chopped), or 1 can
   whole tomatoes
1 quart stock from shrimp

Make stock, put all shrimp shells (and heads if you have them) in 1 1/2 quarts of water; bring to good boil and let boil 30 minutes or more, allow to cool; strain out shells. While stock is cooking, cut onion, bell pepper and celery into pieces the size of your thumb nail. Take medium to large stock pot, sauté onion, bell pepper, and celery in butter until onion is almost clear. Add tomatoes and all dry spices, salt, shrimp and garlic; sauté/cook until shrimp is half cooked (a short time). Add water, allow to simmer 30 to 45 minutes, serve with rice.

NOTE: *Make stock, don't use plain water. *Do not use powdered garlic. *You can substitute scallops, crab, oysters for the shrimp or mix it up. *Do not attempt to substitute for jerk spice (Winn Dixie sells a Caribbean jerk spice that is very good). *This is made to serve with rice, if you want to eat it as a soup you may want to reduce the black pepper. *This will serve 2 to 4 persons, depending on how hungry they are. *This freezes well.

George Barnhill

AUNT DEAN'S CRAB STEW
Mary Dean Crawley's recipe.

1 quart milk
2 tablespoons butter
1 tablespoon flour
1/4 cup ground celery
1 tablespoon ground bell
  pepper

1 tablespoon ground onion
1 tablespoon ketchup
1/2 teaspoon salt
Dash Tabasco
Dash black pepper
1/2 pound crab meat

Melt butter. When butter bubbles, add flour; blend. Add milk. Simmer until smooth, stirring constantly. Boil together for five minutes in one-half cup of water the celery, bell pepper and onion. Combine all ingredients including seasonings and crab meat. Simmer together for five minutes. Serve hot with potato chips, saltines, or cheese crackers, pickles and olives. Serves 4.

Sue Clark

TROUT CHOWDER
Excellent as appetizer with crackers.

4 or 5 large filets of trout
1 quart water
2 large Irish potatoes,
  chopped
1 large onion, chopped
Salt and pepper, to taste

2 or 3 chicken bouillon
  cubes
1 1/2 quarts milk
1/2 to 1 stick margarine
2 (8 ounce) packages light
  cream cheese

Cover trout filets (skinned and boned) with the quart of water and boil until tender (15 minutes). Remove trout and keep stock. Cook potatoes and onions in the fish stock. Add salt and pepper and two or three chicken bouillon cubes. When potatoes get soft, mash potatoes and onions in pot with potato masher. Add flaked fish. Add milk and margarine. Heat well, but do not boil. Just before serving, add cream cheese. Mash with potato masher, but leave it lumpy. (This is the secret ingredient.) Serves 20 plus.

NOTE: If you plan to serve this from a crock pot, warm milk in it while you are cooking potatoes and onions. Then add that mixture to milk.

Genie Fesperman

OYSTER-MUSHROOM STEW

2 (16 ounce) cans oysters
1 (10³/4 ounce) can cream
   of mushroom soup
2 cups oyster liquid and milk
1/4 cup butter or margarine

1/2 teaspoon salt
1 tablespoon sherry
   flavoring (optional)
Paprika

Drain oysters and reserve liquid. Combine all ingredients except oysters and sherry in a 3 quart saucepan. Heat, stirring occasionally. Add oysters. Heat 3 to 5 minutes longer or until edges of oysters begin to curl. Add sherry. Sprinkle with paprika. Makes 6 servings.

Jewell Kopp

GOLDEN OYSTER STEW

16 ounces of oysters,
   undrained
1/2 cup chopped onion
1/2 cup diced celery
1/4 cup margarine or butter
2 cups sliced fresh
   mushrooms
1/4 cup all-purpose flour
1 teaspoon salt
1/4 teaspoon pepper (black)

2 cups milk
11/2 cups grated sharp
   Cheddar cheese
1 (10³/4 ounce) can cream
   of potato soup
1 (2 ounce) jar diced
   pimientos
1/4 teaspoon liquid hot
   pepper sauce

Remove any remaining shell particles from oysters. Cook onions and celery in margarine until tender. Add mushrooms and cook 1 minute. Over low heat, stir flour, salt and pepper into vegetable mixture. Add milk gradually and stir until thickened. Add cheese; stir until melted. Add oysters, soup, pimiento and liquid hot-pepper sauce. Heat for 5 to 10 minutes or until oysters begin to curl. Makes 6 servings.

Marie McDonald

CAMP CATFISH STEW

1 stick butter	1 bunch green onions
5 catfish	4 tablespoons flour
1 potato, diced fine	Salt
1 pint half and half cream	Pepper
1 quart milk	

In a large skillet, meal and fry catfish. When fish are done, remove and pour off grease; melt butter in pan. Add flour, brown, add cream and milk and potatoes. Replace fish in skillet. Simmer stew on low heat (bubbling) for awhile until fish separate from bones. Remove and scrape meat from bones into stew. Remove bones. Salt and pepper to taste. Add chopped green onions when done. Serve over toast, English muffins or biscuit.

Ben Smith

CATFISH STEW

1/2 pound bacon	5 or 6 large potatoes
3 pounds channel catfish	1 stick butter
4 large onions	

Fry bacon in 6 quart pot. Remove bacon (to be used later). Pour off most of bacon grease. In the remaining grease, brown about 1/2 onion, chopped up small. Slice potatoes and onions. To start stew, put 1 layer of fish cut in 2 inch steaks; then a layer of potatoes and a layer of onions. Salt and pepper. Begin another layer of fish, potatoes and onions and season. Continue this until all ingredients are used. Place bacon and pats of butter on top. Start cooking on simmer for about 1 hour 15 minutes or until potatoes are done. Serve with hush puppies and slaw.

Patty Mallard

BROCCOLI SOUP

2 (14¹/2 ounce) cans cream
    of potato soup
2 (14¹/2 ounce) cans cream
    of celery soup
1 cup milk
2 teaspoons Dijon mustard

1 teaspoon thyme
¹/2 teaspoon dry mustard
¹/2 teaspoon dried basil
2 (10 ounce) boxes of frozen
    chopped broccoli

Combine all ingredients in a large saucepan or crock pot and heat on medium temperature. Stir often to prevent sticking.

Lyn Gaston

ENGLISH BEEF SOUP

1 pound ground beef
2 medium onions, chopped
1 cup chopped celery
1 (14¹/2 ounce) can tomatoes
1 tablespoon Worcestershire
    sauce

1 teaspoon salt
1 (12 ounce) can V-8 juice
¹/2 cup uncooked rice
12 cups water
12 beef bouillon cubes

Brown ground beef and drain well. Mix together beef, onion, celery, tomatoes, Worcestershire, salt, and V-8 juice. Cook until vegetables are tender. Add rice and cook additional 30 minutes.

Lylburn Booker

VEGETABLE-BEEF SOUP

1½ to 2 pounds lean top
  round ground beef
1 package dry onion soup
  mix
1 (10 ounce) package frozen
  mixed vegetables
1 (46 ounce) can V-8 juice

Brown meat in Dutch oven. Drain off any grease. Add V-8 juice. Add frozen vegetables. Add onion soup mix. Bring to a boil. Simmer 25 to 30 minutes.

NOTE: May add chili powder, onion powder, pepper, to taste.

Nelle Pinson

HELEN'S CHEESE SOUP

2 cups potatoes, chopped
1 cup onion, chopped
6 cups water
1 pound bag frozen broccoli,
  cauliflower, carrot mix
1 (14½ ounce) can cream
  of mushroom soup
1 (14½ ounce) can cream
  of chicken soup
1 pound Velveeta cheese,
  cubed (lite Velveeta is
  good too)
Pepper, optional

In soup pot, mix water, potatoes and onion. Cook 10 minutes. Add frozen vegetables. Cook 20 minutes. Add cream soups and mix well. Slowly add Velveeta cubes. Stir until all of the cheese melts. Serves lots.

NOTE: This soup freezes well.

Mary Winn Pruet

CREAM OF POTATO SOUP

4 tablespoons butter
1 onion
6 to 7 medium potatoes
Garlic salt
Salt

Pepper
1 can cream of chicken soup
3/4 pound Velveeta cheese
1 1/2 to 2 soup cans of milk

Chop onion and sauté in melted butter. Peel potatoes and cut into small cubes. Add to onions and barely cover with hot water. Season with garlic salt, salt, and pepper. Cook until mushy. Stir in one can of cream of chicken soup. Cut cheese into thin slices and stir into mixture. Stir until cheese is melted. Stir in 1 1/2 to 2 soup cans of milk, depending on thickness desired. Correct seasoning. Heat until warm. Stir frequently as this soup sticks easily. May be made a day or two before serving.

Susan Engram

LEE PARKER'S CABBAGE SOUP
Good to freeze for a rainy day.

1 1/2 pounds ground beef
1 (10 3/4 ounce) can cream
    of tomato soup
1 (10 3/4 ounce) can celery
    soup
2 (14.5 ounce) cans
    tomatoes

1 package Lipton's dried
    onion soup mix
4 cups water
1 medium cabbage,
    shredded

Cook ground beef, do not brown. Add remaining ingredients as listed above. Simmer in oven or on stove for 2 hours. Serves 12. Preparation time: 20 minutes.

Ellen Council

NAVY BEAN SOUP

1 pound (2 cups) Michigan
   dry edible navy beans
6 cups water
1 pound ham hocks
2 cups water
1 bay leaf
4 peppercorns
3 whole cloves
1 cup coarsely chopped
   fresh spinach

1/2 cup chopped onion
2/3 cup mashed potato
   flakes
1 (28 ounce) can whole
   tomatoes
2 cloves garlic, minced
1 teaspoon basil
1 teaspoon oregano
1 teaspoon salt
1/2 teaspoon pepper

Place navy beans in a large soup pot with 6 cups water. Bring to a boil. Boil 2 minutes; remove from heat. Allow to stand 1 hour. Add ham hocks, 2 cups water and bouquet garni made from bay leaf, peppercorns and cloves. Simmer over medium heat 1 to 1 1/2 hours or until beans are tender. Stir in spinach, onion, potato flakes, tomatoes, garlic, basil, oregano, salt and pepper. Continue to simmer 20 to 30 minutes. Remove ham hocks and bouquet garni. Trim meat from ham hocks, dice and return to soup. Makes 3 1/2 quarts.

Jewell Kopp

TACO SOUP

4 chicken breasts, with
   bones
42 ounces water
2 (16 ounce) jars of picanté
   or salsa, mild

Cilantro or parsley
Mozzarella cheese
Corn or taco chips

Cook chicken in 42 ounces water. Cool and chop. Add picanté or salsa. Serve with cheese, cilantro or parsley and chips. (Chips on bottom, soup next, then cheese and parsley.) Can be frozen before adding cheese, parsley and chips. Serves 8 to 10.

Jean Hancock

CHILLED LEMON CUCUMBER SOUP

1 cup chicken broth
1 teaspoon salt
Dash garlic powder
1 teaspoon fresh grated
   lemon peel

2 tablespoons fresh lemon
   juice
1/4 cup chopped onion
1/2 teaspoon dill weed
   (double if fresh)

Combine broth, salt, garlic powder, lemon juice and peel, onion, and dill in blender and blend until smooth. To this, add:

1 cup plain yogurt   1 cup sour cream

Whirl this together a few times. Add:

2 cucumbers, peeled,
   seeded and chopped

Blend cucumber in by turning blender quickly on and off. Chill mixture one hour. Serve garnished with thin slices of lemon and cucumber. Yield: 4 to 6 servings.

Velma Bell

CURRIED CREAM OF CHICKEN SOUP

1 (14 1/2 ounce) can Campbells
   cream of chicken soup

1 soup can of milk
1 teaspoon curry powder

Blend or puree. Chill and serve very cold. A delicious "quickie".

Christine Shields

109

GAZPACHO

2 garlic cloves, minced
2 green peppers, diced fine
3 celery stalks, diced fine
1 onion, diced fine
3 cups tomatoes, peeled,
   seeded and chopped
3 cups chicken broth
1 tablespoon salt
1 teaspoon paprika

1/2 teaspoon cracked black
   pepper
1 tablespoon Worcestershire
   sauce
1 cucumber, diced fine
3 tablespoons lemon juice
3 tablespoons olive oil
1/2 cucumber, sliced

In a food processor, blend the garlic; half the green peppers, half the celery, and half the onions with the tomatoes. Pour into a large bowl. Blend in the chicken broth, seasonings, diced cucumber, lemon juice and the oil. Add the remaining green peppers, celery, and onions. Chill 24 hours. Pour into chilled soup cups. Garnish with sliced cucumber. Serves 6.

Pam Barnhill

NONE BETTER VICHYSSOISE

3 medium leeks, chopped fine
1 medium onion, chopped fine
2 tablespoons water
4 medium potatoes, peeled
   and sliced thinly

4 cups chicken stock
1 to 2 cups heavy cream
Salt
Pepper
Chives

Sauté leeks and onions in butter. Add potatoes and chicken stock and cook in pot for 15 minutes. Remove to blender, and in 3 stages, puree with equal amounts of cream to desired thickness. Add salt, pepper and chives to taste. Serve hot or cold. Serves 6.

NOTE: My children love this and I get at least 2 meals out of it - the first one hot (with Cheddar cheese on top), the next time I serve it cold. You can get by with 1 cup whipping cream.

Lynn Sims Ford

BLUEBERRY AND BANANA SOUP
(Kitty's Cream)

12 bananas
9 tablespoons lemon juice
18 cups apple juice
3/4 cup sugar
41/2 tablespoons cornstarch

11/2 teaspoons cinnamon
71/2 cups heavy cream
Blueberries, for garnish (I
    will bring)

In a food processor or blender, puree bananas with lemon juice. Place in a pot and bring to a boil with half of the apple juice. Add the sugar, set aside. Blend the cornstarch into the remaining apple juice. Add to the soup. Simmer for 2 minutes. Remove and chill. (This portion can be made ahead.) Add the cinnamon to the cream. Whip into soup. Add blueberries for garnish.

NOTE: This can be made ahead up to adding the cream. The cream needs to be added just before you serve.

Pam Barnhill

NOTES

Breads

Breads

ANGEL BISCUITS

5 cups self-rising flour
1/3 cup sugar
1 teaspoon baking soda

1 cup shortening
2 packages yeast
2 cups buttermilk

Dissolve yeast in 1/4 cup warm water. Combine flour, soda, and sugar; cut in shortening and stir in yeast mixture and buttermilk. Place in a greased bowl. Cover and place in refrigerator for at least 2 hours. When ready to use, roll out and cut into desired size. Bake at 450° for about 10 minutes, or until lightly browned.

NOTE: Dough will keep in refrigerator for a week.

Betsy Flanders

CRANBERRY BUTTER

2 sticks butter, softened
1/2 cup whole cranberry
** sauce**

3 tablespoons orange
** marmalade**

Whip butter, add cranberries and marmalade. Serve with hot breads. This is excellent for the holiday seasons!

BISCUITS

2 cups Bisquick
3 tablespoons shortening

1/2 cup COLD water

Stir Bisquick, shortening and water until well mixed. Spread cutting board with flour. Flour hands well and knead dough a few times until it is easy to handle. Pat out to 1/2 inch thick. Cut with small cutter. Bake on ungreased cookie sheet at 425° for 8 to 10 minutes or until light brown. Makes 27 to 28. (For freezing, place uncooked biscuits on cookie sheet and freeze until firm. Pack in plastic bags. Defrost and cook as directed.)

Caroline Herzig

CLARA'S BISCUITS

2 cups plain flour, sifted
1/2 teaspoon salt
4 teaspoons baking powder
1 teaspoon sugar

1/2 teaspoon cream of tartar
1/2 cup Crisco
2/3 cup milk

Combine flour, salt, baking powder, sugar, and cream of tartar and sift together twice. Cut in Crisco to a coarse crumbly mixture. Add milk at one time, stirring only until dough seems to follow fork around the bowl. Pour out onto a pastry cloth or board that has been lightly floured, and knead about one half minute. Roll out to desired thickness (1/2 to 3/4 inches). Cut with small biscuit cutter. Place on an ungreased baking pan, and cook in preheated oven at 450° for about 10 minutes or to desired browness. Additional tip: these are even better leftover. Slice while still fresh, and store in plastic bag. When ready to serve, add pat of butter and heat until crisp and lightly brown.

Sue Clark

OLD FASHIONED HANDMADE BISCUITS

6 cups self-rising flour
1 cup milk

1/2 cup shortening

Sift flour into a large mixing bowl. Make a well in the center and add shortening and half of the milk. Mix by bringing flour to the center with your fingers. Work the shortening into some of the flour. Keep the mixture wet and soft; add milk as needed. (You will not use all the flour.) Pinch off a portion of the dough, dip it in flour and then work it in the palm of your hand until smooth. Place biscuits close together on ungreased pan. Bake at 475° for 10 minutes or until golden brown.

NOTE: 1 cup of buttermilk may be used. If so, add 1/2 teaspoon of soda for 1 cup of buttermilk.

Arlie Nall

116

HONEY BUTTER

1/2 cup butter or margarine, softened

1/2 cup Georgia honey

Let butter stand at room temperature until softened. Gradually add the honey, beating until the honey is well blended with the butter. Keep refrigerated.

PEPPER BISCUITS
The pepper makes these biscuits special. Makes 12 biscuits.

2 cups sifted flour
1 tablespoon baking powder
1/2 teaspoon salt
1 tablespoon coarsely CRACKED black pepper

1/2 teaspoon soda
1/4 cup shortening (cut into four pieces)
3/4 to 7/8 cup buttermilk

Preheat oven to 450°. Fit metal blade in processor bowl. Sift together the flour, baking powder, soda, salt, and pepper and place in the processor bowl. Add the shortening cut into 4 pieces. Process 4 times using quick on/off turns. Mixture will resemble corn meal. With processor running, pour the buttermilk through the feed tube, processing 5 seconds. The entire amount of buttermilk may not be needed. Do not over process. Over processing and heavy handling of the dough will result in a tough biscuit. Dough should be soft and spongy. Remove dough to a lightly floured board and gently fold and knead 3 or 4 times. Pat or roll out to 1/2 inch thickness. Lightly flour cutter and cut out biscuits. Be careful not to twist the cutter. Place on a heavy baking sheet. Bake 10 to 12 minutes.

NOTE: Self-rising flour may be substituted - if so, omit baking powder, salt and soda.

Susan Sweat

CHEDDAR NUT BREAD

3 3/4 cups Bisquick
1 1/2 cups sharp Cheddar
   cheese, shredded
1/4 teaspoon salt

1 egg, slightly beaten
1 cup evaporated milk
1/2 cup water
1/2 cup pecans, chopped

Combine Bisquick, cheese, and salt. Set aside. Combine egg, milk, water and add to dry ingredients, stirring until moistened. Stir in pecans and spoon batter into lightly greased loaf pan. Preheat oven to 350°. Bake 55 to 60 minutes. Remove from pan and cool on wire racks.

Marie Carroll

DILLY-CASSEROLE BREAD

1 (1/4 ounce) package yeast
1/4 cup warm water
1 cup creamed cottage
   cheese, heated lukewarm
2 tablespoons sugar
1 tablespoon instant minced
   onion

1 tablespoon butter
2 teaspoons dill seed
1 teaspoon salt
1/4 teaspoon soda
1 unbeaten egg
2 1/2 cups all-purpose flour

Soften yeast in water, combine cottage cheese, sugar, onion, butter, dill seed, salt, soda, egg, and softened yeast in bowl. Add flour to form a stiff dough, beating well after each addition. Cover, let rise in warm place, until light and doubled in size (50 to 60 minutes). Stir down dough, turn into well greased 1 1/2 quart casserole; let rise in warm place until light (about 30 minutes). Bake at 350° for 40 to 50 minutes.

Amy Stewart

UNBELIEVABLE GARLIC BREAD

1 cup mayonnaise
6 cloves garlic, minced
3/4 cup grated Parmesan
cheese
1/2 cup grated Cheddar
cheese

1 tablespoon light cream
1/4 teaspoon paprika
1 loaf French bread

Mix mayonnaise, garlic and Parmesan cheese in a small bowl. In a saucepan, melt Cheddar cheese, cream and paprika, stirring constantly. Blend mayonnaise mixture into cheese mixture. Cut French bread in half, lengthwise. Toast lightly. Spread cheese on French bread. Broil in oven for 2 to 3 minutes. This mixture will keep indefinitely in the refrigerator in an airtight container. Serves 8.

Deborah Strickland

KHACHAPURI

Khachapuri is a very popular cheese bread eaten in Soviet Georgia. It is delicious served as a dinner bread or as a snack. This recipe is shared from a wonderful trip to Tbilisi, Soviet Georgia with the Friendship Force.

2 cups unbleached
all-purpose flour
1/2 teaspoon salt
1 1/2 sticks of cold butter
2 eggs

1/4 cup plain yogurt
2 cups of each Muenster and
Havarti cheese, mixed
1 egg yolk, beaten

Mix flour and salt in medium bowl. Cut in butter until mixture resembles coarse corn meal. Beat 1 egg and stir in yogurt. Add to flour mixture. Shape into a ball and chill for 1 hour. Grate cheese and combine with 1 beaten egg. Roll dough into a rectangle (about 12 to 16 inches). Spread cheese mixture on half of dough then fold the other half of dough over to enclose it. Seal and crimp the edges. Transfer to baking sheet and brush with beaten egg yolk. Bake at 350° for 50 minutes. Serve warm. Delicious!

Happie Stewart

MY BREAD

1 teaspoon sugar
2 packages dry yeast

1 cup warm water

In small bowl, sprinkle sugar and yeast over water and set aside.

1/3 cup sugar
2 1/2 teaspoons salt
1/3 cup shortening

1 cup boiling water
1 beaten egg
About 6 cups flour

Put everything but egg in large bowl and stir to dissolve sugar, salt, and shortening. Cool to lukewarm and add egg and dissolved yeast mixture, which should be bubbling up by now. Stir in flour. Knead well and let rise until double in bulk. Punch down and let rise a second time.* Punch down and knead again and shape in three small (or two regular size) greased loaf pans. Let rise again and bake at 400° for 20 minutes and at 350° for 15 minutes.

* The second rising will make a better quality loaf, but it can be omitted.

Eddie Mae Spear

PAT'S CHEESE BREAD

1 loaf French bread
Sliced processed Swiss
    cheese
1 cup melted margarine
1 teaspoon mustard (I prefer
    Dijon)

3 teaspoons lemon juice
1 tablespoon dried onion
3 tablespoons poppy seeds
1 teaspoon seasoned salt

Slice bread on diagonal, part way through. Place a cheese slice between each slice of bread. Combine margarine, mustard, lemon juice, onion, poppy seeds and seasoned salt. Brush each slice of bread with butter mixture. Wrap in foil and bake at 350° for 15 minutes or until cheese melts. May be made ahead and frozen.

Cathy McGee

PULL-APART SUPPER BREAD

3 (8 ounce) cans Pillsbury
  crescent rolls

1 stick margarine
Parmesan cheese, to taste

Melt margarine in Bundt cake pan in 375° oven. Sprinkle cheese into melted margarine. Place unrolled rolls in cake pan forming a circle. Pinch ends together. Bake for 30 to 35 minutes. Pull apart and enjoy! Great with chili suppers.

NOTE: Herbs may be substituted for cheese.

Joy Craft

TOMATO CHEESE BREAD

1 medium onion, minced
2 tablespoons butter
1/2 cup dairy sour cream
1/4 cup mayonnaise
4 ounces shredded Cheddar
  cheese
3/4 teaspoon salt

1/4 teaspoon pepper
2/3 cup milk
2 cups Bisquick
3 medium tomatoes, peeled,
  seeded and sliced 1/4
  inch
Paprika

Sauté onion in butter until tender. Blend sour cream, mayonnaise, cheese, salt, and pepper together; set aside. Stir milk into Bisquick to make a soft dough. Turn dough onto a well floured board; knead lightly for 10 or 12 times. Pat dough over bottom of a 13x9 inch pan, pushing dough up sides of dish. Arrange tomato slices over dough. Spoon and spread on cream mixture; sprinkle with paprika. Bake at 400° for 25 minutes. Let stand 10 minutes before cutting. Cut into squares.

Paula Stewart

SAUSAGE BREAD

2 loaves frozen bread
1 (16 ounce) package hot
  sausage
1 (16 ounce) package mild
  sausage
1 (16 ounce) package
  mozzarella cheese,
  shredded

2 tablespoons barbecue
  sauce
1 egg white

Thaw bread and let rise. Fry sausage together and drain grease. Let cool and mix with cheese and barbecue sauce. (Reserve some cheese for top of loaves.) Roll out dough flat. Spread sausage mixture over dough, using 1/2 of sausage for each loaf. Roll up dough like a jelly roll. Brush top of each loaf with egg white and sprinkle with reserved cheese. Bake on cookie sheet at 350° for 30 to 35 minutes. Makes 2 loaves.

NOTE: Eat it all up!

Patti White

BROCCOLI CORNBREAD

1 (10 ounce) package frozen
   broccoli, chopped and
   thawed
1 (8½ ounce) package
   cornbread mix
3 eggs, beaten
1 medium onion, chopped

1 cup (4 ounces) shredded
   Cheddar cheese
½ cup butter, melted
½ teaspoon salt
¼ teaspoon garlic powder
¼ teaspoon red pepper

Press broccoli between paper towels to remove excess moisture. Combine cornbread mix, eggs, chopped onion, cheese, butter, and seasonings; stir well. Stir in broccoli. Pour mixture into a greased 8 inch square pan. Bake at 375° for 25 to 30 minutes. Cool slightly and cut into squares.

Paula Stewart

JOY' CORNBREAD

2 eggs
1 cup sour cream
1 small (8¾ ounce) can
   cream corn

¼ cup oil
1¼ cup Martha White
   self-rising corn meal with
   hot rise

Mix together eggs, sour cream, corn, oil, and corn meal. Pour into a greased skillet and bake at 375° until golden brown.

NOTE: You may add chopped jalapeño peppers, pimientos, or sharp Cheddar cheese.

Landy Rimes

123

NEWELL'S CORN LIGHT BREAD

1 cup flour
2 cups self-rising corn meal
1/2 cup sugar

1/3 cup oil
2 cups buttermilk

Grease 1 loaf pan with bacon grease and place in 350° oven to heat while mixing bread. Mix all ingredients together and pour into HOT pan. Bake at 350° for 45 minutes to 1 hour, until brown. Remove from pan and cool on wire rack. Bread freezes well and is perfect with barbecue. This is a family recipe, served numerous times at my grandmother's and great aunt's home in Franklin, Tennessee.

Mary Ann East

OLD FASHIONED CORN BREAD

1 cup self-rising flour
1 tablespoon sugar
2 teaspoons baking powder
1/2 teaspoon salt
1 cup corn meal

1 1/2 cups milk
1 egg
4 tablespoons melted
   shortening

Sift flour, sugar, baking powder, and salt together. Stir in corn meal. Add milk, egg and melted shortening. Blend together and pour into a greased, hot iron frying pan. Bake in a hot oven (425°) for 25 minutes.

NOTE: May also bake in iron corn stick pan.

Jane Gillis

SPOON BREAD

3 cups milk
1 cup yellow corn meal
  (stone ground)
1 teaspoon salt

1 teaspoon baking powder
1 tablespoon sugar
2 tablespoons oil
3 eggs, separated

Preheat the oven to 350°. Heat 2 cups of the milk in a saucepan. When milk begins to simmer, add the corn meal and continue to cook, stirring until mixture is thick. Remove from heat and add salt, baking powder, sugar, oil, and remaining cup of milk. Beat the egg yolks lightly and add to corn meal mixture. Beat egg whites until stiff, but not dry, and fold into corn meal mixture. Pour into a buttered two-quart soufflé dish. Bake one hour or until well puffed and brown on top. Yield: 6 to 8 servings.

Mary Dean Lott Lee

BEST-EVER OATMEAL MUFFINS

1 cup quick-cooking oats,
  uncooked
1 cup buttermilk
1 egg, beaten
1/2 cup firmly packed brown
  sugar

1/2 cup vegetable oil
1 cup all-purpose flour
1 teaspoon baking powder
1/2 teaspoon baking soda
1/2 teaspoon salt
1/2 cup raisins

Combine oats and buttermilk in a large bowl; let stand 1 hour. Add egg, sugar, and oil, stirring well. Combine remaining ingredients, except raisins, in a medium bowl; add to oats mixture, stirring just until moistened. Stir in raisins. Spoon into greased muffin pans, filling 3/4's full. Bake at 400° about 18 minutes.

Deborah Stickland

BLUEBERRY MUFFINS

1 egg
1/2 cup milk
1/4 cup cooking oil
11/2 cups self-rising flour

1/2 cup sugar
Pinch of salt
1 cup fresh blueberries or 3/4 cup
  canned blueberries, drained

Beat slightly with fork, 1 egg. Stir in 1/2 cup milk, 1/4 cup cooking oil. Sift together and add 11/2 cups self-rising flour, 1/2 cup sugar, and pinch of salt. Stir just until moistened, will be lumpy. Gently blend in blueberries. Fill muffin tins (greased) 2/3 full. Bake at 400° for 20 minutes. Makes 12 muffins.

Cindy Coppage

MATTIE'S HUCKLEBERRY MUFFINS

1/2 stick softened margarine
2/3 cup + 2 tablespoons
   sugar
2 cups plain flour
2 heaping teaspoons baking
   powder

2 eggs, beaten
1/2 cup milk
1 pint huckleberries

Sift flour and baking powder, set aside. Beat butter and sugar; add beaten eggs. Add flour and milk alternately ... beginning and ending with flour. Fold in one pint (2 cups) fresh or frozen (if frozen, do not thaw) huckleberries. Bake at 375° for 20 minutes or until brown. Makes 2 dozen regular size or 4 dozen miniature size muffins.

Anna Fesperman

QUICK AS A WINK MUFFINS

1 cup self-rising flour
1 egg

Vegetable oil
1/2 cup sweet milk

Put flour in a small bowl. Stir one egg in a glass measuring cup; fill cup up to 1/2 cup line with cooking oil; fill cup up to 1 cup line with sweet milk. Combine liquid and flour. Pour into greased muffin tins. Bake in 375° oven for 10 to 15 minutes or until lightly browned. Yield: 12 muffins. These muffins are SO easy and SO good.

Bunny Winge

6 WEEK BRAN MUFFIN MIX

9 cups (15 ounce box) Raisin
   Bran flakes or fruit and
   nut cereal
2 cups sugar
5 cups flour

5 teaspoons baking soda
1 teaspoon salt
4 eggs, well beaten
1 cup oil
4 cups buttermilk

Mix cereal, flour, soda and salt in very large container. Add eggs, oil and milk. Stir to mix well. Store in covered container and use as desired. Batter will keep up to 6 weeks. Line muffin tins with paper liners - fill 2/3 full - bake at 400° for 15 to 20 minutes. May also bake in greased tins. Makes 7 to 8 dozen.

Jane Crawley

CORN MUFFINS

1 box Jiffy corn muffin mix
1/2 teaspoon salt
2 tablespoons flour (plain)
1 egg, beaten

1 pinch baking powder
2 tablespoons Mazola oil
1 cup buttermilk

Preheat oven to 375°. Grease muffin tins. Mix all ingredients. Pour muffin mixture into tins. Bake for 15 to 20 minutes until brown.

Deborah Strickland

POPOVERS THAT POP!

1 cup all-purpose flour,
  sifted
1/4 teaspoon salt
3/4 cup plus 2 tablespoons
  milk

2 eggs (room temperature)
1/2 teaspoon melted butter

Sift flour and salt; add milk gradually to make a smooth batter. Beat eggs until light. Add eggs to batter mixture, add melted butter; beat two minutes. Fill greased large muffin tins or custard cups 2/3 full. Bake at 425° for 30 minutes. Lower oven temperature to 350° and bake 10 more minutes. Makes 8 popovers.

Anna Fesperman

SOUR CREAM MUFFINS

1 cup butter (do NOT
  substitute), melted
1 (8 ounce) container sour
  cream

2 cups self-rising flour

Blend butter and sour cream. Add flour and drop by a teaspoon into ungreased miniature muffin pans. Bake at 450° for 15 minutes. Yield 2 1/2 dozen.

NOTE: For variations, top each muffin with dill weed, or poppy seed. Add 1 cup of sharp Cheddar cheese to mixture for cheese muffins.

Happie Stewart

APPLE CINNAMON ROLLS

1 teaspoon ground cinnamon
1/2 cup sugar
1 (8 ounce) can refrigerated
    crescent rolls
2 large apples (Granny
    Smith), peeled, cored and
    cut into 8 wedges

2 tablespoons butter, melted
1/4 cup orange juice

Preheat oven to 400°. In a small bowl, mix the cinnamon and sugar. Unroll crescent roll dough; separate into 8 triangles. Cut each in half lengthwise to make 16 triangular strips. Place an apple wedge on the wide end of each strip and roll-up. Arrange rolls in a 9x13 inch dish. Drizzle melted butter; sprinkle with cinnamon-sugar. Pour orange juice or water into baking dish but NOT over rolls. Bake for 30 minutes until golden brown.

Paula Stewart

BUNNY ROLLS

1 cup shortening
1 cup sugar
1 1/2 teaspoons salt
1 cup boiling water

2 eggs
2 packages yeast
1 cup warm water
6 cups flour

Pour boiling water over shortening, sugar, and salt. Blend and cool; add eggs. Dissolve yeast in warm water for 5 minutes then add to mixture. Add flour, blend well. Place dough in a large greased mixing bowl, cover, and place in refrigerator overnight or for at least 4 hours. About 3 hours before using, make rolls in desired shapes, using enough extra flour to make them easy to handle, place in greased pans, and let rise until double in bulk. Bake at 400° for 12 to 15 minutes. Brush lightly with melted butter while warm. Serve immediately. Yield: 10 dozen small rolls.

Bunny Winge

BUTTERFLAKE CHEESE ROLLS
Delicious for a luncheon.

1 cup chopped black olives
4 slices bacon, cooked and
  crumbled
1 cup shredded sharp
  Cheddar cheese
1 green onion, chopped

1/4 cup mayonnaise
2 to 3 drops Worcestershire
  sauce
1 dozen brown-and-serve
  butterflake rolls

Combine black olives, bacon, Cheddar cheese, green onion, mayonnaise and Worcestershire sauce. Pull rolls apart slightly, and stuff with cheese mixture. Place in muffin tins and bake at 375° for 15 to 20 minutes. Yields: 1 dozen.

Marguerite Oldenbuttel

BASIC YEAST ROLLS

1 package dry yeast
1/4 cup very warm water
1/2 cup milk, scalded
2 tablespoons sugar
3/4 teaspoon salt

2 tablespoons melted butter
1 egg, beaten
2 1/2 cups White Lily plain
  flour

Dissolve dry yeast in warm water. Add milk (which has been cooled to lukewarm), sugar, and salt. Let stand 5 minutes. Add butter and egg. Mix well. Stir in flour and beat until dough forms a ball. Place dough in large bowl. Brush top of dough with melted butter. Cover with waxed paper. Put in a warm place and let rise until doubled in size. Turn out on floured cloth and knead 1/2 minute. Shape dough into rolls, and let rise again. Bake at 400° for 10 to 12 minutes.

Eunice Burns

CAROLYN'S QUICK AND EASY ROLLS

1 package active dry yeast
  (2¼ teaspoons)
1 cup warm water
2 tablespoons sugar

2¼ cups flour
1 egg
3 tablespoons shortening
1 teaspoon salt

In mixing bowl, dissolve yeast in warm water. Measure flour. Stir sugar, half of the flour and salt into yeast. Beat with spoon until smooth. Add egg and shortening. Beat in the rest of the flour until smooth. Scrape down sides of bowl and cover with a cloth. Let rise in warm place (85°) until double, about 30 minutes. Grease 12 large muffin cups. Stir down raised dough. Fill the cups 1/2 full. Again let rise in a warm place until dough reaches top of cup (20 to 30 minutes). Heat oven to 400°. Bake for 15 to 20 minutes. Makes 12.

Elizabeth May

POTATO REFRIGERATOR DOUGH

1 package active dry yeast
1½ cups warm water (105°
  to 115°)
2/3 cup sugar
1½ teaspoons salt
2/3 cup shortening

2 eggs
1 cup lukewarm mashed
  potatoes (instant potatoes
  may be used)
7 to 7½ cups all-purpose
  flour

Dissolve the yeast in warm water. Stir in sugar, salt, shortening, eggs, potatoes, and 4 cups of the flour. Beat with mixer until smooth. Mix in enough of the remaining flour to make dough easy to handle. Turn the dough onto lightly floured board; knead until smooth and elastic, about 5 minutes. Place in greased bowl; turn greased side up. Cover bowl tightly; refrigerate at least 8 hours or until ready to use. Dough can be kept up to 5 days in the refrigerator at 45° or below. Keep covered. Punch down dough; shape as desired and let rise 1½ hours before baking. Heat oven to 400°. Bake rolls 15 to 25 minutes.

Landy Rimes

APPLE BREAD

2 cups sugar
1 cup vegetable oil
3 eggs
3 cups flour
1 teaspoon salt
1 teaspoon cinnamon

1 teaspoon soda
1 teaspoon vanilla
3 cups apples, chopped and
   peeled
1 cup nuts, chopped

Beat together sugar, oil, and eggs. Sift together flour, salt, cinnamon, and soda. Fold dry ingredients into first mixture. (Dough will be stiff.) To this, add vanilla, apples, and nuts. Beat well and pour into two (8x4 inch) regular bread pans that have been greased and floured. Sprinkle with sugar. Bake 1 hour at 350°.

Lisa Fesperman

AUNT CINDY'S BANANA BREAD

2 or 3 medium, ripe
   bananas, mashed
2 eggs
1 3/4 cups unsifted plain flour
1 1/2 cups sugar
1 cup chopped pecans, if
   desired

1/2 cup vegetable oil
1/4 cup plus 1 tablespoon
   buttermilk*
1 teaspoon baking soda
1 teaspoon vanilla
1/2 teaspoon salt

Preheat oven to 325°. Grease and flour a 9x5 inch loaf pan. Combine all ingredients in large bowl, mix well. Transfer to prepared pan. Bake until golden brown and splits slightly. DO NOT DOUBLE recipe. Yield: 1 loaf.

* I use whole or skim milk and add 1 tablespoon vinegar for buttermilk. Also, I bake in Bundt pan for 50 minutes or until it springs back when pressed on top.

NOTE: Barnes Ford's godmother from Tulsa sent this to me for the cookbook. I bet I've made 10 since she sent it - it's wonderful!

Lynn Sims Ford

BELGIUM WAFFLES

1 (¼ ounce) package dry
   yeast
2 cups lukewarm milk
4 eggs, separated
1 teaspoon vanilla

2½ cups sifted flour
½ teaspoon salt
1 tablespoon sugar
½ cup melted butter

Sprinkle yeast over warm milk. Stir to dissolve. Beat egg yolks. Add to yeast mixture with vanilla. Stir together flour, salt, and sugar and add to liquid ingredients. Stir in melted butter and combine thoroughly. Beat the egg whites until stiff and carefully fold into batter. Let the mixture stand in a warm place about 45 minutes or until mixture doubles in bulk. When ready to prepare, preheat waffle iron and use ⅞ cup of mix per waffle. Makes 5 Belgium waffles.

Landy Rimes

CREAM CHEESE DANISH

2 cans crescent dinner rolls
2 (8 ounce) packages cream
   cheese
1 egg, separated

¾ cup sugar
Juice of ½ lemon
1 teaspoon vanilla

Cover a large cookie sheet with aluminum foil. Open one can of crescent rolls, roll out on foil, and pinch together at slits. Beat together cream cheese, egg yolk, sugar, lemon juice, and vanilla. Spread on top of rolls. Place the remaining can of rolls over mixture, pinching slits together. Brush the top with egg white. Bake at 325° for 30 minutes or until golden brown. Let cool and cut into squares.

Sharon Moseley

C C C (CLIFFORD'S COFFEE CAKE)

2 ripe bananas
1/2 cup butter
1/2 cup brown sugar
1/2 cup granulated sugar
2 eggs
1 teaspoon vanilla
3/4 cup all-purpose flour

3/4 cup whole wheat flour
3/4 cup rolled oats
1 teaspoon baking powder
3/4 teaspoon baking soda
1/2 teaspoon salt
1/2 cup sour cream

Mash bananas to make a cup; set aside. Cream butter and sugars until fluffy. Beat in eggs, vanilla; add bananas, dry ingredients and sour cream, mix thoroughly. Pour in 10 inch pan sprayed with non-stick vegetable spray.

TOPPING:
1/3 cup brown sugar, packed
3 tablespoons flour
2 tablespoons butter,
    softened

1/4 cup chopped pecans

Mix all ingredients except pecans until well blended. Sprinkle topping over batter, then nuts. Bake at 375° for 25 to 30 minutes. Ice while still warm with below:

1 cup powdered sugar
1/2 teaspoon vanilla
3 tablespoons margarine or
    butter

1 to 3 tablespoons any
    flavoring you like

Deborah Strickland

LEMON-BLUEBERRY BREAD

1/4 cup plus 2 tablespoons
   margarine, softened
1 cup sugar
2 eggs
1 1/2 cups plain flour
1 teaspoon baking powder

Pinch of salt
1/2 cup milk
2 teaspoons grated lemon
   rind
1 cup fresh blueberries

Cream butter, gradually add 1 cup sugar until blended. Add eggs, one at a time, beating well after each. Combine flour, baking powder and salt, add to creamed mixture alternately with milk, beginning and ending with flour mixture. Stir in grated lemon rind, then fold in blueberries. Pour batter into greased 8x4x8 inch loaf pan. Bake in preheated oven at 350° for 55 minutes, or until broom straw comes out clean. Yield: 1 loaf.

TOPPING:

1/3 cup sugar

3 tablespoons lemon juice

Combine in saucepan and heat until sugar dissolves. As soon as bread comes out of oven, puncture top with toothpick all over, pour lemon mixture over warm bread. Cool bread in pan for 30 minutes.

NOTE: I adore this recipe. I bake it, freeze it, give it. May be made in miniature loaves as long as the fresh blueberries last. I consider this my best recipe.

Lynn Sims Ford

MAGGIE'S PERSIMMON OR PEACH BREAD

2½ cups plain flour
2 teaspoons baking soda
½ teaspoon salt
2 teaspoons allspice
2 teaspoons cinnamon
1½ cups butter or oleo

2½ cups sugar
3 eggs
2 cups persimmon purée or
  2 cups peaches
2 cups chopped pecans

Peel fresh persimmons, when in season, and purée in blender. (Puréed pulp may be frozen as is.) Sift flour, soda, salt, allspice, and cinnamon. Cream butter and sugar and add eggs and mix well. Gradually add dry ingredients to egg mixture, and also the thawed persimmon purée, and chopped pecans. Prepare 3 small loaf pans (9x5x2¾ inches) by greasing well and lining the bottoms with greased waxed paper. Bake for 1½ hours at 325° or until the top is firm. This may also be baked in a tube pan or 2 large loaf pans (9½x6 inches). Yield: 3 loaves.

Sue Clark

SOUR CREAM COFFEE CAKE

1 butter recipe cake mix
1 (3.4 ounce) box vanilla
  instant pudding
4 eggs
1 (8 ounce) container sour
  cream

½ cup oil
¼ cup white sugar
¼ cup brown sugar
1 teaspoon cinnamon
1 cup grated nuts

Mix together cake mix, pudding, eggs, sour cream, and oil. In a separate bowl, mix sugar, brown sugar, and cinnamon together. Add the sugar, brown sugar and cinnamon mixture to batter except for 3 tablespoons. Place batter in ungreased tube pan, sprinkle the remaining 3 tablespoons of sugar mixture on top of batter and spread nuts. Bake in 325° oven for 1 hour and 15 minutes. Check after one hour. Cake is ready when toothpick inserted comes out clean.

Susan Engram

STRAWBERRY BREAD

This bread is delicious any time of the year. The recipe makes two loaves - - one to keep and one to give away.

3 cups all-purpose flour
1 teaspoon salt
1 teaspoon baking soda
1 tablespoon cinnamon
1¼ cups oil

2 cups sugar
4 eggs, beaten
1 cup chopped pecans
1 (10 ounce) package frozen
   strawberries, thawed

Sift flour, salt, baking soda, and cinnamon. Mix oil and sugar. Add eggs, then flour mixture. Stir in nuts and fold in strawberries. Bake in two greased 9x5 inch loaf pans at 325° for one hour to one hour and 15 minutes.

Georgia Woodard

GRIDDLE CAKES

1¼ cups sifted all-purpose
   flour
2½ teaspoons baking
   powder
3 tablespoons sugar
¾ teaspoon salt

2 to 3 tablespoons wheat
   germ (optional)
1 egg, beaten
¼ cup milk
3 tablespoons salad oil

Sift together flour, baking powder, sugar and salt. Combine egg, milk and oil to dry ingredients all at once, beating with spoon or electric beater until smooth. Drop batter with a spoon on hot griddle which has been greased. Spread cakes out with a spoon. Cook on one side until puffed and full of bubbles; then turn over.

Pauline Hopkins

CALLAWAY GARDENS MUSCADINE BREAD

1/2 cup butter
1 cup sugar
2 eggs
1/2 cup milk
1 cup muscadine sauce

1/2 cup pecans, chopped
2 cups flour
1 1/2 teaspoons baking
  powder

Cream butter and sugar until light and fluffy. Add eggs, beating in one at a time. Sift flour and baking powder together. Add dry ingredients alternately with milk and muscadine sauce into the egg mixture. Stir in nuts. Bake in greased and floured loaf pan at 325° for 50 to 60 minutes, until toothpick inserted in center tests clean.

MUSCADINE SAUCE:
10 pounds VERY ripe grape
  hulls and pulp
9 pounds sugar
2 cups vinegar

3 tablespoons cinnamon
1 1/2 tablespoons mace
1 1/2 tablespoons cloves

Wash and pulp grapes, separating hulls and pulp. Cook hulls until tender. Heat pulp until seeds separate; run through colander to remove seeds; add to hulls. Weigh and use above stated proportions. Boil together with sugar, vinegar, cinnamon, mace and cloves until thick. Pour HOT into HOT jars, leaving 1/2 inch head space in each jar. Adjust lids. Process in boiling water bath for 5 minutes.

NOTE: The country store at Callaway Gardens sells muscadine sauce, as do other stores across the state. The telephone number is 1-800-280-7524.

Georgine Smith

MAPLE SYRUP
A tradition at First Methodist.

2 cups sugar
1 cup boiling water

1½ teaspoons Mapleine (or
maple flavoring)

Boil sugar and water until sugar is dissolved. Add Mapleine and cook slowly. Serve warm over pancakes or waffles. To keep this syrup for a period of time, add ½ cup light Karo syrup while cooking.

NOTE: This is a favorite recipe of Jack Lott. He makes this for the church pancake suppers. To prepare for crowd, always use 2 parts sugar to one part water.

Jack Lott

Vegetables

and

Side Dishes

Vegetables and Side Dishes

MIGHTY GOOD VEGETABLE CASSEROLE

1 stick oleo
1½ rolls of Ritz crackers, crushed
1 small onion, chopped
1 cup celery, chopped
1 (8 ounce) can sliced water chestnuts, drained
2 (16 ounce) cans Veg-All, drained
1 (10¾ ounce) can cream of mushroom soup
¾ cup mayonnaise
8 ounces sharp Cheddar cheese, grated

Melt margarine and mix with crushed crackers. Line the bottom of a 2 quart caserole dish with half the cracker mixture, saving the other half for the topping. Mix the onion, celery, water chestnuts, Veg-All, soup, mayonnaise, and cheese. Pour into casserole over cracker mixture and top with remaining cracker mixture. Bake at 350° for 25 to 30 minutes or until bubbly.

Patty Mallard

ASPARAGUS CASSEROLE I

1 stick butter
2 tablespoons flour
1 cup milk
¾ tablespoon Worcestershire sauce
1 tablespoon lemon juice
2 ribs celery, chopped
½ green pepper, chopped
1 pimiento, chopped or 1 (2 ounce) jar
1 (4 ounce) can mushrooms, undrained
12 almonds, chopped
2 (15 ounce) cans asparagus
Cracker crumbs

Melt margarine over slow heat. Add flour and stir until smooth. Add milk and stir over slow heat until mixture thickens. Mix well. Remove from heat and add celery, green pepper, pimiento, undrained mushrooms and almonds. Layer asparagus and cream sauce mixture. Top with cracker crumbs. Bake at 350° for about 30 minutes or until casserole bubbles and cracker crumbs brown.

Carol Harley

143

ASPARAGUS CASSEROLE II

3 (15 ounce) cans asparagus
1 (8 ounce) can LeSueur
   peas
1 (4 ounce) jar mushrooms
1 (8 ounce) can water
   chestnuts, drained and
   sliced

1 (10¾ ounce) can
   mushroom soup
1½ cups of grated cheese
1 (2.8 ounce) can French
   fried onions

Place a layer of asparagus in the bottom of a 2 quart oblong casserole. Add peas, mushrooms, water chestnuts, mushroom soup and cheese in layers. Repeat layers until all ingredients are used. Bake at 350° for 30 to 40 minutes. Then top with French fried onions and cook about 10 minutes.

Clyde King

"WINK'S FAVORITE CASSEROLE"

1 (11 ounce) box Tid-Bit
   crackers
1 stick margarine, melted
2 (15 ounce) cans garden
   green peas, drained

2 (15 ounce) cans cut green
   asparagus, drained
1 (10¾ ounce) can cream
   of mushroom soup
1 package slivered almonds

Crush crackers and soak in melted margarine; set aside. In a 2 quart casserole, layer peas, soup, almonds and crackers. Begin next layer with asparagus, soup, almonds and crackers. Repeat layers until all ingredients are used. Top with crackers. Bake at 350° for 25 minutes. Serves 6 to 8.

Nancy Lee

GREEN BEANS EXCELLENT

4 pounds fresh green beans
2 small onions, thinly sliced
2 tablespoons vegetable oil
4 (4 ounce) jars sliced
    pimiento, undrained

1 cup apple cider vinegar
1 cup vegetable oil
8 tablespoons sugar
4 teaspoons salt

Wash beans; remove ends. Cook in boiling water to cover 8 minutes or until crisp-tender; drain. Plunge into ice water; drain and set aside. Cook onion in 2 tablespoons oil in a large skillet over medium heat, stirring constantly until tender. Drain on a paper towel, set aside. Drain pimiento, reserving 8 tablespoons of liquid. Combine reserved pimiento liquid, vinegar, oil, sugar, and salt. - whisking until blended. Set dressing aside. Combine green beans, onion, and pimiento, add dressing, tossing to coat. Cover and refrigerate at least 2 hours.

NOTE: Can be made the night before.

Pam Barnhill

JERRY GAY'S BBQ BEANS

1 (53 ounce) can pork and
    beans
1/2 pound bacon
1 pound Polish Kielbasa
    sausage
1 small onion, chopped
1 small green pepper,
    chopped

1/2 pound dark brown sugar
1/2 (18 ounce) bottle
    barbecue sauce
Dash of Worcestershire
    sauce
Tabasco, to taste
Jalapeño peppers (optional)

Drain beans. Fry bacon and sausage. Then sauté onion and green pepper in drippings until tender. Add brown sugar, barbecue sauce, Worcestershire sauce, Tabasco, and jalapeño peppers. Mix all together with beans. Stir well. May be baked in a baking dish at 350° for 45 minutes, or simmer in a crock pot several hours. Serves 6 to 8 people.

Kim Gibson

BAKED BEANS FOR 75 PEOPLE

2 (114 ounce) cans baked
  beans
1 large large green pepper,
  diced
4 large yellow onions, diced
1/4 pound salt bacon, sliced
  in thin strips
1 (28 ounce) bottle Kraft
  smoky barbecue sauce

1/4 (6 ounce) French's
  mustard
1/8 (16 ounce) Liquid Smoke
1/2 (25 ounce) bottle South
  Georgia cane syrup
1/2 (32 ounce) package of
  light brown sugar
Salt and pepper, to taste

Mix beans, pepper, onion, bacon, barbecue sauce, mustard, Liquid Smoke, syrup, brown sugar, salt, and pepper. Cook in 375° oven for approximately two hours. Turn off oven and leave in oven until ready to serve.

Walt Miller

BEETS WITH PINEAPPLE

2 (15 ounce) cans tiny whole
  beets, drained (reserve
  liquid)
1 (20 ounce) can pineapple
  tidbits, drained (reserve
  liquid)

2 tablespoons cornstarch
2/3 cup sugar
2 tablespoons white vinegar

Combine reserved juice from beets and pineapple in saucepan with cornstarch, sugar and vinegar, stirring constantly until mixture thickens. Add beets and pineapple. Cook slowly for about 30 minutes. Serve hot or cold! Refrigerate leftovers. Can be reheated. Will keep for several days.

Jean Hancock

BROCCOLI CASSEROLE

2 (16 ounce) packages
   frozen chopped broccoli
1 (10¾ ounce) can cream
   of mushroom soup
2 eggs, beaten
1 cup mayonnaise

2 tablespoons minced onion
1 cup shredded Cheddar
   cheese
½ cup Ritz crackers,
   crushed
2 or 3 tablespoons butter

Cook broccoli in salted water for 5 minutes. Drain. Mix soup, eggs, and mayonnaise. Combine broccoli, soup mixture, onions, and cheese. Top with cracker crumbs. Dot with butter and bake at 350° for 30 minutes in a 2 quart casserole dish. Serves 8.

Mary Jane Lott

BROCCOLI RICE CASSEROLE

½ cup chopped onion
½ cup chopped celery
4 tablespoons margarine
1 cup uncooked rice
1 (10¾ ounce) can cream
   of mushroom soup
2 (10 ounce) packages
   frozen chopped broccoli,
   barely cooked and
   drained

1 (8 ounce) jar Cheez Whiz
1 (4 ounce) can water
   chestnuts, diced and
   drained

Sauté onions and celery in margarine. Cook rice according to package directions. Mix onion, celery, cooked rice, soup, broccoli, Cheez Whiz and water chestnuts together. Pour into 2 quart baking dish. Bake at 350° for 25 minutes or until bubbly. Serves 8 to 10.

Georgia Woodard

STIR-FRY CABBAGE

2/3 cup onion, chopped
1 clove garlic, minced
1/4 teaspoon ground ginger
   (optional)
2 tablespoons butter or
   margarine, melted

4 cups cabbage, coarsely
   shredded
1/2 cup grated carrot
2 teaspoons soy sauce
1/4 teaspoon black pepper
1/8 teaspoon paprika

Sauté onion, garlic, ginger in butter in large skillet for 2 minutes. Add cabbage and carrot; stir-fry over medium heat for about 5 minutes. Stir in soy sauce, pepper, and paprika. Serve immediately.

Jane Hart

GREEN BEANS INDIA

8 slices bacon, fried
1/2 medium onion, chopped
1/2 cup sugar
1/2 cup vinegar
3 tablespoons sweet pickle relish

1 (2 ounce) jar pimiento, drained
2 (16 ounce) cans French-style
   green beans, drained and
   rinsed

Fry bacon until crisp. Crumble and set aside. Sauté chopped onion in bacon drippings. Drain. Combine onions, sugar, vinegar, relish, pimiento, and beans. Mix together well. Pour into casserole dish and cover with foil. Bake at 275° for 1 1/2 hours. Remove foil and sprinkle crumbled bacon on top just before serving.

Cookbook Committee

STUFFED CARROTS

6 large carrots
1 teaspoon Durkees dressing
1/2 cup New York cheese, grated

1 teaspoon sugar
1 teaspoon Worcestershire sauce
Buttered bread crumbs

Clean carrots and boil until tender. Scoop out more than half of the cooked carrot and mix with Durkees, cheese, sugar, and Worcestershire sauce. Stuff carrot and top with bread crumbs. Bake at 350° for 15 minutes.

Amy Stewart

CARROT CASSEROLE

1/2 pound carrots
1 cup mayonnaise
1 tablespoon grated onion
1 tablespoon horseradish

1/4 cup grated Cheddar cheese
2 tablespoons buttered bread crumbs

Cook carrots until crisp and tender. Drain and reserve 1/4 cup of the liquid. Mix liquid with mayonnaise, onion, and horseradish. Stir in carrots. Pour into casserole dish and top with cheese and bread crumbs. Bake at 350° for 20 minutes or until hot throughout.

Georgianne McGee

CARROT CASSEROLE II

1 pound carrots
1 small onion, diced
1/2 cup grated cheese
Dash salt

1 cup mayonnaise
1 cup herb stuffing
Butter

Cook carrots until tender. Mash and add onion, cheese, salt, and mayonnaise. Blend well. Place in greased casserole dish, cover with herb stuffing, dot with butter, and bake at 350° until brown.

Sue Brown

149

PENNY CARROTS

2 pounds carrots, cooked
1 medium size onion
1 bell pepper
1 (10¾ ounce) can tomato
  soup
½ cup white vinegar

¾ cup sugar
½ cup vegetable oil
1 teaspoon dry mustard
¼ teaspoon salt
¼ teaspoon pepper

Slice carrots and cook in salted water until tender. Drain well. Cut up onion and pepper. In saucepan, combine onion, pepper, soup, vinegar, sugar, oil, mustard, salt, and pepper. Bring to a boil and pour over carrots. Let marinate overnight in refrigerator. Drain before serving or serve with slotted spoon.

NOTE: Note; This is an excellent, colorful, delicious side dish!

Binky Farris

CAULIFLOWER CASSEROLE

1 large head cauliflower
½ teaspoon salt
1 (10¾ ounce) can cream
  of chicken soup
1 cup grated Cheddar
  cheese

1 teaspoon curry powder
⅓ cup margarine, softened
¼ cup buttered bread
  crumbs

Break up cauliflower and cook 5 minutes in boiling, salted water. Drain well. Mix together the soup, cheese, curry powder, and margarine. Add cooked cauliflower and pour into 2 quart casserole. Top with bread crumbs and bake at 350° for 40 minutes. Serves 8.

Margaret Lott

CORN PUDDING AU GRATIN

2 tablespoons margarine,
  melted
2 tablespoons flour
1 teaspoon salt
1/4 teaspoon pepper
1 cup milk
1 tablespoon sugar

1 cup sharp Cheddar
  cheese, diced
2 cups canned corn (white
  shoepeg or niblets)
2 eggs
1/2 cup buttered bread
  crumbs

Melt margarine over slow heat. Add flour and stir until smooth. Add milk and stir over slow heat until mixture thickens. Add salt, pepper, sugar, and cheese. Stir in corn and slightly beaten eggs. Pour into casserole dish and top with bread crumbs. Bake at 350° for 15 minutes.

Mary Hood

PEG O' MY HARTS
Shoepeg corn, the family name, and an "oldie" song title combined to name this casserole - a favorite at the Hart house!

2 cups white shoepeg corn
  (canned)
1 cup American cheese,
  diced
2 eggs, beaten
2 tablespoons butter or
  margarine

2 tablespoons flour
1 cup milk
1 teaspoon salt
1 tablespoon sugar
1/8 teaspoon black pepper
Bread crumbs

Partially drain corn and mix with cheese and eggs. Pour into 11/2 or 2 quart casserole dish. Over medium heat, melt butter and stir in flour. Add milk. Cook until thickened, stirring constantly. Add salt, sugar, and pepper. Pour sauce over corn mixture and cover with bread crumbs. Bake at 350° until bubbly - about 25 minutes.

Jane Hart

JOE'S SAVANNAH GRILLED CORN

**Fresh corn that still has the
husk (green leaves)
around the ears**

Soak corn in a pan of water for at least an hour. Try to pull silk off first. When charcoal coals are white and ready for cooking, put ears of corn on rack about 4 inches above coals. Let cook for 1/2 hour, turning 3 or 4 times. To serve, pull the husk off for each person (or let them do it!). Serve with butter, salt and pepper. Be sure to soak it first! The water that seeps in really steams the corn. THIS IS DELICIOUS!

TIP: The fresher the corn, the sweeter the corn.

Joe East

CREAMED FRIED CORN

**4 large ears fresh corn
4 slices bacon
1 1/4 cups water
1 tablespoon sugar**

**1 teaspoon salt
1 tablespoon cornstarch
2 tablespoons cold water**

Cut just the tips from the corn kernels, using a sharp knife; scrape down the remainder of the corn and the pulpy liquid from the cobs with the back of the knife. There should be 2 cups. Cook the bacon until crisp in a 9 or 10 inch skillet over low heat; drain on paper; break into large pieces and set aside. From the skillet, drain off all but 2 tablespoons of the bacon drippings. Stir the corn into the drippings. Add 1 1/4 cups water, sugar, and salt, and bring to a boil. Cover and simmer for 20 to 25 minutes, stirring occasionally. In a small container, stir together the cornstarch and 2 tablespoons cold water. Stir until smooth. Stir into corn mixture, stirring constantly, bring to a boil and boil 1 MINUTE. Add bacon pieces. Makes about 4 servings. DELICIOUS!

Imogene Hatfield

SOUTHWESTERN CORN CASSEROLE

4 cups corn, drained
1 cup grated Cheddar
  cheese
1 (8 ounce) package cream
  cheese, softened

1 (4 ounce) can green chilies
2 teaspoons chili powder
2 teaspoons ground cumin

Mix corn, cheese, cream cheese, chilies, chili powder and cumin together. Pour into casserole dish and bake at 300° for 30 minutes. Serves 8.

Mary Kathryn Murray

EGGPLANT CASSEROLE

2 or 3 eggplants
2 tablespoons chopped
  onion
2 tablespoons chopped bell
  pepper

1 egg
1/3 cup bread crumbs
8 ounces sharp Cheddar
  cheese

Peel eggplant and boil in salted water until tender; drain. Mix eggplant with bell pepper, onion, and egg. Add bread crumbs to mixture; pour into casserole dish and cover with grated cheese. Bake at 350° about 1/2 hour or until cheese is melted.

Jane Crawley

CRAB AND SHRIMP STUFFED EGGPLANT

2 large cloves garlic,
    chopped
1/2 cup chopped onion (or to
    taste)
1/2 cup chopped celery (or to
    taste)
1 stick butter
4 large eggplants
3 cups milk
2 teaspoons salt
1/4 teaspoon pepper
1 tablespoon Worcestershire
1 1/2 cups Parmesan cheese
2 teaspoons dry mustard
2 tablespoons Dijon mustard
Dash Tabasco
1/2 cup sherry flavoring
4 eggs
2 cups bread crumbs
Juice of 1 lime
Large pinch mace
1 (2 ounce) jar diced
    pimientos
1 1/2 pounds crab meat (or
    imitation crab)
1 pound shrimp, roughly
    chopped
1 (14 ounce) can artichoke
    hearts, chopped
Lemon slices, for garnish
Paprika, for garnish

Sauté garlic, onion, and celery in butter. Parboil WHOLE eggplants for 5 minutes, turning often. Slice whole eggplant lengthwise and scoop out meat. Cook eggplant meat until done and mash. Combine eggplant, sautéed vegetables, milk, salt, pepper, Worcestershire, cheese, mustards, Tabasco, sherry flavoring, eggs, bread crumbs, lime juice, mace, pimientos, crab, shrimp, and artichoke. Turn into baking dish and bake at 350° until hot and lightly browned. Stuff mixture into eggplant halves and garnish with lemon slices and paprika.

NOTE: For extra "zip", may add Creole seasoning to taste.

Edmund Pedrick

TEXAS - COLORADO GRITS CASSEROLE

1 cup grits	1 (4 ounce) can green chilies
3 cups water	8 ounces Monterey Jack
1 1/3 teaspoons salt	cheese, grated
1 cup sour cream	

Cook grits in salted water as usual. Cook 2 minutes more, uncovered. Fold in sour cream and chilies. Pour 1/3 of grits mixture into a 2 quart casserole. Sprinkle with 1/3 of the cheese. Repeat these layers 2 times. Bake at 350° for 30 minutes. Let stand 10 minutes before serving. Serves 8.

Margaret Lott

BAKED CHEESE GRITS

3/4 cup quick or instant grits	1 egg, beaten
3 cups chicken stock	Salt and pepper
1 1/4 cups grated sharp	Pinch of garlic salt
Cheddar cheese	(optional)
1 tablespoon butter	

In a saucepan, cook grits in chicken stock following package directions. Lower heat; stir in cheese, butter, eggs, and seasoning. Continue stirring until cheese melts. Pour mixture into prepared casserole. Bake at 325° for 25 minutes or until golden and bubbly.

NOTE: Quick grits take only minutes to prepare. If you are a traditionalist and insist on slow-cooked "real" grits, prepare them the night before, mix with cheese and other ingredients and refrigerate overnight. Bake 10 minutes longer than called for.

Marie Groover Garrison

HORSERADISH MOUSSE

1/4 cup water
1 package (11/2 teaspoons)
   plain gelatin
1/4 cup mayonnaise
2 tablespoons onion, minced
1/3 cup bottled grated
   horseradish
1/2 teaspoon salt

1/4 teaspoon Worcestershire
   sauce
1/8 teaspoon white pepper
   (or a few dashes cayenne
   pepper)
1 cup heavy cream
   (whipping cream)
1 tablespoon parsley, minced
Small bunch watercress

Oil a 2 or 3 cup mold (or spray with non-stick cooking spray). Place cold water in top of a double boiler. Sprinkle gelatin over water and allow to soften 5 minutes. Meanwhile, combine mayonnaise, onion, horseradish, salt, Worcestershire sauce, and pepper. In mixer, beat cream until it holds a soft shape. Fold in mayonnaise mixture. Heat softened gelatin until dissolved. Cool. Add to mayonnaise mixture. Pour into mold. Cover with plastic wrap, pressing wrap into mousse to prevent skin from forming. Refrigerate 3 hours. Unmold onto watercress. Garnish with parsley. May be prepared 2 to 3 days ahead.

Georgine Smith

MUSHROOM 'TATER TOPPER

2 tablespoons olive oil
8 ounces fresh mushrooms,
   sliced
1 small red bell pepper, cut
   into 1 inch spears
1 large clove garlic, minced

2 tablespoons water
11/2 tablespoons lemon juice
Salt and pepper, to taste
2 medium-size potatoes,
   baked
Parsley, for garnish

Heat oil in skillet. Add mushrooms, bell pepper, and garlic. Toss over high heat until mushrooms brown lightly. Add water and lemon juice. Reduce heat to low. Cook and stir for 3 minutes. Season with salt and pepper. Split and fluff potatoes. Top with hot mushroom mixture. Sprinkle with chopped parsley. This will make 2 large servings or 4 small servings.

Jane Hart

156

MUSHROOM CASSEROLE

6 slices white bread
2 tablespoons margarine
1 pound fresh mushrooms,
  sliced
1/2 large onion, sliced
1/2 cup chopped green
  pepper
1/2 cup celery, chopped

1 (10 3/4 ounce) can cream
  of mushroom soup
1/2 cup Hellmann's
  mayonnaise
2 eggs, well beaten
1 1/2 cups milk
3/4 teaspoon salt
3/4 cup grated Cheddar cheese

Trim bread and cube. Sauté mushrooms, onion, pepper, and celery in margarine. Combine soup, mayonnaise, eggs, milk, and salt. Grease 2 quart casserole dish and place bread cubes in bottom of dish. Pour mixture over bread cubes and stir. Let stand in refrigerator overnight. Bake at 350° for 40 minutes. Cover with cheese and bake 10 minutes more.

Mary Hereford

BAKED ONIONS WITH ROSEMARY

6 large onions, peeled and
  sliced about 3/4 inch thick
3 teaspoons fresh rosemary
6 tablespoons unsalted
  butter

Salt and pepper, to taste
1/3 cup freshly grated
  Parmesan cheese
1/2 cup water
1 teaspoon paprika

Put the onion slices in large buttered baking dish. Place rosemary in between layers. Dot with butter. Salt and pepper as desired and sprinkle with half of the cheese. Add 1/2 cup water to the dish and cover with aluminum foil. Bake at 400° for 30 minutes or until onions are tender. Remove foil, add remainder of the cheese and paprika and bake 10 more minutes, uncovered.

NOTE: Vidalia onions are preferred!

Georgianne McGee

CHERYL'S EGGS AND ONION DISH

4 large onions, sliced
(Vidalia or sweet
Spanish)
2 tablespoons butter or
margarine
6 hard-boiled eggs, sliced
3/4 cup mayonnaise

1/4 cup milk
4 tablespoons grated
Parmesan cheese
1 teaspoon dry mustard
1/4 teaspoon salt
1/8 teaspoon cayenne
pepper

Sauté onions in butter until translucent. Arrange onions and eggs in layers in 9x13 inch casserole. Mix mayonnaise, milk, cheese, mustard, salt, and pepper together well and spread on top of eggs and onions. Broil 3 minutes or until lightly browned and bubbly. Serve immediately. This dish may be prepared ahead and broiled at the last minute. Serves 10.

Cheryl Monroe

VIDALIA ONION CASSEROLE

1/2 cup margarine
4 medium Vidalia onions,
sliced in 1/4 inch rings
15 saltine crackers, crushed
1 (103/4 ounce) can cream
of mushroom soup

2 eggs, beaten
1/2 to 3/4 cup milk
1 cup shredded sharp
Cheddar cheese

Melt butter in a large fry pan. Sauté onions over medium heat until clear. Reserve 3 tablespoons of cracker crumbs for topping and place remaining crumbs in the bottom of a lightly greased 2 quart casserole. Remove onions from pan with a slotted spoon. In the casserole dish, add soup and onions alternating layers. Combine eggs and milk and pour over onions. Top with cheese and remaining cracker crumbs. Bake at 350° for 20 or 30 minutes, until brown and bubbly. Serves 4 to 6.

Martha Mason

LO-FAT SPINACH PASTA

1 medium sweet onion,
  chopped
1 tablespoon olive oil
8 ounces Shitake
  mushrooms, sliced
2 cloves garlic, minced
Fresh herbs (basil and dill
  are good)

3 cups chicken broth
1/2 cup water
Juice of one large lemon
1 1/2 tablespoons cornstarch
10 ounces fresh spinach,
  washed and stemmed
1 pound linguine, cooked al
  dente

Sauté onion in olive oil until translucent. Add mushrooms, garlic, herbs, and 1 cup chicken broth. Bring to a simmer and add 1 1/2 cups more chicken broth, water, and lemon juice; bring to a simmer. Whisk together remaining chicken broth and cornstarch in separate container. Wilt spinach in simmering mixture then slowly add cornstarch mixture. Simmer until mixture thickens. Serve over linguine. Serves 6.

Rick Lynch

ENGLISH PEA CASSEROLE

1 stick butter or margarine
1 cup chopped celery
1/2 cup chopped bell pepper
1 cup chopped onion
2 (15 ounce) cans English
  peas, drained
1 (8 ounce) can water
  chestnuts, chopped

1 (2 ounce) jar pimiento,
  chopped
1 (10 3/4 ounce) can cream
  of mushroom soup
Ritz cracker crumbs
1/2 cup grated Cheddar
  cheese

Sauté in butter the celery, bell pepper, and onion. Combine vegetables with English peas, water chestnuts, pimiento, and mushroom soup. Pour into casserole dish, topping with cracker crumbs and cheese. Bake at 350° for about 45 minutes or until brown and the cheese melts. Serves 12 to 15.

Anna Mayo

BACON CHEESE POTATOES

8 to 10 medium potatoes
1/2 cup finely chopped onion
1 pound Cheddar cheese,
   cubed
1 cup mayonnaise

1/2 pound bacon, cooked and
   crumbled
Parsley (optional)
Paprika (optional)

Peel potatoes, place in saucepan and cover with water. Cook until tender, but firm; drain and cube. In a large bowl, mix potatoes, onion, cheese, and mayonnaise. Pour into an ungreased 9x13x2 inch baking dish. Sprinkle with bacon. Cover and bake at 350° for 30 minutes. Garnish with parsley or paprika.

Gloria Murray

HASH BROWN POTATO CASSEROLE

1 (32 ounce) bag frozen hash
   brown potatoes
2 (10¾ ounce) cans potato
   soup
1 cup sour cream
1 cup sharp Cheddar
   cheese, shredded

1/2 teaspoon garlic salt
2 tablespoons butter
1/2 cup grated Parmesan
   cheese

In a large mixing bowl, mix potatoes, soup, sour cream, Cheddar cheese, and garlic salt. Pour into prepared casserole dish. Dot with butter. Sprinkle Parmesan cheese over top. Bake, uncovered, at 350° for 1 hour.

Kim Gibson

ROASTED POTATOES

2 pounds potatoes
2 tablespoons olive oil
1 teaspoon salt

1/2 teaspoon black pepper
1/2 teaspoon rosemary

Cut potatoes into chunks. Toss in ziplock bag with olive oil, salt, pepper, and rosemary. Line pan with foil. Spread potatoes in one layer. Bake at 400° for 40 minutes. Stir after first twenty minutes.

Kalista Morton

PATRICIAN POTATOES

4 cups mashed potatoes
2 teaspoons salt
3 cups cream-style cottage
  cheese
3/4 cup sour cream
1 1/2 tablespoons finely
  grated onion

2 1/2 teaspoons salt
1/2 teaspoon white pepper
Melted butter
1/2 cup almonds, toasted and
  chopped

Cook potatoes in water seasoned with 2 teaspoons salt. Mash cooked potatoes thoroughly. (DO NOT add milk or water.) Press cottage cheese through sieve and mix with warm potatoes. Add sour cream, onion, salt, and pepper. Mix and pour into buttered shallow 2 quart casserole dish. Brush top with melted butter. Bake at 350° for 30 minutes. Place under broiler to brown top. Sprinkle with almonds. Serves 8.

Lou Turk

161

POTATOES SUPREME

12 medium potatoes, cooked
 and mashed
1 (16 ounce) carton sour
 cream
1 (8 ounce) package cream
 cheese, softened

1/4 teaspoon garlic powder
1/4 cup chopped chives
Salt and pepper, to taste
2 or 3 tablespoons butter

Combine mashed potatoes with sour cream, cream cheese, garlic powder, chives, salt and pepper. Pour into casserole dish and dot with butter. Bake at 350° for 15 minutes.

Isabell Lott

HOT!!! RICE

1 cup uncooked rice
Salt and pepper, to taste
2 (4 ounce) cans green
 chilies
1/2 pound Monterey Jack
 cheese, sliced

1 cup sour cream
1/4 cup Romano cheese,
 grated
2 or 3 tablespoons butter

Cook rice about 15 minutes, until barely tender. Add salt and pepper. Butter a casserole and add half the rice, a layer of green chilies, sliced cheese, and sour cream. Repeat layers until all ingredients are used. Top with Romano cheese and dot with butter. Bake at 350° for 30 minutes.

Mary Kathryn Murray

BAKED PUMPKIN

2 cups fresh pumpkin,
    cooked
2/3 cup sugar
1/4 cup butter, softened

2 eggs, beaten
6 ounces evaporated milk
2 teaspoons butternut
    flavoring

Drain and mash cooked pumpkin in colander. Combine sugar and butter, add pumpkin, beaten eggs, milk, and flavoring. Pour into 1 quart casserole and bake at 350° for 1 hour. Serves 6.

Marie McDonald

MRS. COOLIDGE'S RICE CASSEROLE

2 cups long grain rice,
    uncooked
1 stick butter, melted
1 (14 ounce) can chicken
    broth
1 (6 ounce) can frozen
    orange juice

1/2 teaspoon curry powder
1/2 cup white raisins (soaked
    in sherry flavoring and
    drained)

Combine rice, butter, broth, orange juice, curry, and raisins. Pour into 2 quart casserole dish. Bake at 350° until done, approximately 45 minutes.

Christine Shields

SAVANNAH RED RICE

1/4 pound bacon, chopped
1/2 cup diced onions
1/3 cup diced green peppers
1 cup water
1 (8 ounce) can tomato
    sauce

1 teaspoon brown sugar
1/4 teaspoon salt
1 cup uncooked rice

In a saucepan, sauté bacon, onion, and green pepper until tender. Add water, tomato sauce, brown sugar, and salt. Bring to a boil and add rice. Reduce heat, cover and simmer 15 minutes. Remove from heat and let stand, covered, for 5 minutes before serving. Serves 6.

Edwina Foster

REALLY RICH RICE

1 large onion, diced
2 tablespoons butter
2 cups cooked white rice
2 eggs, beaten
1 cup milk
1 cup shredded Swiss
    cheese

1/4 teaspoon salt
Pepper, to taste
Parsley and paprika, for
    garnish

Preheat oven to 375°. In a large skillet, sauté onion in butter for 5 minutes or until golden. Stir in rice, beaten eggs, milk, cheese, salt, and pepper. Pour into a greased 1 1/2 quart baking dish. Bake for 20 to 25 minutes. Sprinkle with parsley and paprika to garnish.

Paula Stewart

BROWN RICE

4 strips bacon
1 cup uncooked rice
1/2 green pepper, chopped
1/2 onion, chopped

1 (10 1/2 ounce) can chicken
and rice soup
1 soup can of water

Cook bacon until crisp. Set aside. Brown rice in some of bacon drippings. Pour into casserole. Sauté green pepper and onion in same pan. Add to casserole. Add soup and water to casserole. Cook at 350° for 1 hour, covered. Before serving, top with crumbled bacon.

Lylburn Booker

CHINESE RICE

1 pound bacon, cooked and
drained
1 pound sausage, browned
and drained
1 pound shrimp, cooked in
butter and garlic
1/2 head cooked chopped
cabbage
2 cups cooked rice
8 scrambled eggs

1 large onion, chopped and
sautéed in bacon
drippings
1 large bell pepper, chopped
and sautéed in bacon
drippings
3 large carrots, grated
(optional)
Soy sauce
Salt and pepper, to taste

Cook each ingredient separately. Drain in colander. In large bowl, mix all ingredients. Serve hot. Keeps well in refrigerator for several days. Serves 10 to 12.

Sharon Moseley

MEXICAN RICE AND CORN CASSEROLE

1 (10 ounce) package yellow
  rice, cooked
1 medium onion, chopped
1 (8 ounce) can sliced water
  chestnuts, undrained

1 (11 ounce) can Mexicorn
1 cup sour cream
1 (10¾ ounce) can cream
  of chicken soup
Grated cheese

Cook rice. Add onion, water chestnuts, Mexicorn, sour cream, and soup. Pour into a 9x13 inch baking dish. Top with grated cheese. Bake at 350° for about 25 minutes.

Sharon Moseley

ELEGANT WILD RICE

RICE MIXTURE:
2 packages R. M. Quiggs
  long grain and wild rice
1 (14 ounce) can beef broth

1 large box of fresh
  mushrooms, sliced

Cook rice as directed on package, using beef broth for part of liquid necessary. Set aside. Lightly brown mushrooms.

SAUCE:
½ cup butter or margarine
2 tablespoons flour
1 cup milk
½ teaspoon salt

1 (8 ounce) package cream
  cheese, softened
Parsley, for garnish

Melt butter, and stir in flour. Gradually add milk and stir over medium heat until mixture thickens. Add salt and cream cheese and blend until smooth. In a 3 quart casserole dish, spread the cooked rice. Mushrooms may be added to rice. Top with sauce. Bake at 325° for 20 minutes.

NOTE: After cooking casserole mushrooms may be spread down the middle of casserole and topped with parsley for garnish. The mushrooms and parsley make a beautiful presentation.

Coralyn Gaston

RICE CASSEROLE

1 cup uncooked rice	1 stick margarine
1 onion, sliced in rings	1 (4 ounce) can mushrooms,
2 (14½ ounce) cans beef	drained
consomme	

Place rice, onion, consomme, margarine, and mushrooms in a 2 quart casserole dish. Bake at 350° for 1 hour.

Susan Peterman

SPAGHETTI WITH GARLIC AND OIL

½ cup plus 1 tablespoon	1 pound spaghetti
olive oil	Freshly ground pepper, 6 to
2 teaspoons very finely	8 twists of the mill
chopped garlic	2 tablespoons chopped
Salt	parsley

The sauce can be prepared in the time it takes to bring the water for the spaghetti to a boil. When you've turned on the heat under the water, put the ½ cup oil, the garlic, and 2 teaspoons of salt in a very small saucepan. Sauté the garlic over very low heat, stirring frequently, until it slowly becomes a rich, golden color. Drop the spaghetti into the boiling salted water and cook until tender but al dente, very firm to the bite. Drain immediately, transfer to a warm bowl, and add the oil and garlic sauce. Toss rapidly, coating all the strands, adding pepper and parsley. Mix the remaining tablespoon of olive oil into the spaghetti and serve.

Irene Crawford

RUTH HARLEY'S BAKED SQUASH CASSEROLE

2 pounds small young yellow
   squash
1 cup milk
1 stick butter, softened
2 eggs

1 cup cracker crumbs,
   divided
1/2 cup slivered almonds
Salt and pepper, to taste

Cook whole squash until tender. Drain and mash. Stir together milk, butter, almonds, salt and pepper, and 1/2 cup crumbled cracker crumbs. Stir in squash and pour into casserole. Top with remaining cracker crumbs. Bake at 350° for 20 to 30 minutes.

Carol Harley

SOUTHERN SQUASH CASSEROLE

11/2 pounds squash
1 large onion
1/2 teaspoon salt
1/4 teaspoon pepper
1 cup grated Cheddar
   cheese

1/2 cup butter or margarine,
   melted
2 eggs, separated
10 or 15 crackers, crushed
   into crumbs

Cook squash and onion until tender. Drain well and mash fine. Combine salt, pepper, cheese, margarine, egg yolks, and cracker crumbs with cooked squash. Beat egg whites until stiff and fold into mixture. Pour into 2 quart casserole dish.

TOPPING:
3/4 cup crushed cracker
   crumbs
1/4 cup butter or margarine

1/2 cup grated Cheddar
   cheese

Mix cracker crumbs, margarine and cheese. Top casserole with mixture. Bake at 325° for 45 minutes.

Jane Gillis

168

JENNIFER'S SQUASH CASSEROLE

6 or 8 yellow squash, cubed
2 or 3 Vidalia onions, diced
2 or 3 tablespoons butter
Salt and pepper, to taste
1 (10³/₄ ounce) can cream
   of shrimp soup

1 (8 ounce) can water
   chestnuts, sliced and
   drained
Buttered cracker crumbs

Over low heat, sauté squash and onions in butter. Salt and pepper, to taste. Combine soup and water chestnuts with squash and onions and pour into a greased 2 quart casserole dish. Sprinkle crumbs on top and bake at 350° until hot and bubbly.

Nell Pinson

SUMMER SQUASH CASSEROLE

6 cups summer squash,
   diced
1/4 cup chopped onion
1 (10³/₄ ounce) can cream
   of chicken soup
1 cup sour cream
1 cup shredded carrot

1 teaspoon each salt and
   pepper (or to taste)
1 (8 ounce) package
   herb-seasoned stuffing
   mix
1/2 cup margarine (or butter)

Cook squash and onion in salted water for 5 minutes; drain. Combine chicken soup and sour cream and stir in carrot. Fold the drained squash and onion into this mixture. Add salt and pepper. Combine in another bowl the stuffing mix and margarine. Spread half of the stuffing mixture in the bottom of casserole. Spoon squash mixture on top. Spread remaining stuffing mixture over vegetables. Bake in 350° oven about 25 minutes. Serves 8 to 10.

Lisa Fesperman

SQUASH DRESSING

5 medium squash, grated
2 medium onions, grated
1½ sticks margarine,
   melted
2 eggs, beaten
1 (10 ounce) can cream of
   mushroom soup

½ cup self-rising flour
½ cup self-rising corn meal
Pepper, to taste
Grated Cheddar cheese
   (optional)

Mix grated squash and onions with margarine, eggs, soup, flour, meal, and pepper. Put in prepared 9x13 inch baking dish and top with grated cheese. Bake at 350° for about 45 minutes.

Susan Engram

SENATOR RUSSELL'S SWEET POTATO CASSEROLE

3 cups mashed sweet
   potatoes
1 cup granulated sugar
1 tablespoon vanilla

2 eggs, slightly beaten
½ cup butter or margarine,
   melted

Spray 2 quart casserole dish with Pam. Mix together sweet potatoes, sugar, vanilla, eggs, and melted butter. Spread into casserole.

TOPPING:
1 cup light brown sugar,
   packed
1 cup chopped nuts

½ cup flour
⅓ cup butter, softened

Mix brown sugar, flour, nuts, and butter together. Drizzle topping over top of sweet potato mixture. Bake at 325° for 20 to 25 minutes.

Jacqueline McCrary

SHREDDED YAMS

2 pounds sweet potatoes
(raw)
1 tablespoon salt
1 cup sugar
1/2 cup white Karo syrup
1/2 cup water

1 cup pineapple juice (or 6
ounce can pineapple
juice and 2 ounces of
orange juice)
1/2 stick margarine

Shred yams into one gallon water with 1 tablespoon salt. Mix sugar, syrup and water together to make a simple syrup. While syrup is cooking, drain and wash yams well. Put yams into 9x13 inch casserole. Pour fruit juice over yams. Then, pour syrup over yams. Dot yams with margarine. Bake, uncovered, in 350° oven about 35 minutes or until yams are transparent. Serves 12.

June Reese

SWEET POTATO SNOWBALLS

2 cups mashed sweet
potatoes
1/4 cup melted margarine
2 eggs
1/2 cup evaporated milk
3/4 cup sugar

Dash cinnamon, nutmeg, and
allspice
1 (10 ounce) bag
marshmallows
1 (31/2 ounce) can coconut

Combine sweet potatoes, margarine, eggs, evaporated milk, sugar, and spices. Beat until smooth. Cut marshmallows in half and cover with potato mixture. Then, roll potato balls in coconut. Place on greased baking dish and bake at 350° until marshmallow is melted. Remove from baking dish with spatula.

NOTE: This is GREAT for the holiday season!

Sue Brown

171

FRIED GREEN TOMATOES

4 medium green tomatoes	1 teaspoon sugar
1/2 cup flour	1 cup packaged seasoned
1 teaspoon salt, divided	dry bread crumbs
2 eggs	1/2 cup vegetable oil

Cut away thin slice from top and bottom of each tomato, discard. Slice tomatoes in 1/2 inch slices. Combine flour and 1/2 teaspoon salt in a small dish or on waxed paper. In a small bowl, combine remaining 1/2 teaspoon salt with eggs and sugar. Place bread crumbs in another small dish or waxed paper. Dip tomato slices into flour mixture, then egg mixture, and then bread crumbs, coating completely each time. Heat oil, add tomato slices, cooking on each side three minutes or until nicely browned. Add oil as needed. Serve hot.

Genie Fesperman

MARINATED SLICED TOMATOES

4 large tomatoes, peeled and sliced	1/2 teaspoon minced garlic
1/4 cup vegetable oil	1/2 teaspoon salt
1 tablespoon lemon juice	1/2 teaspoon dried oregano leaves

Slice tomatoes in thick slices. Arrange slices in shallow Pyrex dish. Combine oil, lemon juice, garlic, salt and oregano and pour over tomatoes. Chill for 6 hours or overnight. Good served with chicken salad.

NOTE: To peel a tomato for slicing, dip whole tomato in boiling water for a few seconds. The peel will come off very easily.

Pauline Hopkins

TOMATO PIE

1 (9 inch) pie shell, pricked
  with fork
1/4 cup Parmesan cheese
1/2 cup finely chopped fried
  bacon or ham
2 medium tomatoes, sliced

3/4 cup mayonnaise
1 cup grated Cheddar
  cheese
3 tablespoons onion, minced
Salt and pepper, to taste

Bake pie shell 5 minutes at 350°. Sprinkle pie shell with Parmesan cheese and bacon. Add tomatoes. Mix cheese, onions and mayonnaise. Spread on top of tomatoes. Bake at 350° for 30 minutes.

Edwina Foster

VIOLETTE KELLAM'S TURNIP GREENS

1 large bunch of turnip
  greens with roots
4 cups water
1/2 pound smoked or fresh
  pork or ham hock

3 tablespoons bacon grease
1 tablespoon sugar
Salt and pepper, to taste

Remove tough stems and roots of the turnips. Wash greens several times removing all sand and dirt. Peel turnip roots and cut into cubes. Boil meat in water until very tender. Remove meat from broth and add bacon grease, sugar, salt and pepper. Return broth to boiling then add greens. After they wilt, reduce heat to medium and cook about 30 minutes until tender. Add cubed roots and cook another 15 minutes until tender. Remove from heat and let sit in stock until ready to serve. Before serving, cut up using a large fork and sharp knife.

NOTE: This was a special dish at every "church dinner-on-the ground".

Nancy Kellam Witherington

ZUCHINNI CASSEROLE

3 cups zucchini, thinly
  sliced
1/4 cup spring onion
1 pound ground beef
2 cups cooked rice
1 cup (8 ounces) sour cream
2 cups shredded Monterey
  Jack cheese, divided

1/2 teaspoon garlic powder
1 (4 ounce) can green
  chilies, chopped and
  drained
2 teaspoons chili powder
Salt and pepper, to taste
2 or 3 sliced tomatoes

Sauté zucchini and onions in margarine. Cook beef and drain. Combine vegetables, cooked beef, rice, sour cream, 1 cup cheese, garlic powder, chilies, chili powder, salt and pepper. Top with sliced tomatoes and remaining 1 cup cheese. Bake at 350° for 30 minutes.

Margaret Lott

ZESTY ZUCCHINI

4 tablespoons butter
1 large onion, thinly sliced
6 small zucchini, thinly
  sliced
1 large tomato, peeled and
  quartered

1/2 teaspoon salt
1/4 teaspoon Greek
  seasoning
1/4 teaspoon black pepper
1/2 cup hot pepper cheese,
  grated

In a large skillet, melt butter and sauté onion until transparent. Add zucchini and cook for 5 minutes, stirring occasionally. Add tomatoes, salt, Greek seasoning and pepper. Cook 5 minutes more. Transfer to greased 1 quart casserole. Top with cheese and bake at 350° for 25 minutes until browned. Serves 6.

Sarah Harrell

ZUCCHINI AND TOMATO SKILLET

2 tablespoons olive oil
1 large Vidalia onion, thinly
   sliced
1 large zucchini, sliced in
   rounds

1 large or 2 medium
   tomatoes, chopped
Salt and pepper, to taste
1/4 teaspoon garlic salt
3/4 cup grated Cheddar cheese

In skillet, heat oil and sauté onion until wilted. Add zucchini and stir until well-coated and mixed. Place tomatoes on top. Sprinkle salt, pepper and garlic salt over tomatoes. Cover and cook 10 minutes on medium heat. Top with grated cheese and heat until cheese melts.

Edwina Foster

HOLIDAY MARINATED VEGETABLES

MARINADE:
3/4 cup salad oil
1 tablespoon cider vinegar
1/4 teaspoon garlic salt
1 tablespoon Dijon mustard
1 tablespoon Parmesan cheese

1/4 teaspoon dill weed
1/4 teaspoon pepper
1 teaspoon salt
1 green pepper, sliced

Mix oil, vinegar, garlic salt, mustard, Parmesan cheese, dill, pepper, salt, and green pepper for marinade.

VEGETABLES:
1 small onion, sliced
1/2 pound fresh mushrooms,
   sliced
1 (14 ounce) can artichokes,
   drained and sliced

1/2 cup celery, sliced
1 cucumber, sliced thin
1 cup mozzarella cheese,
   cubed
Bacon, crumbled to garnish

Combine onion, mushrooms, artichokes, celery, and cucumber. Pour marinade over vegetables and refrigerate several hours. Garnish with mozzarella cheese and bacon before serving. This is a wonderful buffet dish!

Betsy Clark

MINGLE-MANGLE MARINATED VEGETABLES

MARINADE:

3/4 cup vinegar

1/4 cup vegetable oil

1 cup sugar

1 teaspoon salt

1 teaspoon pepper

1 tablespoon water

Mix vinegar, oil, sugar, salt, pepper, and water in saucepan. Bring to a boil, stirring constantly until sugar dissolves. Cool and pour over well drained vegetables.

VEGETABLES:

1 (11 ounce) can white
  shoepeg corn, drained

1 (15 ounce) can English
  peas, drained

1 (14 1/2 ounce) can
  French-style green
  beans, drained

1 cup celery, chopped

1/2 cup chopped onion

1 (2 ounce) jar diced
  pimiento

Mix vegetables together in bowl. Pour marinade over vegetables. Marinate overnight in the refrigerator. Drain to serve. This keeps well for a week in the refrigerator.

TIP: Marinade vegetables in a large zip-lock bag. When ready to serve, snip corner of bag and drain!

Irene Crawford

VEGETABLES IN CREOLE SAUCE

1 cup mayonnaise
2 hard-cooked eggs, grated
1/2 medium onion, grated
1 teaspoon to 1 tablespoon
  Worcestershire sauce
Dash of Tabasco sauce
4 tablespoons vegetable oil
1 teaspoon to 1 tablespoon
  prepared mustard

1 (15 ounce) can English
  peas, drained
1 (15¼ ounce) can baby
  lima beans, drained
1 (14½ ounce) can whole
  blue lake green beans,
  drained
1 (2.8 ounce) can French
  fried onion rings

Mix mayonnaise, eggs, onion, Worcestershire sauce, Tabasco, oil, and mustard; set aside. In a 2 quart casserole, layer the peas, limas, and beans. Pour sauce over vegetables and bake at 350° for 20 minutes. Top with onion rings and serve.

Missouri Talley

177

BREAKFAST CASSEROLE SUPREME

10 slices white bread
1 pound ground sausage
2 cups sharp shredded
   cheese
2 cups mild shredded cheese

3/4 teaspoon dry mustard
3 cups milk
6 eggs
1/2 teaspoon salt
1/4 teaspoon white pepper

Remove crust from bread; cut into squares. Fry sausage and drain well. Arrange half of bread squares in bottom of lightly greased 13x9 inch casserole. Top with sharp cheese, then sausage, remaining bread squares and then mild cheese. Dissolve mustard in a little of the milk. Beat eggs, add milk, mustard, salt and pepper. Pour mixture over layers. Cover and refrigerate overnight. Bake, uncovered, in a 350° oven for 1 hour or until firm and browned.

Dot Gibson

CHEESE ASPARAGUS STRATA

24 slices white bread
2 (10 ounce) packages
   frozen asparagus, thawed
   (or 2 cans, drained)
4 cups shredded Cheddar
   cheese
1 (4 ounce) jar diced
   pimiento, drained

10 eggs, beaten
6 cups milk
1/2 cup finely chopped onion
2 tablespoons prepared
   mustard
1 teaspoon salt
1/2 teaspoon pepper

Trim crust from bread. Lightly grease two 13x9 inch casseroles. Line the bottom of each with 6 slices of bread. Cut asparagus in 1 inch pieces. Put asparagus, cheese and pimiento evenly over bread in each casserole. Put rest of bread slices on top. Mix eggs, milk, onion, mustard, salt and pepper. Pour 1/2 mixture on each casserole. Refrigerate overnight or up to 24 hours. Bake, uncovered, at 325° for 1 hour. Serves 12.

NOTE: Mother prepared this for Remington's christening.

Mary Ann East

CHEESE PUFF CASSEROLE

4 tablespoons butter or
    margarine
4 tablespoons flour
1 cup milk
1/2 teaspoon salt

1 cup grated American
    cheese, packed firmly
4 egg yolks
4 egg whites, stiffly beaten

Make a cream sauce of butter, flour and milk, adding salt and cheese, stirring until cheese is melted. Remove from heat. Allow to cool slightly and add egg yolks which have been well beaten. Set aside and allow to cool until lukewarm. Then, gently fold in stiffly beaten egg whites, combining thoroughly. Pour into 3 quart casserole. Place dish in a pan of water and bake at 300° for 40 minutes. Remove from oven and allow to cool. (It may be kept in refrigerator overnight or frozen for several days.) Before serving, thaw thoroughly and return to 300° oven, again in the pan of water and bake for 20 minutes more. Serve immediately. Serves 6.

NOTE: This dish is great for a brunch, breakfast, or luncheon. It may be served as is or with cream sauce of chicken, ham, or seafood. It is similar to a soufflé, but the second cooking makes the top crunch and easier to serve to a crowd.

Sue Clark

CHEESE SOUFFLÉ

2 tablespoons melted butter
2 tablespoons flour
1 cup milk
1/4 teaspoon salt
Pinch of paprika

3/4 cup grated Cheddar
    cheese
4 egg yolks, beaten
4 egg whites, beaten until
    stiff and dry

Rub butter in flour until smooth. Add milk, salt, and paprika. Cook sauce until it begins to thicken. Add cheese and beaten egg yolks; mix thoroughly. When mixture has cooled slightly, fold in stiffly beaten egg whites. Bake in buttered casserole about 30 minutes in moderate oven.

Eddie Mae Spear

179

CHILI EGG PUFF

10 eggs
1/2 cup flour
1 teaspoon baking powder
1/2 teaspoon salt
1 pint small curd cottage
   cheese

1 pound Monterey Jack
   cheese, shredded
1/2 cup margarine, melted
2 (4 ounce) cans of mild
   diced green chilies,
   undrained

Beat eggs until light and lemon colored. Add flour, baking powder, salt, cottage cheese, Monterey Jack cheese, margarine, and chilies. Pour into buttered 9x13 inch baking dish. Bake at 350° for 35 minutes. Serves 10 to 12.

Deborah Strickland

GOOD EGG CASSEROLE FOR BRUNCH OR LUNCH

1/2 cup chopped onion
2 tablespoons butter or
   margarine
2 tablespoons flour
1 1/4 cups milk
1 cup grated sharp Cheddar
   cheese

6 hard-boiled eggs
1 1/2 cups crushed potato
   chips
12 slices bacon, cooked

Sauté onion in butter. Add flour, milk and cheese making a sauce. Stir until thickened. In buttered casserole, layer half the eggs, cheese sauce, potato chips, and bacon. Repeat layers until all is used. Bake at 350° for 30 minutes.

Madge Herrin

WORLD'S BEST MACARONI AND CHEESE

1 cup raw macaroni (salt
    after cooking)
1 pound sharp Cheddar
    cheese, grated
1½ cups milk
2 teaspoons butter or
    margarine

1 teaspoon prepared
    mustard
5 eggs, beaten
Salt and pepper, to taste

Cook macaroni. Drain off liquid and add butter while hot. Stir together milk, eggs, cheese, mustard, salt, and pepper. Mix with macaroni and pour into 1 quart flat, 8 inch square baking dish. Top with some of the grated cheese. Bake at 350° about 30 minutes.

NOTE: This was my grandmother's recipe. It is everyone's favorite.

Anne Fesperman

BASIC QUICHE

4 eggs, beaten   1/8 teaspoon pepper
2 cups light cream   1 partially cooked pie shell
1/2 teaspoon salt

Combine eggs, cream, salt, and pepper. Pour over layered fillings in pie shell. Bake at 425° for 15 minutes, then lower oven temperature to 350° and continue cooking for 30 more minutes or until knife inserted in center comes out clean.

QUICHE LORRAINE FILLING:
10 slices bacon, cooked   1/8 teaspoon nutmeg
    crisp and crumbled
11/4 cups grated Swiss
    cheese

SPINACH QUICHE FILLING:
1/2 cup grated Swiss cheese   2 tablespoons onions,
1 cup cooked spinach,   sautéed in 1 tablespoon
    chopped and drained   butter

Add spinach and onion to custard recipe.

HAM AND CHEESE QUICHE FILLING:
2 tablespoons prepared   3/4 cup grated Swiss cheese
    mustard
1/4 or 1/2 cup cooked ham,
    diced

Paint mustard on bottom of pie shell. Add ham and cheese, then add custard recipe.

NOTE: For more variations on a quiche theme, try 11/2 cups of cooked vegetables, slices of ham, sausage, or seafood combinations.

Susan Sweat

Seafood

Seafood

SMOKED WHOLE ATLANTIC SALMON

1 (3 to 4 pound) whole
   salmon, cleaned
Salt
Fresh dill with stems
Mild vegetable oil
2 cups white wine
2 cups water

3 or 4 bay leaves
1/2 cup assorted fresh herbs
   (rosemary, basil,
   oregano, marjoram)
Cream cheese
Fresh dill, for garnish

Soak hickory wood chips in water for 30 minutes. Meanwhile, start the smoker and regulate the temperature to 170° to 190°. Rinse the salmon well and salt the inside. Let it sit, chilled, for 20 to 30 minutes, then rinse out the salt. Stuff the fish with dill and oil the outside well on both sides. Cover the tail and head with aluminum foil. Lay the water-soaked wood over the charcoal fire. Put the wine, water and herbs in a metal bowl and place on a rack under the fish. Place the fish on the top rack of the smoker. Close the smoker. Smoke about 2 hours, until the flesh is pink and firm to the touch. Using spatulas, carefully lift salmon from the smoker. Chill until the flesh is firm and cold. To serve, peel back the top skin and let people pull the meat from the bones. Serve with cream cheese and fresh dill. Makes 8 servings.

Georgianne McGee

GRILLED SALMON

1/4 cup firmly packed brown
   sugar
1/4 cup butter, melted
2 tablespoons soy sauce

2 tablespoons sherry
   flavoring
1 1/2 pound salmon fillet (or 4
   salmon steaks)

Combine brown sugar, butter, soy sauce and flavoring, stirring until sugar dissolves. Place salmon in a shallow dish, add marinade and chill for 1 hour. Remove from marinade. Grill 5 to 8 minutes per side or broil in oven for 5 minutes on each side. Yield: 4 servings.

Coralyn Gaston

BAKED SALMON WITH DILL SAUCE

Salmon fillets or steaks   **Lemon juice**
Melted butter

Place salmon fillets or steaks on a well greased broiler pan (line pan with aluminum foil for a quick and easy clean-up). Brush fish with melted butter and squeeze lemon juice on fillets; lightly salt. Bake at 450° for 7 minutes. DO NOT turn fish during baking. Serve with Dill Sauce.

DILL SAUCE:
1/2 cup mayonnaise   **1 tablespoon lemon juice**
1 teaspoon dill weed   **1 tablespoon milk**
1/2 teaspoon sugar   **Salt and pepper, to taste**
1/4 cup sour cream

Combine mayonnaise, dill weed, sugar, sour cream, lemon juice, milk, salt, and pepper until smooth. Refrigerate until ready to use. Delicious with seafood.

Jim Winge

"LIGHT AS A FEATHER" SALMON CROQUETTES

1 (14³/4 ounce) can red   **2 eggs, beaten**
**   salmon, drained and**   **1/2 cup buttermilk**
**   de-boned**   **1/2 cup flour**
Salt and pepper, to taste   **1/4 teaspoon soda**

Mix salmon, salt, pepper and eggs together. Add buttermilk. Sift flour with soda and mix into salmon. Drop batter from spoon into hot shortening. Fry until golden brown. Drain on paper towels. Buttermilk is the secret to lighter, fluffier croquettes. Yield: 8 to 10 croquettes.

Jane Hart

SALMON LOAF

1 large can salmon,
undrained, but flaked
1½ cups poultry stuffing
(Pepperidge)
¼ cup minced celery

2 tablespoons minced onion
Lemon juice (1 lemon)
2 eggs, slightly beaten
1 can condensed mushroom
soup

Mix and place in lightly greased glass loaf pan. Bake at 350° for 45 minutes. Let sit a few minutes before serving.

Pauline Hopkins

RED SNAPPER IN DILL SAUCE

2 pound fillet of red
snapper, or other firm fish
¾ teaspoon salt
½ teaspoon fresh ground
pepper
½ cup olive oil
1½ tablespoons parsley,
minced

2 tablespoons shallots or
green onions, minced
2 tablespoons snipped fresh
dill or ½ teaspoon dried
dill
¼ teaspoon oregano
½ cup fresh lemon juice

Wipe fish with damp cloth. Sprinkle both sides with salt and pepper. Arrange in single layer in an oiled baking dish. Sprinkle with oil, parsley, shallots, dill, and oregano. Bake at 350° until flesh separates when tested with a dinner knife, 15 to 25 minutes, depending on thickness. Baste occasionally with pan juices. Lift fish to serving plate and keep warm. Stir the lemon juice into the pan drippings, then pour over fish. Serves 4 to 6. This dish is very good using fresh salmon steaks.

Jewell Kopp

BAKED STUFFED FISH

1 big fish (bass or large trout)	1/2 cup chopped celery
	1 onion, chopped
Salt and pepper	2 or 3 slices of bread
1/4 cup margarine, melted	

Salt and pepper cleaned fish 30 minutes before baking. Refrigerate. Sauté celery and onion in margarine. Wet the bread and crumble. Mix celery, onion and bread together. Stuff fish. Place on aluminum foil which has been sprayed with Pam. Bake at 325° for 1 hour.

VARIATIONS: Make bleu cheese stuffing by mixing 1 tablespoon bleu cheese, 2 tablespoons cream cheese, softened, dash garlic salt and 2 chopped cooked shrimp together. Stuff fish.

Genie Fesperman

TUNA CASSEROLE

1 (12 ounce) can pink tuna	1/2 soup can water
A large onion, chopped	Several slices of Cheddar cheese
3 stalks celery, chopped	
1 (3 ounce) can chopped pimiento	Saltine crackers (to line bottom and sides of casserole dish)
3 eggs, hard-boiled	
1 (10 3/4 ounce) can cream of mushroom soup	

Boil onion and celery until tender; drain. Line bottom and sides of 2 quart casserole with saltines. Layer the following over crackers; tuna fish, onions and celery, sliced boiled eggs, and pimiento. Mix mushroom soup and water together and pour over layers. Cover with saltines and slices of cheese. Bake at 300° for 20 minutes.

Judge Ben Smith

188

EASY TUNA CASSEROLE

1 cup uncooked macaroni
1 (8 ounce) jar Cheez Whiz
1 (10¾ ounce) can cream
    of mushroom soup

1 (6½ ounce) can tuna,
    drained
Cracker crumbs

Cook macaroni according to directions and drain well. Melt Cheez Whiz in microwave. Mix together macaroni, cheese, soup, and tuna. Pour into prepared casserole and top with cracker crumbs. Bake at 350° for 25 to 30 minutes.

Joy Craft

SEAFOOD CLARK

4 tablespoons butter or
    margarine
4 tablespoons flour
2 cups milk
½ teaspoon salt
1 cup grated cheese, packed
    (medium sharp or sharp
    American)
1 cup sour cream

1 pound raw, peeled shrimp
1 pound uncooked fish fillets
    or scallops
1 (4 ounce) can sliced
    mushrooms (optional)
½ cup toasted almond
    slivers
Accompanying dish of
    cooked rice

Melt butter in saucepan. Stir in flour until it is a thick paste. Gradually add milk, stirring constantly until it is smooth and thickened. Add salt, and cheese, stirring until cheese has melted. Cool. Fold in sour cream. Spread a thin layer of sauce in a greased two quart Pyrex baking dish. Add uncooked seafood and mushrooms and cover with balance of sauce. Sprinkle with almonds. Bake at 300° for 20 minutes or until fish is just done. Serve with rice. Serves 6 to 8.

Sue Clark

SHRIMP ÉTOUFFÉE
(or crawfish)

2 pounds fresh shrimp, peeled and deveined or 1½ pounds frozen shelled and deveined shrimp, thawed
1 teaspoon salt
½ teaspoon black pepper
¼ teaspoon cayenne pepper
1 large onion, chopped (1 cup)
½ cup finely chopped celery
¼ cup finely chopped green pepper
3 large cloves garlic, minced
¼ cup vegetable oil
1 cup water
1 tablespoon Worcestershire
5 drops liquid red pepper seasoning
1 teaspoon cornstarch
Hot cooked rice

Sprinkle shrimp with salt, pepper and cayenne in a medium-size bowl; reserve. Sauté onion, celery, pepper and garlic in oil in a large saucepan until soft. Add shrimp, ½ cup of the water, the Worcestershire and pepper seasoning. Bring to boiling; lower heat; simmer gently for 15 minutes, or just until shrimp are pink and tender. Stir cornstarch into remaining ½ cup water in a 1-cup measure, then pour into mixture in saucepan. Cook, stirring constantly, until thickened and bubbly. Serve over hot cooked rice. Serves 4.

O.J.'S CRAWFISH (OR SHRIMP) ÉTOUFFÉE:

¾ stick butter
1 red onion
Bell pepper
Onion tops (this means the tops of young green onions)
Parsley
2 tablespoons Worcestershire
Salt and pepper
1 cup water
2 teaspoons cornstarch
Shrimp or crawfish

Papa Lormand was a good Cajun cook, too. He occasionally made étouffée for us, and when I tried to pin him down about what he did, this was the best I could get. He left me on my own to figure out how to put it together.

(continued on next page)

NOTE: These are old Lormand family recipes. The first is from Papa Lormand's cousin's wife, Velma Lormand, and her recipe for étouffée was published in Family Circle magazine years ago.

Fran Spear Lormand

SAUCY SEAFOOD ENCHILADAS

1¼ cups Pace picanté
  sauce
8 ounces imitation crab,
  shredded
3 cups (12 ounces) grated
  Monterey Jack cheese

½ cup sliced green onions
3 ounces cream cheese,
  softened
8 ounces small shrimp
1 small bell pepper, chopped
12 (6 inch) flour tortillas

Combine picanté sauce and cream cheese in large bowl and mix well. Add crab, shrimp, 2 cups cheese, peppers, onion and mix well. Spoon ½ cup of mix evenly down center of each tortillas. Roll up and place seam side down in 13x9 inch baking dish. Spoon remaining ¾ cup picanté sauce evenly over tortillas. Cover tightly with Saran Wrap, venting one corner. Microwave on high 12 to 14 minutes, turning after each 4 minutes. Remove from microwave and sprinkle with remaining cheese. Let stand 5 minutes. (If you prefer, cover casserole with foil and bake at 350° for 15 to 20 minutes.)

NOTE: Optional garnish to be added after serving is shredded lettuce, chopped tomatoes, chopped ripe olives and sour cream.

Margaret Lott

ITALIAN SEA PASTA

1 (8 ounce) package
 imitation crab meat
1 teaspoon lemon juice
1/2 cup chopped celery
1/4 cup chopped onion

1/2 cup chopped green
 pepper
1/2 cup Italian dressing
21/2 cups uncooked Rotini
 (pasta)

Cook rotini according to package directions. Rinse with cool water and drain. Stir lemon juice with crab meat. To the crab meat add celery, onions, pepper, and Italian dressing and mix in a large bowl. Add pasta and gently toss. Chill before serving.

Diana Strickland

SCALLOPED OYSTERS

11/2 pints select oysters
2 cups crushed cracker
 crumbs (saltine)
1/2 cup melted butter
1/2 teaspoons salt

Dash pepper
1/2 cup cream (half and half)
1/2 teaspoon Worcestershire
 sauce

Drain oysters, reserving liquid. Coarsely crush saltines and toss with butter, salt and pepper. Spread 1/3 of crumbs in greased casserole. Cover with half of oysters. Layer crumbs and oysters until all are used. Combine cream, oyster liquid, and Worcestershire sauce. Pour over oysters and crackers. Top with crumbs. Bake at 350° for 30 minutes.

Lillian Stubbs Family

CRAB CASSEROLE

1 stick margarine
1 package Pepperidge Farm
   herb dressing mix
   (reserve 1 cup)
3 tablespoons dried parsley
1 pound fresh crab meat or 2
   (6½ ounce) cans

6 boiled eggs, chopped
1 cup half and half cream
1 cup mayonnaise
1 tablespoon grated onion
1 (8 ounce) can sliced water
   chestnuts
Salt and pepper, to taste

Melt margarine in pan and add herb dressing mix (reserving 1 cup), parsley, crab, chopped eggs, cream, mayonnaise, onion, water chestnuts, salt and pepper. Spread into prepared casserole dish and top with reserved dressing mix. Bake at 350° for 25 to 30 minutes or until bubbly.

Madge Herrin

MAMA CLYDE'S CRAB CASSEROLE

1 pound lump crab meat
½ cup mayonnaise
1 tablespoon Worcestershire
   sauce
2 raw eggs
2 hard-boiled eggs, chopped
   fine
3 tablespoons onion,
   chopped fine
3 tablespoons green
   pepper, chopped fine

2 tablespoons celery,
   chopped fine
1 stick butter, melted
1 teaspoon mustard
Salt and pepper, to taste
¼ cup of milk (if needed)
6 slices white bread, lightly
   toasted on both sides,
   then grated

Mix all ingredients except milk and bread crumbs. Add milk if mixture is too thick. Put into a 2-quart casserole. Top with bread crumbs. Bake at 350° for 35 to 40 minutes.

Clyde King

DEVILED CRAB

1 pound crab meat
1 cup bread crumbs,
   moistened in 3
   tablespoons water
2 eggs, slightly beaten
1/4 cup celery, finely
   chopped
1 small onion, finely
   chopped
1 small green pepper,
   chopped fine

4 tablespoons mayonnaise
1 tablespoon salad cubes
   (or sweet pickle relish)
1 teaspoon Worcestershire
   sauce
4 tablespoons catsup
3 tablespoons margarine,
   melted

Moisten bread crumbs with milk. Mix crab meat, crumbs, eggs, and vegetables. Combine mayonnaise, salad cubes, Worcestershire sauce, and catsup into a sauce and stir into mixture. Pour into crab shells or buttered casserole. Top with melted margarine and bake at 350° until brown (about 30 minutes).

Mary Ann East

CHARLOTT'S DEVILED CRAB

1 to 1½ pounds fresh crab
   meat (claw or white or
   mixture)
2 or 3 slices of white bread
½ teaspoon salt
⅛ teaspoon pepper
1 tablespoon mayonnaise
   (or salad dressing)

1 tablespoon apple cider
   vinegar
½ teaspoon prepared
   mustard
1 egg, well beaten
20 saltine crackers

In a large mixing bowl, flake crab meat, being sure to check crab for shell pieces. Crumble bread into crab, and add salt, pepper, mayonnaise, vinegar, and mustard. Mix well. Add well beaten egg to crab mixture, stirring well. Pour into prepared baking dish. Bake at 400° for 20 to 30 minutes. Serves 8.

Janet Herrin

194

SAVORY CRABMEAT

2 cups crab meat
3 eggs, beaten
1/2 cup butter
Pepper
1 tablespoon minced green
   pepper
1 tablespoon chopped
   parsley

1/2 teaspoon prepared
   mustard
1/2 teaspoon Worcestershire
   sauce
1 teaspoon salt
11/2 cups evaporated milk
1 tablespoon chives
1/2 cup buttered crumbs

Combine all ingredients except the crumbs. Turn into a deep buttered casserole. Sprinkle with the crumbs. Bake at 350° until piping hot and delicately browned. Serve while hot.

Myrrl Young

PAWLEYS ISLAND CRAB CAKES

1 cup mayonnaise
11/2 tablespoons cracker
   crumbs
1/8 teaspoon cayenne
   pepper
1/8 teaspoon dry mustard
1/4 teaspoon fresh lemon
   juice

1 large egg white, slightly
   beaten
1/4 teaspoon celery seed
1 pound lump crab meat
11/4 cups fresh white bread
   crumbs
1/3 cup (5 tablespoons)
   butter

Combine mayonnaise, cracker crumbs, cayenne, celery seed, mustard, lemon juice, and egg white. Stir in crab meat, gently. Form into six 1/2 inch thick cakes and coat cakes with most of fresh bread crumbs. Sprinkle a large plate with the rest of crumbs; transfer cakes to plate and refrigerate (covered loosely) for at least 1 hour and up to 4 hours. Heat butter in large heavy skillet. Sauté 2 or 3 minutes per side, or until golden.

Beth and Tom McCrary, Jr.

CRAB AU GRATIN

1 pound crab meat
1 cup grated Cheddar
   cheese
4 tablespoons butter or
   margarine
4 tablespoons flour
1/4 teaspoon salt

Dash of pepper
1 cup milk
2 (4 ounce) cans
   mushrooms, drained
   (optional)
Paprika

Melt butter in medium saucepan. Add flour mixed with salt and pepper, and stir until well blended and smooth. Pour milk in slowly, stirring constantly. Bring to a boiling point. Boil about 2 minutes. Add 1/2 cup cheese. Remove from heat. Stir in crab meat. Pour into casserole dish and top with remaining 1/2 cup grated cheese. Sprinkle with paprika. Bake at 350° for 15 to 20 minutes, until hot and cheese starts to brown.

NOTE: This recipe may also be used for Seafood Au Gratin. Use same ingredients, changing the pound of crab meat to 1/2 pound crab meat plus 1/2 pound boiled shrimp and 1/4 pound of sautéed scallops.

Jane Gillis

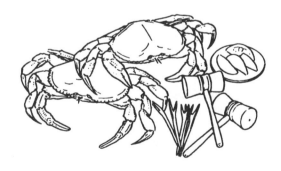

SHRIMP-CRAB CASSEROLE

1 cup chopped bell peppers
1 cup chopped onion
1 cup chopped celery
1 (8 ounce) can chopped
   water chestnuts

1 cup boiled shrimp,
   chopped
1 cup cooked crab meat
1 cup mayonnaise
1 cup buttered bread crumbs

Mix peppers, onion, celery, water chestnuts, shrimp, and crab meat. Stir in mayonnaise; mix well. Pour into 2 quart baking dish. Top with bread crumbs and bake at 350° for 30 minutes. Makes four to six servings. May be served hot or cold.

Jimmy McDonald

SHRIMP CREOLE

2 pounds shrimp (cooked
   and peeled)
1 cup chopped celery
1 medium onion, chopped
1/2 bell pepper, chopped

1 clove garlic, minced
1 (28 ounce) can diced
   tomatoes
4 slices bacon

Fry bacon until crisp. Remove bacon from pan and leave enough drippings in pan to sauté celery, onion, pepper, and garlic until tender. Add tomatoes and simmer for 30 minutes. Salt and pepper to taste. Add shrimp, white sauce and crumbled bacon. Serve over rice.

WHITE SAUCE:
2 tablespoons butter, melted
2 tablespoons flour
1/4 teaspoon salt

1 cup milk
Dash white pepper

Melt butter, stir in flour, and gradually add milk - stirring until mixture thickens. Add salt and pepper and set aside.

Jane Crawley

PATSY'S SHRIMP CREOLE

6 slices of bacon, cooked
2 large onions, chopped
1 1/4 green peppers, chopped
1 clove garlic, minced
1 (28 ounce) can tomatoes
1 small can tomato paste
1 teaspoon Worcestershire
    sauce
Salt and pepper, to taste

1 bay leaf
1 1/2 tablespoons brown
    sugar
1/2 teaspoon basil
2 pounds shrimp, cooked
    and peeled
2 tablespoons butter
1 (4 ounce) can mushrooms,
    drained

Cook bacon, set aside. Sauté onions, peppers and garlic in bacon drippings until clear. Add chopped tomatoes, tomato paste, Worcestershire sauce, salt, pepper, bay leaf, sugar, basil and simmer for about 1 hour. Before serving, add shrimp, butter and mushrooms. Serve over rice. Top with crumbled bacon.

Patsy Paulk

SHRIMP ELEGANTE

3 pounds fresh or frozen
    shrimp in shells (50 large
    shrimp)
Boiling water
2 (6 ounce) packages frozen
    snow peas
3 chicken bouillon cubes
2 1/2 cups boiling water

1/2 cup sliced green onion
    with tops
3 tablespoons soy sauce
1 teaspoon salt
1/4 cup cold water
1/4 cup cornstarch
4 medium tomatoes, cut into
    eighths

Thaw shrimp if frozen. Peel and devein shrimp; set aside. Pour a little boiling water over pea pods and carefully break apart with fork; drain immediately and set aside. In a large saucepan or Dutch oven, dissolve bouillon cubes in the 2 1/2 cups boiling water; add shrimp, green onion, soy sauce, and salt. Return to boiling; cook for 3 minutes, stirring occasionally. Slowly blend cold water into cornstarch; stir into shrimp mixture. Cook, stirring constantly, until mixture is thick and bubbly. Add tomatoes and pea pods. Cook until tomatoes are heated through, about 3 minutes longer. Serves 12. Good served over hot cooked rice.

Jewell Kopp

UNCLE BEN'S SHRIMP CREOLE

2/3 cup olive oil
1/2 cup flour
1 large Bermuda (red) onion,
  chopped lengthwise
3 stalks celery (Frenched or
  sliced diagonally)
1/2 bell pepper, chopped
1 teaspoon minced garlic
1 sliced lemon
1 (8 ounce) can small
  English peas (LeSeurs)
1 (16 ounce) can tomato
  sauce
1 fresh tomato, chopped
2 pounds shrimp, medium
  size (peeled)

1 teaspoon salt
1 teaspoon pepper
1 teaspoon thyme
2 tablespoons chili powder
1/2 teaspoon cayenne
  pepper
1 tablespoon wine vinegar
1 tablespoon Worcestershire
  sauce
1 tablespoon sugar
2 tablespoons dry sherry
2 bay leafs
1/2 teaspoon celery seed

In a large iron skillet, make a roux with flour and olive oil (brown flour in hot oil). Add onions and celery to roux - sauté on low heat - add garlic and bell pepper. Add tomato sauce, chopped tomato and sliced lemon. Add shrimp and English peas. Add seasonings and water to cover. Simmer over slow heat - cover skillet from time to time - for 1/2 hour to 45 minutes. Serve with rice and French bread.

NOTE: Guacamole or some kind of avocado salad is ideal with this dish.

Judge Ben Smith

SHRIMP SPECIAL

2 pounds shrimp, cleaned
  and deveined
3/4 stick butter
8 ounces fresh mushrooms,
  sliced
1 cup finely chopped onion
1 teaspoon seasoned salt
2 teaspoons lemon pepper

2 tablespoons chopped parsley
1 tablespoon Worcestershire
  sauce
1/2 cup grated Romano cheese
4 ounces chopped ripe
  olives (optional)
8 ounces vermicelli or
  angel hair pasta

Melt butter over moderate heat. Sauté shrimp, mushrooms, and onions in butter for about 5 to 8 minutes. Transfer to mixing bowl. Add lemon pepper, parsley, Worcestershire sauce, 1/4 cup cheese, and olives. While preparing shrimp, cook vermicelli "al dente" (about 9 minutes). Drain. Add to shrimp mixture while warm. Place in 2 quart baking dish and top with remaining 1/4 cup cheese. Bake at 350° for 20 to 30 minutes or until warmed through. This dish is best if made a few hours in advance to allow flavors to blend. Bake just before serving. Serves 6 to 8.

Georgine Smith

SHRIMP NEWBURG

2/3 cup chopped onion
2/3 cup chopped celery
2/3 cup chopped green pepper
2/3 cup butter or margarine
11/3 cups evaporated milk
2 (101/2 ounce) cans cream
  of potato soup

Red food coloring
1 cup grated sharp Cheddar
  cheese
2 tablespoons lemon juice
11/2 pounds cleaned shrimp
  (I cook mine in above)
Hot cooked rice or patty shells

In large saucepan on medium heat, sauté onion, celery and green pepper in butter until just tender; blend in milk and potato soup. Add few drops of coloring to make pretty pink. Reduce temperature to low. Add cheese, stirring until melted, then lemon juice and shrimp, cook slowly until shrimp are done. Serve over rice or patty shells.

Madge Herrin

SHRIMP STROGANOFF

1 (8 ounce) package
   fettuccine
2 tablespoons butter
2 tablespoons chopped
   onion
1/2 pound shrimp, peeled
1 (103/4 ounce) can
   condensed cream of
   shrimp soup

1/2 cup milk
1/2 cup sour cream
1/4 teaspoon paprika
Salt and pepper, to taste

Cook fettuccine according to directions on package. Drain. Melt butter in pan and sauté onion. Add shrimp and cook until done. Blend in soup and milk. Heat. Stir in sour cream and paprika. Be careful not to let mixture boil. Serve over hot fettuccine.

Kalista Morton

SHRIMP AND GREEN NOODLES

1/2 (8 ounce) package
   spinach noodles
2 pounds shrimp, peeled and
   deveined
1 (103/4 ounce) can cream
   of mushroom soup
1 cup sour cream

1 cup mayonnaise
1/2 teaspoon Dijon mustard
1 teaspoon chopped chives
4 tablespoons sherry
   flavoring
1/2 cup grated sharp
   Cheddar cheese

Cook noodles as directed on package. Line casserole with noodles and make into a nest. In a large frying pan, sauté shrimp in 1/2 cup clarified butter until pink and tender (about 5 minutes). Cover noodles with shrimp. Combine soup, sour cream, mayonnaise, and chives. Add mustard and flavoring. Pour sauce over shrimp and sprinkle with cheese. Bake at 350° for 30 minutes until cheese melts and is bubbly. Serves 6 to 8.

Nancy Lee

SHRIMP AND ARTICHOKE CASSEROLE

7 tablespoons butter
5 tablespoons flour
3/4 cup milk
3/4 cup heavy cream
Salt and pepper to taste
1 (14 ounce) can artichoke
  hearts, drained
1 pound shrimp, cooked,
  shelled and deveined

1/2 pound fresh mushrooms,
  sliced
1/2 cup dry sherry
1 tablespoon Worcestershire
  sauce
1/2 cup freshly grated
  Parmesan cheese
Paprika

In a small saucepan, melt 5 tablespoons of the butter and stir in flour to blend well; gradually add the combined milk and cream, stirring constantly with wire whisk until thickened and smooth. Season to taste with salt and pepper. Arrange drained artichoke hearts over bottom of buttered 2 quart baking dish and scatter shrimp over them. Sauté sliced mushrooms in remaining 2 tablespoons of butter for about 6 minutes. Spoon over artichokes and shrimp. Add sherry and Worcestershire sauce to cream sauce and pour over layered ingredients in baking dish. Sprinkle with Parmesan cheese and paprika. Bake at 375° for 30 minutes. Serves 6.

Jewell Kopp

BBQ SHRIMP

2 or 2 1/2 pounds raw shrimp
1 1/2 sticks margarine
1 1/2 teaspoons pepper
2 teaspoons rosemary
1 teaspoon thyme

2 teaspoons celery salt
1/2 teaspoon cayenne pepper
1/2 teaspoon Worcestershire
1 teaspoon olive oil
Lemon juice

Melt margarine. Add shrimp, pepper, rosemary, thyme, celery salt, cayenne pepper, Worcestershire, olive oil, and lemon juice. Marinate 6 hours. Bake at 350° in 2 quart Pyrex dish for 20 to 30 minutes, until shrimp are pink.

NOTE: Line table with newspaper. Serve at table with a green salad and French bread. Peel, eat, and use wonderful sauce for a dip. Messy, but GREAT!

Lynn Sims Ford

MARINATED SHRIMP

1 tablespoon basil
1 tablespoon oregano
1 tablespoon olive oil
2½ quarts of water
3 pounds of peeled fresh
    shrimp
1 purple onion
2 cups vegetable oil
1 cup red wine vinegar
1 teaspoon coriander
1 teaspoon salt

1 teaspoon coarse ground
    pepper
1 teaspoon crushed red
    pepper flakes
1 teaspoon sugar
3 cloves crushed garlic
1 (3 ounce) jar capers,
    drained
1 tablespoon Worcestershire
    sauce
1 tablespoon lemon juice

Combine basil, oregano and olive oil and set aside. Bring water to a boil and cook shrimp for 3 minutes. Peel and devein. Put shrimp in bowl with onion. Combine vegetable oil, Vinegar, coriander, salt, pepper, red pepper flakes, sugar, and garlic. Bring to a boil and let simmer 3 minutes. Stir in the herb mixture, capers, Worcestershire, and lemon juice. Pour over shrimp. Cover and chill for eight hours.

Bettie Mayo

LOW COUNTRY BOIL

Shrimp
Smoked sausage
Corn on the cob

1 stick margarine
Tabasco
Salt and pepper

On an outside cooker, fill a large pot half full of water. To this add 1 stick margarine, lots of Tabasco, salt and pepper. Bring to a boil. Add corn (either fresh or frozen) and cook for 5 minutes. Then, add sausage and cook for 5 minutes. To all of this add shrimp (with shells) and cook for 3 minutes. Delicious!

NOTE: Serve with salad and hot bread. This is a fun meal and it is so GOOD!

Cookbook Committee

GOURMET SHRIMP

2 pounds fresh shrimp
4 tablespoons butter or
  margarine

¼ cup chopped parsley
1 clove garlic, minced
¾ teaspoon salt

Wash shrimp in strainer under cold, running water. Remove shell and vein. Place in bowl and chill until ready to cook. Just before serving, melt butter in medium-sized frying pan. Add parsley, garlic, salt and shrimp. Sauté, stirring often, 2 to 4 minutes, or until shrimp are firm and pink. Time carefully, overcooking makes shrimp tough.

NOTE: 1 package of Good Seasons Italian dressing mix may be substituted for parsley, garlic and salt.

Carol Harley

SHRIMP CASSEROLE I

3 pounds boiled shrimp
6 tablespoons butter or
  margarine
4½ cups cooked rice
4½ cups grated Cheddar
  cheese
1½ cups light cream (half
  and half)

6 tablespoons chili sauce
Dash of Worcestershire
1 (8 ounce) can mushrooms,
  drained
Salt and pepper, to taste

Sauté mushrooms in butter. Stir together mushrooms, shrimp, rice, cheese, cream, chili sauce, Worcestershire, salt, and pepper. Pour into lightly greased 2 quart casserole. Bake at 350° for 25 minutes. Serves 8 to 10.

Lou Turk

SHRIMP CASSEROLE II

2¹/₂ pounds cooked shrimp
1 pound cooked rice
³/₄ cup white raisins
¹/₂ cup toasted almonds
1 (9 ounce) bottle chutney
1 small onion, chopped

1¹/₂ sticks margarine
1 teaspoon curry powder
1 teaspoon white pepper
1 teaspoon celery salt
6 slices of cooked bacon

Melt margarine in skillet. Sauté onion in margarine. Add curry, white pepper, and celery salt. Mix together rice, shrimp, raisins, almonds and chutney. Add onions. Mix all together well. Pour into 9x13 inch casserole and sprinkle with crumbled bacon. Bake at 350° for 30 minutes.

Martha Mason

SHRIMP AND RICE CASSEROLE

2 pounds fresh shrimp
6 cups of water
2 tablespoons margarine
1 cup chopped celery
1 cup chopped onion
1 cup cooked rice
1 cup milk
1 (10³/₄ ounce) can cream
   of mushroom soup

1 (8 ounce) can water
   chestnuts, drained and
   chopped
¹/₂ cup mayonnaise
1 teaspoon dried parsley
   flakes
¹/₄ teaspoon salt
¹/₂ teaspoon pepper

Boil water, add shrimp and cook 3 to 5 minutes or until shrimp turn pink. Drain, peel, and devein shrimp. Melt margarine in large skillet over medium high heat. Add celery and onion and cook, stirring constantly, until tender. Stir in rice and then add milk, mushroom soup, water chestnuts, mayonnaise, parsley, salt, and pepper. Spoon mixture into lightly greased 2 quart casserole. Bake at 350° for 30 minutes or until bubbly.

Jane Gillis

NOTES

Entrées

Entrées

BAR-B-QUED BRISKET

1 (5 to 6 pound) fresh
  brisket of beef
1 (5 ounce) bottle Liquid
  Smoke
Onion salt

Garlic salt
Celery salt
Salt and pepper
Worcestershire sauce
1 bottle barbecue sauce

Pierce beef with fork. Sprinkle with onion, garlic and celery salt. Pour 1/2 bottle (or more) Liquid Smoke to cover brisket. Cover tightly with foil and refrigerate overnight. The next morning trim off fat. Sprinkle with salt and pepper and Worcestershire sauce. Wrap tightly with foil and bake at 275° for 5 hours. Remove cover and pour 6 ounces barbecue sauce over meat on both sides. Bake 1 hour longer.

Cheryl Monroe

OVEN STEW

1 1/2 pounds beef stew, very
  lean
3 medium potatoes, peeled
  and quartered
3 medium onions, peeled
  and quartered
3 carrots, scraped and
  quartered

1 bell pepper, cut in small
  pieces
3 medium stalks celery, cut
  in small pieces
3 tablespoons Minute
  tapioca
1 (12 ounce) can V-8 juice

Place meat in a flat baking dish. Add vegetables - mix tapioca and juice and pour over top. Cover. Bake at 350° for 3 hours. Don't peek!

Hazel Cook

209

BEEF STROGANOFF

1½ pounds lean stew beef
1 (4 ounce) can sliced
   mushrooms
½ cup chopped onion
1 small clove garlic
1 stick margarine
1 (10½ ounce) can beef
   broth

1 (8 ounce) carton sour
   cream
⅓ cup cooking sherry
   (optional)
1 package noodles, cooked
2 teaspoons poppy seeds

Brown beef and cook until tender. Cool and cut into smaller pieces and remove all fat. Sauté onion and garlic in margarine until tender. Add broth and thicken with cornstarch or flour. Add beef and mushrooms. Simmer until flavors blend and add sour cream and heat. (Do NOT let mixture come to a boil after adding sour cream.) Serve over hot noodles which have been tossed with poppy seeds.

Lisa Fesperman

ROULADEN (BEEF ROLLS)

6 slices beef (have butcher
   cut ⅛ inch thick slices
   from flank or sirloin)
½ cup finely chopped
   crunchy dill pickles

½ cup finely chopped
   onions
3 slices of bacon, chopped
Salt and pepper
6 toothpicks

Sauté bacon and onions together until onions are tender. Drain and discard any grease from bacon. Add pickles and mix with bacon and onion mixture. Lay out slices of beef, lightly salt and pepper, spread mixture on each slice. Roll up from narrow side, close with toothpick. Brown Rouladen on all sides in hot vegetable oil or shortening. Place in baking dish (large enough to hold Rouladen and 2 cups of gravy). Make a good brown gravy, about 2 cups, and pour over Rouladen. Cover and simmer in 300° F. oven for 30 to 45 minutes, depending on size of Rouladen. Serve with noodles or whipped potatoes. Serves 6.

Hildegard Amspacher

210

FLUFFY, SPICY MEATLOAF

3 pounds lean ground beef
2 cups Pepperidge Farm
   seasoned bread dressing mix
2 1/2 cups milk
2 eggs, beaten
1/2 cup minced onion
1 1/2 teaspoons salt
1/2 teaspoon pepper
1/2 teaspoon dry mustard
1/2 teaspoon sage
1/2 teaspoon celery salt
1/2 teaspoon garlic salt
2 tablespoons
   Worcestershire sauce

Mix thoroughly all ingredients. For better browning, shape into three 1 pound loaves on a long, shallow baking sheet. Bake at 350° for 1 1/2 hours.

NOTE: For a catsup-topped loaf, spread 3 tablespoons catsup on top of loaves before baking.

NOTE: This is still a favorite of our grown children and their families.

NOTE: From the Cookbook Committee - Try creole sauce with meat loaf.

Cynthia Raynor

COMPANY BEEF CASSEROLE

1 pound ground beef
1 small onion, chopped
1 (14 ounce) can tomatoes
1 tablespoon catsup
Dash Worcestershire sauce
1/4 cup green pepper
2 tablespoons parsley
1/2 teaspoon salt
1/4 teaspoon pepper
1 cup macaroni, uncooked
1 (10 3/4 ounce) can cream
   of celery soup
1 cup grated Cheddar
   cheese

Brown and drain ground beef. To the beef add onion, tomatoes, catsup, Worcestershire sauce, green pepper, parsley, salt and pepper. Simmer for 30 minutes, stirring occasionally. Cook macaroni according to package directions. Drain. Stir macaroni into beef mixture. Add soup and pour into a baking dish. Top with cheese. Bake at 350° for 30 minutes.

Madge Herrin

GROUND BEEF CASSEROLE SUPREME

1½ pounds ground beef
½ stick margarine
1 medium onion, chopped
1 bell pepper, chopped
½ cup chopped celery
1 cup raw rice, washed
1 (14½ ounce) can beef
   consomme

1 (12 ounce) can tomato
   juice
1 (4 ounce) can mushrooms,
   drained
Dash garlic salt
2 teaspoons Worcestershire
   sauce
Dash pepper

Sauté onion, pepper, and celery in margarine. Add ground beef and brown. Season lightly with garlic salt, pepper, and Worcestershire sauce. Drain off grease. Spray casserole with "Pam" and spread washed rice in the bottom of casserole. Add a layer of mushrooms, then ground beef mixture. Pour consomme and tomato juice over casserole. Cover with foil and bake at 350° for 1 hour.

Cindy Hitt

GRECO
Inexpensive and different.

1 pound lean ground round
   or chuck
1 yellow onion, chopped
1 green pepper, chopped
1 or 2 (3 ounce) cans
   mushrooms, drained

2 cups shell macaroni
3 (8 ounce) cans tomato
   sauce
1 (16 ounce) can cream style
   corn
1 cup sharp cheese, grated

Sauté onion and green pepper in small amount of oil. Add beef, stirring until brown. Drain. Add mushrooms. Remove from heat. Boil macaroni until tender. Drain. Combine macaroni, beef mixture, tomato sauce and corn. Mix well. Place in greased casserole and refrigerate. When ready to bake, top with grated cheese. Bake in 300° oven for 1 hour. Serves 6.

Hannah Fesperman

HAMBURGER PIE

1 pound ground chuck
1/2 teaspoon minced garlic
1/2 cup chopped onions
1/2 package slivered
    almonds

1 can tomato soup
1 cup cooked green beans
3 medium Irish potatoes,
    cooked and mashed

Sauté meat until brown. Season with garlic, salt, and pepper. Add onions and almonds. Add tomato soup. Simmer about 10 minutes. Add beans. Put in a 1 quart casserole. Top with mashed potato patties. Bake in a 350° oven until potatoes begin to brown. Take out and serve hot.

Lynn Smith

BEEF BROCCOLI PIE

1 pound ground beef, very
    lean
1/4 onion, chopped
2 teaspoons salt
1/2 teaspoon garlic powder
2 tablespoons flour
1 (3 ounce) package cream
    cheese
1 cup milk

1 (10 ounce) package frozen
    chopped broccoli, cooked
    and drained
2 eggs, beaten
1 (5 ounce) package
    Monterey Jack cheese
    slices
2 pie shells

Cook ground beef and onion until brown. Drain well. Add salt, garlic and flour. Cook on low heat on top of stove. Add cream cheese and milk and heat until cheese is melted and smooth. Stir in cooked and drained broccoli. Stir a little of beef mixture into beaten eggs to warm them. Then, add eggs to whole pan of beef mixture. Cook over low heat until mixture is thick. Pour into one pie crust. Place cheese slices on top. Put second pie crust on top and seal edges. Bake at 350° for 25 to 30 minutes. Cool 10 minutes before serving.

Elizabeth Copeland

213

KERNEL JOE

1 pound ground beef
1/4 cup chopped onion
1 clove garlic, minced
1 (17 ounce) can creamed
    corn
1 (8 ounce) can tomato
    sauce

1 package chili seasoning
    mix
Salt and pepper
1 (15 ounce) can pinto
    beans, undrained
Cornbread or hamburger
    buns

In large skillet, brown meat with onion and garlic. Drain. Add corn, tomato sauce, seasoning mix, salt, and pepper. Cover and simmer 15 minutes. Add beans and heat through. Serve over split buns or cornbread. Top with grated cheese.

Velma Bell

BASIC MEAT SAUCE WITH VARIATIONS

1 pound lean hamburger
    meat (or ground turkey)
1/2 tablespoon vegetable oil
1 (14.5 ounce) can stewed
    tomatoes

1 (8 ounce) can tomato sauce
1 cup water or optional
    flavoring
1/4 cup parsley, chopped
Salt and pepper, to taste

Brown the beef in oil. Drain well. Add stewed tomatoes, tomato sauce, water and parsley. Cook about 5 minutes. Add salt and pepper. Cover and simmer 35 to 40 minutes.

FOR SPAGHETTI SAUCE: Add 1 (4 ounce) can mushroom pieces, drained. Serve with pasta of choice. Top with Parmesan cheese.

FOR CHILI: Add 1 (16 ounce) can of Bush's chili hot beans and 1 tablespoon chili powder.

FOR BRUNSWICK STEW: Add 1 (8 1/2 ounce) can lima beans, 1 (8 3/4 ounce) can whole kernel corn, 3/4 cup diced potatoes and dash of Tabasco.

Mary Winn Pruet

SPAGHETTI - PIZZA STYLE

1 cup milk
2 eggs
1 pound thin spaghetti,
   cooked and drained

2 cup shredded mozzarella
   cheese
1 jar Ragú sauce
1 package sliced pepperoni

Beat milk and egg together; toss with spaghetti. Spread mixture in roasting pan. Top with Ragú sauce. Arrange pepperoni in rows over sauce. Sprinkle with cheese. Bake for 30 minutes in 350° oven. Let stand 5 minutes before cutting into squares.

Susan Peterman

SPAGHETTI PIE

1/2 (12 ounce) package
   vermicelli
2 tablespoons of butter
1/3 cup grated Parmesan
   cheese
2 eggs, well beaten
1 pound of ground beef
1/2 cup chopped onion
1/4 chopped green pepper
1 (8 ounce) can tomato paste
1 can stewed tomatoes,
   undrained

1 teaspoon sugar
3/4 teaspoon dried oregano
1/2 teaspoon salt
1/2 teaspoon garlic salt
1 cup cream-style cottage
   cheese
1/2 cup shredded mozzarella
   cheese
12 small pepperoni slices
3 teaspoons fresh parsley

Cook vermicelli according to package directions; drain. Stir butter and Parmesan cheese into hot vermicelli. Add eggs; stir well. Spoon mixture into a ten inch glass pie plate. Shape the spaghetti into a pie shell. Microwave on High, uncovered, for three minutes. Set aside. Crumble beef in a two quart casserole. Stir in onion, green pepper, tomatoes, tomato paste and seasonings. Spread cottage cheese evenly over pie shell. Top with the meat sauce. Garnish with pepperoni slices and parsley. Cook in 350° oven until pie is bubbly.

Bettie Mayo

215

LAYERED ENCHILADAS

FILLING:

2 pounds ground sirloin
1 onion, chopped
1/2 green bell pepper,
   chopped
1/4 teaspoon coriander
1/2 teaspoon chopped garlic
1 (8 ounce) can tomato
   sauce
1/8 teaspoon hot pepper
   sauce

1/4 cup picante sauce
1 teaspoon Worcestershire
   sauce
1 tablespoon chili powder
1/2 cup chopped ripe olives
12 to 15 tortillas, quartered
2 cups grated Cheddar
   cheese

Sauté ground sirloin, onion and bell pepper. Drain, then add remaining ingredients except tortillas and cheese.

SAUCE:

1/2 cup butter, melted
2 tablespoons flour

1 1/2 cups milk
2 cups sour cream

In a small saucepan, combine butter and flour and mix well. Slowly add milk and cook until thickened and smooth. Cool, then add sour cream. Spread a little of the sauce in the bottom of a 9x13 inch baking dish. Place one-half of the tortilla quarters over sauce and follow with one-half of meat mixture, one-half of white sauce, and one-half of cheese. Repeat layers, and bake at 375° for 20 minutes. Serves 6 to 8.

Deborah Strickland

"PASTA IN A POT"

1½ pounds ground beef
1 medium chopped onion
2 minced garlic
1 (14 ounce) jar Ragu sauce
1 (11 ounce) can of diced
   tomatoes
1 (3 ounce) can of sliced
   mushrooms

1½ pints sour cream
1 (4 ounce) package grated
   provolone cheese
1 (4 ounce) package grated
   mozzarella cheese
1 (8 ounce) box shell
   macaroni, cooked
Parmesan cheese

Brown ground beef with onion and garlic. Drain. Add Ragu, tomatoes, mushrooms. Simmer 30 minutes. Put ½ of macaroni in a dish. Cover with ½ of meat mixture and ½ of the sour cream. Top with provolone cheese. Repeat macaroni, meat sauce and sour cream. Top with mozzarella cheese. Sprinkle with Parmesan cheese. Bake at 350° for 35 to 45 minutes.

Cathy McGee

TACO PIE

1 pound ground beef
1 (1¼ ounce) package taco
   seasoning mix

2 (8 ounce) cans refrigerated
   crescent rolls
4 cups shredded Monterey
   Jack cheese (divide in ½)

TOPPINGS:
Sour cream
Lettuce
Olives

Salsa
Cheese
Jalapeño pepper slices

Brown ground beef in a skillet. Drain well. Add taco seasoning mix according to package directions. Set meat mixture aside. Spread 1 can of crescent rolls on the bottom of a greased 9x13 inch Pyrex dish. Sprinkle with 2 cups of cheese. Spread ground beef-taco mixture on cheese. Sprinkle with remaining 2 cups of cheese. Top with second can of crescent rolls. Bake at 400° for 15 minutes or until browned. Serve with any variety of toppings.

Cathy McGee

BACHELOR'S PIE

1 pound ground beef	Hickory smoked salt
1/2 jar chopped garlic	Pickapepper Sauce
Black pepper	

Mix ground beef, garlic, pepper and salt into microwave safe bowl. Spread Pickapepper Sauce on top. Cook in microwave with Saran Wrap cover until meat separates from bowl. Pour off fat. Serves 2.

NOTE: Prepare for long-time bachelorhood if you eat this too many times a week.

Dr. S. William Clark, III

SWEDISH MEATBALLS

1 pound lean ground beef	1 (14 ounce) can chicken
2 slices bread, broken	and rice soup
1/2 cup evaporated milk	1 (14 ounce) can cream of
1 egg, beaten	tomato soup
1 teaspoon salt	1 can water
Vegetable oil	1 minced onion

Mix together beef, bread, milk, egg, and salt. Form into meatballs. Brown meatballs in oil. Drain. Stir in chicken and rice soup, tomato soup, water, and onion. Simmer until ready to serve (about 20 to 30 minutes). Serve with hot rice or noodles.

Barbara Orr

PAELLA

4 ounces Italian sausage, sliced
8 chicken legs and wings (4 each)
1 medium onion, chopped (1/2 cup)
1 small sweet red or green pepper, cut into chunks
1 clove garlic, minced
3/4 cup long grain rice, uncooked
1 1/2 teaspoons instant chicken bouillon granules

1/4 teaspoon ground turmeric
3 cups hot water
4 baby carrots or 3 carrot chunks
1 (10 ounce) package frozen peas
1 (10 ounce) package frozen artichoke hearts
1/4 cup pitted ripe olives
6 cherry tomatoes, halved

In a 12 inch skillet or 4 quart Dutch oven, brown sausage over medium heat about 10 minutes. Drain, reserving drippings in pan; set sausage aside. Season chicken with salt and pepper. Brown chicken in reserved drippings; remove chicken, reserving 1 tablespoon drippings in pan. Add onion, red or green pepper, and garlic to pan; cook until onion is tender. Stir in uncooked rice, bouillon granules, turmeric, and water; bring to boiling. Add sausage and carrots. Arrange chicken atop. Reduce heat; cover and simmer 20 minutes. Meanwhile, rinse peas and artichokes under hot tap water to separate. Arrange peas, artichokes, and olives atop chicken. Cover and cook 15 to 20 minutes more or until rice and chicken are tender. Just before serving add tomatoes; heat through. To serve, toss mixture gently together. Serves 4.

Dan and Cheryl Lott

SAUSAGE AND VEGETABLE MEDLEY

1½ pounds Hillshire Farm
smoked sausage
1 cup uncooked rice
1 (14½ ounce) can chicken
broth
1 (4 ounce) can mushrooms,
undrained
1 package New England
style frozen mixed
vegetables (broccoli, red
peppers, corn)

1½ tablespoons Lipton
onion soup mix
Salt and pepper, to taste
½ cup grated Cheddar
cheese

Pre-cook sausage and cut in 1½ inch pieces. Combine sausage with rice, chicken broth, mushrooms, and mixed vegetables. Add onion soup mix, salt, and pepper and mix to season. Cover with foil and bake at 350° for 45 minutes or until rice is done. Remove foil, top with grated cheese and bake until cheese melts.

Carol Mathison

HAM AND CHICKEN ROLLS

8 chicken breast halves
2 (10.2 ounce) packages
cooked ham slices
1 package Pepperidge Farm
herb stuffing mix

1 pound roll of hot sausage,
cooked and drained
1 jar ham glaze

Mix stuffing with hot water as directed on package. Add cooked sausage and mix well. Clean chicken and pat dry. (Chicken may be deboned and flattened by pounding. This makes a pretty party dish.) Leave skin on chicken as rolls should be crisp. Pack stuffing-sausage mixture into chicken cavities. Using 2 slices of ham, place a large spoonful of mix onto ham and roll into ¾ inch rolls. Place in baking dish, alternating ham and chicken. Top with ham glaze. Bake 1 hour at 350°.

Mary Winn Pruet

LUCK OF THE IRISH STEW

1 envelope onion soup mix
3/4 cup water
2 tablespoons brown sugar, firmly packed

1/2 teaspoon ground cinnamon
1/4 teaspoon ground nutmeg

Mix the above ingredients together.

4 cups potatoes, thinly sliced (sprinkled with salt and pepper)
4 medium apples, peeled and sliced

4 or 6 pork chops, cut 1/2 inch thick

In a greased 2 quart baking dish, layer half of potatoes and apples. Cover with half "mix". Add chops. Top with remaining apples and potatoes and "mix". Cover and bake at 375° for 1 1/2 hours, or until potatoes and chops are tender.

NOTE: Male types like this!

Anna Mayo

GRILLED PORK TENDERLOIN

1 boneless pork loin (or 2 pork tenderloins)
1 cup orange juice
1/4 cup olive oil

1/3 cup soy sauce
2 tablespoons rosemary
1/2 cup red cooking wine

Place tenderloin in large heavy duty Zip-loc plastic bag. Combine orange juice, oil, soy sauce, rosemary and cooking wine, stirring well. Pour marinade over tenderloin. Seal bag securely. (Tenderloin may be marinated in a pan.) Let tenderloin marinate in refrigerator for 8 hours. Turn occasionally. Remove tenderloin from marinade, reserving marinade. Grill, covered, over medium heat 20 to 30 minutes, turning and basting frequently.

Coralyn Gaston

CURRIED PORK

1 pound boneless pork
1 tablespoon cooking oil
1/4 teaspoon salt
1/4 teaspoon grated ginger
1 clove garlic
1 large apple, cored and
   chopped

1/4 cup sliced onions
2 teaspoons curry powder
1 (10 3/4 ounce) can cream
   of mushroom soup
3/4 cup milk
1 (8 ounce) carton sour
   cream

Partially freeze pork. Cut on the bias into thin bite-size strips. Preheat a large skillet over high heat. Add oil. Stir-fry pork. Remove from skillet reserving drippings. In the same skillet cook apple, onion, curry powder, ginger and garlic, cooking until onion is tender. Add meat, soup and milk. Cook over medium heat about 30 minutes, stirring occasionally. Stir in sour cream and heat through. Do not boil. Serve over hot cooked rice.

Diana Strickland

COUNTRY STYLE RIBS

3 pounds country style ribs
1 medium onion, chopped

2 tablespoons butter

Sauté onion in butter until onion is clear. Wash ribs, boil until tender and drain. Place in a casserole dish and cover with sauce and onion. Bake at 350° for 1 hour.

SAUCE:
2 tablespoons vinegar
2 tablespoons brown sugar,
   packed
2 tablespoons lemon juice
2 tablespoons
   Worcestershire sauce

Dash Tabasco sauce
1 teaspoon prepared mustard
1/4 teaspoon pepper
1 teaspoon salt
1/2 cup chopped celery
1 small bottle catsup

Mix all ingredients together. Fill catsup bottle with water and add to sauce.

Sue Brown

222

PORK TENDERLOIN WITH BEARNAISE SAUCE
Very simple, very elegant, very good!

1 pound whole pork tenderloin	1 tablespoon butter
1 tablespoon vegetable oil	Freshly ground black pepper

Combine vegetable oil and butter in heavy skillet over medium heat, stirring to mix as butter melts. Add tenderloin and cook until brown on all sides, turning occasionally. Sprinkle with freshly ground black pepper.

1/4 cup water	1/4 cup red cooking wine

Add water and red wine to skillet. Cover tightly and cook over low heat for 45 to 60 minutes or until done.

1/4 cup white wine vinegar with tarragon	1/4 teaspoon dried tarragon leaves
2 tablespoons white cooking wine	1/4 teaspoon parsley flakes
1 green onion with tops, sliced	

Combine vinegar, white wine, green onions, tarragon and parsley flakes in a small saucepan. Cook over medium-high heat for 10 to 15 minutes or until reduced by half. Set aside.

3 egg yolks	1/2 cup butter, melted
1/4 teaspoon dry mustard	Fresh basil, to garnish

Beat egg yolks with a wire whisk about 1 minute in the top of a double boiler. Add dry mustard and vinegar mixture, beating well. Place yolk mixture over simmering water. Gradually add melted butter in a slow, steady stream, beating constantly. Continue beating until thickened. Pour sauce onto heated serving platter. Place whole tenderloin on top. Garnish with fresh basil.

Kathy Hackel

223

HAM TOMATO PIE

Pastry for 9 inch pie crust   **2 tablespoons Dijon mustard**

Bake pie crust. Cool slightly, then brush inside with mustard and allow to dry.

FILLING:

1 1/2 cups coarsely ground ham
5 tablespoons minced fresh
   parsley
3 tablespoons minced onion
2 tomatoes, peeled, cored
   and thickly sliced

1 1/2 cups shredded sharp
   Cheddar cheese
1/2 cup mayonnaise
2 tablespoons crushed
   crackers
1/2 teaspoon basil

In a small bowl, combine ham, 1 tablespoon of the parsley and 1 tablespoon of the onion. Spread in pie shell. Cover with tomato slices. In a bowl, blend cheese, mayonnaise, remaining parsley, remaining onion, cracker crumbs, and basil. Spread cheese mixture over filling. Bake in a 400° oven for 30 to 35 minutes or until hot and bubbly. Serve immediately.

Jean Hancock

CROCK POT BAR-B-QUE PORK

18 ounces Kraft hickory
   smoke barbecue sauce
4 to 5 pound pork roast, with
   fat

2 white onions, sliced
6 whole cloves
2 cups water (enough to
   almost cover)

Place one onion, sliced, in bottom of crock pot, then roast, then other sliced onion with cloves on the top. Almost cover the roast with water. Cook on low 10 to 12 hours. Remove everything from pot. Return only the meat to the crock pot after removing fat and bones. Pour sauce in with the meat and cook on low for 3 to 4 more hours, stirring often.

Lisa Fesperman

PORK LOIN WITH CRANBERRY GLAZE

5 to 8 pound boneless pork loin

Garlic salt
Onion salt

Sprinkle pork loin generously with garlic and onion salt. Place fat side up on rack of roasting pan, adding 2 cups of water to pan. Roast, uncovered, in 325° oven for 25 minutes per pound.

GLAZE:

2 tablespoons margarine
3/4 cup chopped onions
1 (16 ounce) can whole cranberry sauce
1/4 cup brown sugar, packed
1/2 cup water

2 tablespoons lemon juice
1/3 cup chili sauce
2 teaspoons prepared mustard
1/4 cup soy sauce
3 drops Tabasco

Melt margarine and add onions, cooking until tender. Add cranberry sauce, sugar, water, lemon juice, chili sauce, mustard, soy sauce and Tabasco; simmer 15 minutes. (Cool and refrigerate if made a day ahead.) When pork has cooked required time, drain any fat from pan and place loin in pan. Cover with 1/2 cranberry glaze. Return to oven for 30 minutes, basting often. Slice and serve with extra warmed glaze on the side.

Bunny Winge

ROAST BEEF

1 (2½ to 3 pound) boneless
   rump roast
Vinegar

Salt and pepper
Garlic salt

Preheat oven to 450°. Wipe roast with damp cloth. Pour about one tablespoon vinegar over roast. Sprinkle with salt and pepper and garlic salt. Put roast in a small roasting pan and cook for 30 minutes, uncovered. Reduce heat to 350°, cover pan and bake for 2½ hours. To make gravy, take roast out of pan and put pan on top of stove. Dissolve 3 tablespoons plain flour in two cups water. Add slowly to juices in pan and stir until thickened.

Betty Hopkins

STANDING RIB ROAST SUPREME

1 (6 pound) prime rib roast
   (eye or round or boneless
   top sirloin may be used)

1 clove garlic or garlic
   powder
Salt and pepper

Preheat oven to 500°. Rub roast with garlic and sprinkle with salt and pepper. Place roast in a Dutch oven or heavy pan. Put in HOT oven and roast, uncovered, for 30 minutes. Then, turn heat OFF. Do NOT open oven door for exactly 2 hours. Then, remove roast from oven. Allow roast to stand for 15 minutes before carving for easier slicing. Thirty minutes roasting time will make a rare roast. For more well-done meat, roast for 35 minutes at 500° before turning heat off. The general rule is: 5 minutes per pound for rare, and 6 minutes per pound for more well done roast.

NOTE: This roast tastes like those in fine restaurants! Because of the use of high cooking temperature, do not leave unattended. Delicious serve with Yorkshire Pudding.

Jane Hart

YORKSHIRE PUDDING

2 eggs
1 cup milk
1 cup flour, sifted

1/2 teaspoon salt
2 tablespoons roast beef
   drippings

Blend this mixture at least four hours before cooking! Place milk in a blender and add eggs, one at a time, flour and salt. Blend on high for 1 minute or until WELL blended. Refrigerate until ready to cook. Pour roast beef drippings in a 10 inch pie plate. Tilt to cover surface. Run in hot oven a few minutes so dish will be quite hot. Pour mixture into hot pie plate and cook 25 minutes at 425° or until it is a deep golden brown. Serve immediately with roast beef.

Georgianne McGee

QUICK AND EASY POT ROAST

3 to 5 pound chuck roast
1 package Lipton's onion
   soup mix

1 (10 3/4 ounce) can cream
   of mushroom soup

Sprinkle the onion soup mix in the bottom of a Dutch oven. Place the roast in and pour the undiluted can of soup over the meat. Put a tight fitting lid on and bake at 325° for 2 1/2 to 3 hours. Roast may be turned once.

NOTE: This is good with quartered potatoes and/or carrots added to pot about 35 minutes before the meat is done. It makes its own gravy and is SO good!

Roy A. Jensen

227

STUFFED ROAST

1 (3 pound) eye of round
 roast
1½ pounds pepperoni
 sausage
2 medium onions, cut into
 quarters

1 clove garlic, cut
1 large green pepper, cut
2 or 3 strips of bacon, cut in
 half

With a large sharp knife, cut down the middle of the roast and stuff alternately with sausage, onion, green pepper, and garlic. Brown roast well on top of stove in a heavy skillet. Place in roasting pan with bacon strips over top. Bake at 350° for about 2 hours. This is very pretty when sliced.

Happie Stewart

ROAST BEEF PROVENÇALE

6½ pound boneless beef
   (rib eye)
2 cups fresh white bread
   crumbs
½ cup chopped parsley
2 cloves garlic, crushed

2 teaspoons salt
½ teaspoon pepper
4 tablespoons Dijon-style
   mustard
½ cup butter or margarine,
   melted

Preheat oven to 325° F. Wipe roast with damp paper towels. Place in open roasting pan. Combine bread crumbs, parsley, garlic, 2 teaspoons salt and ½ teaspoon pepper. Spread mustard over top of roast. Firmly pat crumb mixture into mustard. Drizzle with butter. Insert meat thermometer into center of roast. Roast, uncovered, 2 to 2¼ hours, or until meat thermometer registers 140° F., for rare; or 2¼ to 3 hours 160° F. for medium. Let roast stand 20 minutes, for easier carving.

BROWN GRAVY:
2 tablespoons meat
   drippings
3 tablespoons flour
1 (10½ ounce) can
   condensed beef broth,
   undiluted

¼ teaspoon salt
Dash pepper

Make brown gravy by pouring off drippings in roasting pan. Return 2 tablespoons drippings in pan. Stir in the flour, to make a smooth mixture; brown over low heat, stirring in order to loosen any brown bits that are in the pan. Add water to beef broth to measure 2 cups; slowly stir into flour mixture; add salt and pepper. Bring to boiling, stirring gravy until smooth and bubbly. Makes 2 cups. Nice served with cauliflower and broccoli spears. Makes 12 servings.

Jean Hancock

229

SISTER'S LEG OF LAMB

1 (5 pound) leg of lamb
Salt, pepper and flour
1 (15 ounce) jar spiced
   peaches, reserve juice

1 cup sugar
1 teaspoon whole cloves

Sprinkle the lamb roast with salt, pepper, and flour. Sear in a 500° oven for 15 minutes. Reduce heat to 350° and cook for about 2 hours or until tender. Baste with the spiced peach juice, reserving half of the juice. While roast is cooking, combine the sugar, cloves and half of peach juice; cook until slightly thickened. Add the peaches and simmer for 15 minutes. Remove peaches and set aside to be used later around the roast as a garnish, AFTER you have fried them in butter.

SAUCE FOR LAMB ROAST:
1 cup stock from lamb roast
2 tablespoons butter
1 small onion, sliced
Juice of one lemon

1 tablespoon vinegar
1 tablespoon Worcestershire
   sauce
3/4 cup prepared mustard

Sauté sliced onion in butter. Mix together lemon juice, vinegar, Worcestershire sauce, and mustard and stock from roast. Add to onions and simmer slowly for 15 minutes. Serve sauce with the roast. Garnish roast with fried peaches.

NOTE: This was a special recipe of my sister, Mrs. Q. L. Garrett. She was also the director of music at First United Methodist Church for many years.

Georgia McDonald

BUTTERFLY LEG OF LAMB

1 (5 or 6 pound) boned leg of lamb
2 tablespoons Dijon mustard
1 teaspoon rosemary

1 teaspoon ginger
1 clove of garlic, crushed
2 tablespoons olive oil
2 tablespoons soy sauce

Mix together the mustard, rosemary, ginger, garlic, olive oil and soy sauce. Marinate the roast overnight in mixture. Broil in oven or on grill for 10 to 15 minutes on each side. Serve pink.

Susan Sweat

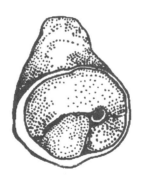

VEAL SCALLOPINI

2 pounds veal cutlets, sliced
   thin
2 tablespoons flour
1¼ teaspoons salt
¼ teaspoon pepper
¼ cup vegetable oil

1 clove garlic
½ pound mushrooms, thinly
   sliced
½ cup water
1 cup California burgandy
   (optional)

Pound cutlets, and sprinkle lightly with flour, salt, and pepper. Brown cutlets in oil. Place in a baking dish. In the same oil, sauté mushrooms and garlic. Add water and burgandy; simmer for 2 minutes. Pour over cutlets and bake at 350° for about 25 minutes or until cutlets are tender. Baste occasionally.

Virginia Holtzendorf

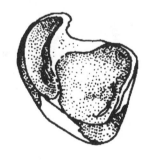

POPPY SEED CHICKEN

6 chicken breasts
2 (10¾ ounce) cans cream
   of chicken soup (or cream
   of mushroom)
1½ cups sour cream

30 to 40 Ritz crackers,
   coarsely crushed
2 tablespoons poppy seeds
½ cup melted butter

Poach chicken breast with celery leaves and onions to season. Discard vegetables and skin and bone chicken. Reserve broth. Cut chicken into bite-sized pieces. Combine soup, sour cream, chicken and 1 to 2 cups chicken broth. Separately combine cracker crumbs, butter and poppy seeds.

Layer chicken mixture then cracker mixture in a 2 quart buttered baking dish. Layer twice, ending with crackers. Bake at 350° for 30 minutes. Serve over rice.

OPTION: Add a layer of broccoli that has been steamed five minutes.

Tillie Lynch

APRICOT CHICKEN

1½ fryers, cut in pieces
1 bottle Russian salad
   dressing
1 (10 ounce) jar apricot
   preserves

1 package dry onion soup
   mix

Place chicken pieces in prepared baking dish. Mix salad dressing, apricot preserves and dry onion soup mix together. Pour over chicken. Bake at 350° for 1 hour and 15 minutes.

NOTE: For sweet and sour chicken use same recipe, substituting French salad dressing for the Russian dressing.

Claire Smith

SOUTHWEST CHICKEN WITH BROWN RICE

¾ pound boneless chicken
breast, cut into short, thin
strips
1 teaspoon ground cumin
1 teaspoon chili powder
½ teaspoon salt
1 tablespoon olive oil
1 small onion, sliced and
separated into rings
1 clove garlic, minced

1 (8 ounce) can tomatoes
(cut into wedges)
⅓ cup salsa (or picante
sauce)
1 cup instant brown rice
1 (8 ounce) can kidney
beans, drained
¼ cup shredded Monterey
Jack cheese

Sprinkle chicken with cumin, chili powder, and salt. Heat oil in large (10 inch) skillet over medium heat. Add chicken and stir, cooking until chicken is no longer pink. Stir in onion and garlic and cook for 2 minutes. Drain tomatoes, reserving liquid. Coarsely chop tomatoes and set aside. Add enough water to reserved tomato liquid to equal ¾ cup. Add liquid and salsa to skillet and bring to a boil. Stir in rice, reduce heat and cover tightly. Simmer for 5 minutes. Stir in beans and chopped tomatoes. Cover and remove from heat. Let stand about 5 minutes until all liquid is absorbed. Sprinkle with cheese.

Elizabeth Copeland

LEMON CHICKEN

4 to 6 chicken breast halves
5 tablespoons lemon juice
(fresh or bottled)

10 tablespoons water
1 teaspoon salt

Mix lemon juice, water and salt and pour into deep skillet. Add chicken breasts and bring to a boil. Lower heat and cook (medium heat) uncovered, turning several times until liquid is gone (about 20 to 25 minutes). Cover and cook until chicken is brown and crisp.

G. Frank Pruet

BROCCOLI CHICKEN CASSEROLE

4 chicken breasts, cooked
   and deboned
2 (10 ounce) packages
   frozen broccoli
2 (10 3/4 ounce) cans cream
   of chicken soup
1 cup mayonnaise
1 teaspoon lemon juice

3/4 teaspoon curry powder
1/2 cup shredded sharp
   cheese
1/2 cup toasted bread
   crumbs
1 tablespoon margarine,
   melted

Cook broccoli according to package directions and drain. Layer chicken and broccoli in large prepared casserole. Combine soup, mayonnaise, lemon juice, and curry powder together and pour over chicken. Sprinkle with cheese. Combine bread crumbs and margarine and put on top of casserole. Bake at 350° for 30 minutes.

Bettie Mayo

CALIFORNIA CHICKEN

4 chicken breasts (deboned)
1 (8 ounce) package cream
   cheese, softened
4 scallions, chopped

1 (10 3/4 ounce) can cream
   of mushroom soup
8 strips bacon

Combine cream cheese and scallions. Stuff breasts with cheese mixture and wrap each breast with 2 strips of bacon. Place in prepared baking dish and pour soup over breasts. Bake at 350° for 1 hour.

NOTE: This is great served with rice!

Harriet James

"CATHERINE'S CHICKEN DISH"

6 breasts of chicken (cooked
   and cut up)
1/2 cup cream of chicken soup
2 cups chopped celery
1 cup of mayonnaise
1 cup sour cream
1 (8 ounce) can of water
   chestnuts, sliced and drained
1/2 pound fresh mushrooms
   (or one 31/2 ounce can),
   drained

1/2 cup toasted slivered
   almonds
2 tablespoons of lemon juice
1 teaspoon curry powder
2 tablespoons minced onion
1 teaspoon salt
1/2 teaspoon pepper (black)
1 cup grated Cheddar cheese
1 (31/2 ounce) can fried
   onion rings

Mix all ingredients except cheese and onion rings with the chicken. Put in 13x9 inch casserole dish. Top with cheese. Bake at 350° for 30 minutes. Put onion rings on last 5 minutes. Serves 12.

NOTE: This recipe made the rounds in Virginia and at the Pentagon before I retired in '85. The dish can be made ahead and not wait until the last minute which, on that one point, most every one liked very much.

Thad Dean Kelly

CHEESY CHICKEN CRESCENT SQUARES

1 chicken, cooked, deboned
   and diced
1 cup shredded Cheddar cheese

1 can cream of chicken soup
2 (8 ounce) cans crescent rolls
3/4 cup milk

In a large bowl, mix diced chicken and 1/2 cup cheese. In saucepan, combine soup, milk, and 1/4 cup cheese. Heat until cheese melts. Pour 1/2 of soup mixture into 9x13 inch baking dish. Separate rolls into triangles. Place 2 to 3 tablespoons of chicken mixture on wide end of roll. Then, roll up and close ends. Arrange filled rolls over soup in pan. Bake at 375° for 20 to 25 minutes, until golden brown. Pour remaining soup over rolls and sprinkle with remaining 1/4 cup cheese. Return to oven until cheese melts. Serve hot.

Joy Craft

CHEESE CHICKEN SUPREME

3 cups diced cooked
  chicken
1 (8 ounce) package lasagne
  noodles
1 recipe mushroom sauce
1½ cups cream style
  cottage cheese

1 (8 ounce) package
  processed American
  cheese slices, shredded
½ cup grated Parmesan
  cheese

MUSHROOM SAUCE:
½ cup chopped onion
½ cup chopped green
  pepper
3 tablespoons butter
1 (10¾ ounce) can cream
  of chicken soup

⅓ cup milk
1 (6 ounce) can sliced
  mushrooms, drained
½ teaspoon basil

To prepare sauce, sauté chopped onion, green pepper in butter. Stir in soup, milk, mushrooms, and basil. Cook until well blended and smooth. Set aside. Cook noodles according to package directions until tender. Drain and rinse in cold water. Place half of cooked noodles in a 9x13 inch prepared baking dish. Cover with half each of mushroom sauce, cottage cheese, chicken, American cheese and Parmesan cheese. Repeat layers. Bake at 350° for 45 minutes. Serves 10.

Eleanor Harrison

CHICKEN BREAST SAUTÉ WITH WILD RICE
This is one of my favorite recipes, it's so good!

10 chicken breasts
1 stick butter
Salt, to taste

White and Wild Rice Bake
Toasted almonds

Melt butter, sauté chicken until brown, salt to taste. Place in baking dish, cover and bake at 325° for 30 minutes. Serve over "Rice Bake".

WHITE AND WILD RICE BAKE:

3 cups cooked long grain
   white and wild rice
1 stick butter
1 cup green onions, chopped
1 green pepper, chopped
2 cloves garlic, minced

1 (8 ounce) can sliced water
   chestnuts
1 cup sliced mushrooms
1 cup chopped celery
1/2 cup slivered almonds, toasted
2 cups chicken broth
3/4 cup Dales steak seasoning

Melt butter. Add onions, pepper, garlic, water chestnuts, mushrooms, and celery. Cook to clear color. DO NOT brown. Add cooked rice, chicken broth, and Dales seasoning. Bake in 3 quart casserole, covered, in 350° oven for 20 minutes or until liquid is absorbed. Sprinkle toasted almonds over chicken breasts before serving. Serves 10.

Happie Stewart

LOW FAT CHICKEN CASSEROLE

5 to 6 boneless chicken
   breasts, cooked
1 (10¾ ounce) can Healthy
   Request cream of
   mushroom soup
1 cup fat-free sour cream

1/2 cup skim milk
1 sleeve fat-free saltine
   crackers, crushed
2 tablespoons poppy seeds
Fat-free margarine

Cut chicken into pieces and place in a prepared 2 quart casserole dish. Mix soup, sour cream, and milk. Pour over the chicken. Top with crushed crackers and poppy seeds. Dot with margarine. Bake at 350° for about 25 minutes.

Claire Smith

CHICKEN CASSEROLE

4 to 6 chicken breasts,
   cooked and deboned
1½ sticks margarine, melted
1 (12 ounce) package
   cornbread stuffing mix
1 (10¾ ounce) can cream
   of chicken soup

1 (10¾ ounce) can cream
   of mushroom soup
2 cups chicken broth
2 boiled eggs, sliced (optional)

Melt margarine and stir in cornbread stuffing mix. Put half of this mixture in buttered 9x13 inch casserole. Stew chicken breasts. Keep broth. Take chicken off bones and chop coarsely. Place chopped chicken over the stuffing mix. Stir together chicken soup, mushroom soup, and chicken broth. If using eggs, add them at this time. Pour over chicken. Spread remaining stuffing over top of casserole. Bake at 350° for 45 minutes.

Cheryl Monroe

CHICKEN AND DUMPLINGS

1 (4 to 5pound) hen, cooked
3 cups flour
½ cup milk

2 eggs, beaten
Salt and pepper, to taste

Cook hen (boil) until tender. Remove skin and bones and set meat aside. Save the broth for cooking the dumplings. To make dumplings, put flour in a bowl. Make a "well" in the center of the flour. Stir together the milk and eggs and pour into the flour "well". Blend with a spoon until dough is very stiff. Place dough on a floured surface and knead 2 or 3 times. Roll out with rolling pin until dough is very thin. (If dough sticks to the rolling pin, sprinkle it with flour.) Let dough dry for several hours. Cut into small squares. Add enough water to the chicken broth to make about 3 quarts of liquid. Season to taste with salt and pepper. Bring broth to a rolling boil and drop dumplings in. Stir once or twice. (DO NOT over-cook at this point.) Add chicken, turn off heat and cover tightly. Dumplings will simmer until done. Leave in broth for at least 20 minutes.

Bonnie Lynn

239

HOT CHICKEN SANDWICH

2 cups hot boiled chicken
1 (10¾ ounce) can cream
   of mushroom soup
1 (10¾ ounce) can cream
   of chicken soup
2 tablespoons chopped pimiento
1 (8 ounce) can chopped
   water chestnuts

Dash of curry
Little grated onion
14 slices bread (edges trimmed)
4 eggs
2 cups milk
Potato chips, crushed
Slivered almonds

Cut up chicken. Mix chicken, soups, pimiento, water chestnuts, curry, and onion. Spread on bread to make sandwiches. Wrap individually in foil and freeze immediately. When ready to serve, unwrap and dip into mixture of eggs and milk, beaten together. Then, roll in crushed potato chips and sprinkle with slivered almonds. Bake on greased cookie sheet for 30 to 45 minutes at 300°.

NOTE: These sandwiches are ideal for a luncheon plate.

Coolie Hughes

DILLED CHICKEN

4 chicken breast halves
⅓ cup flour
1 teaspoon salt
½ teaspoon paprika
2 tablespoons oil

¼ cup fresh dill weed
   (or ⅛ cup dried)
2 cups chicken broth
8 new potatoes
12 ounces fresh asparagus
1 tablespoon lemon juice

Wash and clean asparagus, partially peel potatoes; set aside. Mix flour, salt, and paprika together. Coat chicken breast with mixture. Pour oil into large skillet and brown chicken. Remove chicken and drain oil from skillet. Add remaining flour mixture to broth. Return chicken and broth to skillet with ½ dill weed. Cover and simmer 10 minutes. Add potatoes. Simmer 10 more minutes, covered. Lay asparagus on top of meat and potatoes and simmer for another 10 minutes, covered. Remove from heat and add the lemon juice and remaining dill.

Mary Winn Pruet

FIRST UNITED METHODIST CHURCH
CHICKEN CASSEROLE

3 cups cooked diced chicken
4 hard boiled eggs, chopped
2 cups cooked rice
1 cup mayonnaise
1 package slivered almonds
1½ cups chopped celery
2 (10¾ ounce) cans cream
   of chicken soup

1 teaspoon salt
1 small onion, chopped
2 tablespoons lemon juice
1 cup buttered, browned
   bread crumbs
2 tablespoons melted
   margarine

Combine chicken, eggs, rice, mayonnaise, almonds, celery, soup, salt, onion, and lemon juice. Mix well. Pour into a 3 quart casserole dish. Brown bread crumbs in melted margarine and sprinkle over the top of casserole. Bake at 350° for 35 to 40 minutes. Serves 12.

NOTE: This is the recipe we have used for our luncheon during the Arts and Crafts Bazaar. The women of the church hope you will enjoy this recipe as much as we have!

Cookbook Committee

CHICKEN CASSEROLE SPECTACULAR

1 box wild and white rice,
   cooked
2 cups (or more) chopped
   cooked chicken
1 (15 ounce) can French
   style green beans, drained
1 medium onion, chopped

1 (8 ounce) can sliced water
   chestnuts, drained
1 (3 ounce) jar chopped pimiento
½ cup mayonnaise
1 (10¾ ounce) can cream
   of celery (or mushroom) soup

Combine cooked rice, cooked chicken, beans, onion, water chestnuts, pimiento, mayonnaise, and soup. Place in a prepared 11x14 inch casserole. Bake at 350° for approximately 45 minutes.

Danita Cannon

HURRY CURRY CHICKEN

4 chicken breast halves	1 tomato, cut into wedges
1 (10 ounce) can cream of	1/2 cup raisins
chicken soup	1 tablespoon curry powder
1/2 (12 ounce) can	1 tablespoon dried onion
evaporated milk (for more	flakes
sauce)	1/8 teaspoon garlic powder

Arrange chicken breasts in 8 inch square baking dish (meatier portions toward edge of dish). Combine soup, milk, tomato, raisins, curry powder, onion flakes and garlic powder. Spoon evenly over chicken. Cover and cook in microwave on High power for 32 minutes, or until tender. Let stand, covered, for 5 minutes. (If using boneless breasts, cook 20 minutes only - then let stand for 5 minutes.) Remove chicken and place on serving platter. Stir sauce until smooth. Serve hot over rice.

NOTE: Pineapple chunks, coconut, nuts, and grated cheese may be added or served as a complement to this dish.

Ginger Groover Lang

CHICKEN PICANTE

6 to 8 pieces of chicken	8 ounces sour cream
(breast, thigh, leg)	1/3 cup milk
1 (10 3/4 ounce) can cream	Paprika, for color
of mushroom soup	

Place chicken in a 9x13 1/2 casserole. Mix together soup, sour cream and milk. Pour over chicken, covering all pieces. Sprinkle generously with paprika and bake in 350° oven for 1 hour or until done. Serve with yellow or Spanish rice. Serves 6 to 8.

NOTE: The chicken may be prepared as early as the night before, WITHOUT the paprika. Sprinkle paprika on chicken just before baking. This makes a wonderful dish for a ladies luncheon. When using smaller, boneless chicken, less baking time is required then.

Hildegard Amspacher

MITTIE ROOSEVELT'S COUNTRY CAPTAIN

16 chicken breast halves
Flour, salt, and pepper
3 to 4 onions, finely chopped
3 green peppers, chopped
4 small garlic buds, minced
2 tablespoons salt
White pepper
4 tablespoons curry powder
  (more if you wish)
6 (20 ounce) cans peeled
  tomatoes

2 tablespoons parsley
1 tablespoon thyme
3 cups toasted slivered
  almonds
1 cup currants, plumped in
  tomato juice
8 cups cooked rice
Parsley, for garnish

Roll chicken in seasoned flour. Brown in ¼ cup shortening or oil. Remove from pan and keep hot. (This is secret of the dish's success!) Cook onions in same pan. Add peppers and garlic, stirring constantly. Drain off fat and season with salt, pepper and curry powder. Add tomatoes, parsley and thyme. Put chicken in roaster or large (4 quart) covered casserole and pour mixture over it. Rinse skillet with a little water and pour this over chicken. Cover roaster. Bake at 375° for about 45 minutes or until chicken is tender. Serve over a mound of rice. Add currants to sauce mixture and pour over rice. Scatter toasted almonds over top. Garnish with parsley. Serves 16.

NOTE: A recipe for Country Captain was included in "Miss Leslie's New Cookery Book" written by Eliza Leslie in 1857. It was thought to have crossed the Atlantic with Anglo-Saxon settlers as a recipe from home. British soldiers developed a taste for this curried chicken dish while in India and brought it home with them. It works well for "company" because the finished chicken holds well and can be served over rice at the last minute.

Georgine Smith

PUFF PASTRY CHICKEN

1 box Pepperidge Farm puff
   pastry sheets, 2 sheets
6 chicken breasts, whole,
   boned raw
6 tablespoons cream
   cheese, mixed with 1
   tablespoon minced garlic

6 teaspoons stone ground
   mustard or Dijon mustard
1 egg yolk

Let pastry come to room temperature, about 30 minutes. Roll each sheet out (with a little flour if necessary) into a large square. Cut pastry into 8 squares (4 from each sheet), if any seams open, moisten with a few drops of water, then roll out more. Put dollop of mustard (1 teaspoon) in middle of each square. Put chicken breast in middle of square. Put 1 tablespoon of cream cheese in center of breast. Wrap pastry around breast and seal edges with drops of water. Have a cookie sheet with foil, sprayed with Pam ready, place each breast, wrapped side under, on cookie sheet. Using 2 remaining squares, decorate; cut in thin strips and make pastry into a bow and place on top of chicken bundle, or take a strip at a time, twist and criss-cross over each bundle. For Valentines Day, cut hearts ... etc. Mix egg yolk with 1 tablespoon water, brush all over each bundle with pastry or small paint brush. Bake 25 minutes, at 375°. Let sit 5 minutes before serving. (If browning too quickly, lay a piece of foil just on top for remainder of cooking time.) Serves 6.

Lynn Sims Ford

SUNDAY CHICKEN CASSEROLE

4 tablespoons butter
1 cup chopped onion
1 cup chopped celery
2 cups cooked rice
3 chicken breasts, cooked
   and sliced
1 (10 ounce) can cream of
   chicken soup

1/2 cup milk
1 (10 ounce) package frozen
   chopped broccoli,
   undercooked
1 small jar cheese or 4 to 6
   slices American cheese

Sauté onion and celery in butter until tender. Mix soup and milk. Place rice in buttered casserole; cover with onions and celery. Pour on soup and milk. Layer chicken; cover chicken with broccoli. Spread cheese over the broccoli. Bake at 350° for 30 minutes or until cheese is bubbly. Flavor is better if casserole is made the night before and baked just before serving.

Lucy Mason

CHICKEN ZESTA

1 stick butter or margarine
1/2 cup diced celery
1/4 cup diced green pepper
1/2 cup diced onion
3 cups cooked diced
   chicken
1 (103/4 ounce) can cream
   of chicken soup
1 (2 ounce) jar pimiento

1 (12 ounce) can evaporated
   milk (large)
1 (3 ounce) can sliced
   mushrooms
1/2 teaspoon salt
1/4 teaspoon pepper
2 cups cooked rice
1/2 cup grated Cheddar
   cheese

Sauté celery, green pepper and onion in butter or margarine. Add chicken, cream of chicken soup, pimiento, evaporated milk, mushrooms, salt, pepper, and cooked rice. Mix together and put in large casserole dish. Top with grated cheese. Bake in 350° oven for 35 minutes or until firm. Serves 10 to 12 people.

Alex Hood

CHICKEN KIEV

6 chicken breasts, boned
   and pounded flat
Salt and pepper
1 stick ice cold butter
1 tablespoon finely chopped
   parsley

6 cloves garlic
2 cups wheat germ
3 eggs, beaten until frothy

Salt and pepper chicken breasts on both sides. In the center of each, place a sliver of butter about the size of your little finger, 1/2 teaspoon chopped parsley, 1 clove garlic, peeled and crushed. Now fold the two shorter ends of the breast toward the center, then the two longer ends, overlapping one end over the other - envelope style to make as TIGHT a package as possible (so the butter won't ooze out). Skewer firmly shut (use picks). Roll breasts in wheat germ, then in beaten egg, then again in wheat germ. Roast breasts uncovered, in a moderately slow oven, 325° for about 1 hour. Near end of roasting time, baste chicken with a little melted butter and sprinkle with salt and pepper. When breasts are golden brown and tender, they're done! Serves 6.

Georgine Smith

BAKED SESAME CHICKEN

4 chicken breasts or a whole
   chicken, cut up
1/4 cup butter or margarine,
   melted
1/2 cup milk
1 large egg, slightly beaten
1/2 cup flour

1/4 cup sliced almonds
1 tablespoon paprika
3 tablespoons sesame
   seeds
1 1/2 teaspoons salt
3/4 teaspoon pepper
1/4 teaspoon baking powder

Place melted butter in a 9x13 inch baking dish or pan and set aside. Stir together milk and egg in a small bowl. Combine flour, almonds, paprika, sesame seeds, salt, pepper, and baking powder in a bowl, stirring together. Dip chicken pieces in egg mixture, then place chicken pieces in flour mixture, coating thoroughly. Place chicken in prepared pan and bake, uncovered, at 350° for 50 to 55 minutes.

Dale James

EASY CHICKEN PIE

1 medium sized chicken, cooked
2 cups chicken broth (saved
   from chicken)
1 (10³/4 ounce) can cream
   of chicken soup

1 stick margarine, melted
¹/2 teaspoon pepper
1 cup self-rising flour
1 cup buttermilk

Cook and debone chicken, reserving broth. Cut chicken into bite-size pieces and put in a well greased 2 quart casserole or baking dish. In a saucepan, mix the soup with 2 cups of chicken broth. Bring to a boil and pour over chicken. For the crust, combine melted butter with pepper, flour and buttermilk. Mix well to form batter. Spoon over the top of the chicken. Bake at 425° for 25 to 30 minutes.

NOTE: Boiled eggs, English peas, mushrooms, pimientos, or mixed vegetables can be used in this chicken pie. These should be drained before adding to mixture.

Kaye Pendley

CHICKEN SPAGHETTI

4 or 5 chicken breasts (or 1
   fryer)
1¹/2 green peppers, chopped
2¹/2 onions, chopped
2 (3 ounce) jars pimiento
1 (8 ounce) package vermicelli
2 (10³/4 ounce) cans cream
   of mushroom soup

¹/4 cup milk
1 (4 ounce) can mushrooms
Salt and pepper, to taste
American cheese, shredded
   (as much or as little as
   you like)

Boil chicken in a large pot for 30 to 45 minutes until tender. Sauté onions and green pepper in small amount of margarine until soft. Add soup, pimiento, milk, and mushrooms. Cut chicken into small pieces and add to the soup mixture. Pour all into a 2 quart casserole. Boil vermicelli in chicken broth, drain and put on top of chicken mixture in casserole. Salt and pepper to taste. Sprinkle shredded cheese on top. Bake at 350° for 45 minutes. Freezes well.

Isabell Lott

247

CHICKEN TETTRAZINI

1 large chicken, cooked and
  diced
Broth from cooked chicken
1 (12 ounce) wedge sharp
  Cheddar cheese, grated
1/2 medium onion, diced
1/4 green pepper, diced
1 (2 ounce) jar pimiento,
  chopped

1 (10-3/4 ounce) can cream
  of mushroom soup
1 (8 ounce) jar sliced
  mushrooms (fresh is
  better)
Salt and pepper, to taste
1 (4 ounce) package
  vermicelli pasta

Cook vermicelli in chicken broth and drain. Combine chicken, cheese (reserve 1/4 cup for topping), onion, pepper, pimiento, mushrooms, and soup. Salt and pepper to taste. Toss together with vermicelli. Place in greased baking dish and bake at 350° for 30 minutes or until bubbly and browned around the edges. Top with cheese the last few minutes of baking.

Julie Tomlinson

SMOKED TURKEY VERONIQUE
(The Cat's Meow)

9 cups diced smoked turkey
  (cut in cubes)
3 cups seedless green
  grapes
1-1/2 cups cashew nuts
1 cup mayonnaise

1 cup lemon flavored yogurt
9 tablespoons honey
6 teaspoons cracked black
  pepper
Romaine lettuce
Grape clusters, for garnish

Toss turkey, grapes, and cashews together. Blend together the mayonnaise, yogurt, honey and pepper. Combine dressing mix with turkey mixture. Wash Romaine lettuce leaves and grapes, arrange on serving platter and put turkey in the middle.

NOTE: To make ahead, prepare dressing and diced turkey the day before. DO NOT add cashews and grapes until just before serving.

Pam Barnhill

248

SOUTHERN DEEP FRIED TURKEY

1 (10 to 12 pound) turkey	**Ground cayenne pepper**
Creole seasoning	**Peanut oil**

Thaw, clean and dry turkey. Cover turkey inside and out with creole seasoning. Refrigerate overnight. When ready to cook, using a LARGE pot on an outside cooker, fill pot half full of peanut oil and heat to 350°. Pot should be large enough for whole turkey to fit and oil must cover bird completely. Just before cooking, coat the turkey well with cayenne pepper - until the bird is RED! Put whole turkey in the pot slowly, being careful not to splash the hot oil. Fry 4 minutes per pound.

NOTE: This is a marvelous way to cook a turkey. The deep frying seals in all the juices. It is delicious! You may cook whole Cornish hens this way adjusting your cooking time to the size of the bird.

Revenal Winge

GRANDMOTHER'S ROAST TURKEY AND TWO DRESSINGS

1 (8 to 12 pound) turkey	**Turkey giblets**
Salt and pepper	**2 to 3 hard boiled eggs**
3 to 4 tablespoons flour	**Melted butter**

Wipe outside of turkey with melted butter, then salt and pepper bird inside and out. Dredge outside of turkey with flour. (This makes a nice crust during roasting time.) Cook in covered roasting pan at 325° for 3½ hours or about 30 minutes per pound. (I always put an old plate under the bird to keep it from sticking to the pan, then add about 2 cups of water to the bottom of the pan.) Uncover the last ½ hour to brown. To make giblet gravy, after removing the turkey from the roasting pan, add 3 to 4 tablespoons flour to the liquid and brown in pan on top of the stove. Add to this the giblets and broth that have been cooked separately. Add diced hard boiled eggs.

Marion Fesperman, by Genie Fesperman

OYSTER DRESSING

2 pints or more oysters   **Water**
3 packages Uneda biscuits
  or saltine crackers

Heat oysters in own juice until oysters begin to curl. Remove from heat. Crumble crackers and mix with liquid. Add enough water to soften crackers. Salt and pepper to taste and stuff bird before roasting.

Genie Fesperman

CORNBREAD DRESSING

6 tablespoons melted butter   **4 cups chicken or turkey**
1/2 cup chopped celery and   **broth**
  leaves   **3 eggs, beaten**
1/2 cup chopped onion   **Salt**
6 cups cooked crumbled   **Pepper**
  cornbread   **Pinch of sage, thyme and**
3 slices day old bread,   **cilantro**
  crumbled

Sauté celery and onion in butter until tender. Combine crumbled cornbread and bread crumbs in a large bowl. Add celery, onions, and broth and mix well. Stir in beaten eggs and spices. Stuff into bird and roast.

NOTE: This can be baked in a 9x13 inch baking pan at 400° for 25 to 30 minutes.

Genie Fesperman

BAKED CORNISH HENS

8 Cornish hens
Salt and pepper
8 whole medium onions
3/4 cup butter or margarine

1/4 cup Kitchen Bouquet
1 (8 ounce) jar orange
  marmalade

Clean and dry hens. Season inside and out with salt and pepper; refrigerate overnight. When ready to bake, insert a whole onion in cavity of each hen and place in open roasting pan, leaving space between them. In small saucepan, put butter, Kitchen Bouquet, and orange marmalade; heat together until butter has melted and mixture is blended. Spoon over the hens and bake at 350° until hens are tender, about 1 1/2 hours, basting often. If sauce cooks down before hens are done, add a little hot water to the pan to assure having some of the delicious sauce left to accompany the hens. If hens appear to be getting dry during the baking, place a piece of foil loosely over the pan to retard the browning. Yield: 8 servings.

NOTE: For entertaining, onions should be removed from hens before serving; but for family enjoyment, leave them there!

Deborah Strickland

CHICKEN MAYONNAISE DELIGHT
Excellent for luncheons!

2 cups diced white meat
  chicken
1 (8 ounce) can English
  peas, drained
3 hard boiled eggs, chopped
1 cup diced celery

2 tablespoons pickle relish
2 tablespoons diced olives
1 cup sliced blanched almonds
2 cups chicken broth
2 envelopes gelatin
1 cup mayonnaise

Soften gelatin in chicken broth. Heat until gelatin dissolves. Cool thoroughly. Add chicken, peas, eggs, celery, relish, olives, and almonds. Fold in mayonnaise last. Mold in loaf pan or oblong casserole. Slice and serve. Serves 12.

Dot Gibson

CHICKEN AND WILD RICE SALAD
Great luncheon entrée!

1½ cups wild and white rice
  blend
2 cups water
½ teaspoon salt
3 large chicken breasts,
  cooked and cut bite-size
½ cup chicken broth
1 Granny Smith apple,
  unpeeled and chopped

½ small red onion, chopped
1 large red bell pepper,
  chopped
½ cup currants
2 tablespoons balsamic
  vinegar
2 tablespoons olive oil
Salt and pepper, to taste
½ cup toasted pecan pieces

Cook rice in water with salt until tender. Cool. Mix cooled rice with chicken, chicken broth, apple, onion, bell pepper, and currants. Add balsamic vinegar and olive oil. Salt and pepper to taste. Best if marinated overnight and served at room temperature. Sprinkle with toasted pecans.

NOTE: Serve over red leaf lettuce with fresh fruits or marinated vegetables.

Myrtle Sands

CHICKEN SALAD

1 fryer
2 teaspoons minced garlic
2/3 cup celery
1/2 cup dill pickle

Mayonnaise
Garlic salt, to taste
Sprinkle of black pepper
3 hard cooked eggs, grated

Cut up fryer. Spray large frying pan with Pam or oil. Heat pan until hot and place chicken skin side down. Brown skin side and turn and brown other side. Add garlic (minced) over the chicken and cover. Turn the heat to medium and cook until tender and done. Skin chicken and debone, then chop. Cut up celery and pickle. Grate the eggs. Mix chicken, celery, eggs and mayonnaise. Season with black pepper and garlic salt. Stuffed olives may be added if desired.

Blanche Kroell

SAVORY CHICKEN SALAD

2 cups chicken, chopped
   (light and dark meat)
1/2 cup finely chopped
   celery
3/4 cup finely chopped
   crunchy dill pickles

7 to 8 tablespoons
   mayonnaise
1 teaspoon Worcestershire
Salt and pepper, to taste

Combine chicken, celery, pickle, mayonnaise, Worcestershire, salt, and pepper. Chill in refrigerator for several hours. Serve on a bed of lettuce (dress-up with tomato and cooked egg wedges) or spread on sandwiches. Serves 6 to 8.

Hildegard Amspacher

CHINESE CHICKEN SALAD

4 large chicken breasts (or 1
   whole chicken), cooked
1/3 cup vegetable oil
1/4 cup vinegar
1/4 cup sugar
1/4 cup chopped green
   onions

1 1/2 teaspoons salt
1 large crisp heat of lettuce
1/2 cup slivered almonds,
   toasted
1/4 cup sesame seeds,
   toasted
8 Won Ton skins, fried

Marinate cooked chicken in oil, vinegar, sugar, onions, and salt overnight. Cut chicken into small strips or bite-size pieces. Wash and break lettuce into bite-size chunks. Toss chicken, lettuce, almonds, sesame seeds, and Won Tons together. Serve on bed of curly lettuce. Serves 8.

Lou Turk

HOT CHICKEN SALAD

2 cups cooked, chopped
   chicken
1 cup celery, finely chopped
1/2 cup sliced almonds,
   toasted
1/2 cup Ritz cracker crumbs
1/2 cup onion, finely chopped

1 (10 3/4 ounce) can cream
   of chicken soup
1/2 cup mayonnaise
1 cup sharp Cheddar
   cheese, grated
1 cup crushed potato chips

Combine chicken, celery, almonds, cracker crumbs, onion, chicken soup, mayonnaise, and cheese. Toss gently. Place in 1 1/2 quart baking dish. Bake at 375° for 15 minutes. Sprinkle potato chips on top and bake 15 additional minutes. Serves 4 to 6.

Virginia Sims

HOT CHICKEN SALAD

3 cups cooked chicken,
cubed
1 1/2 cups chopped celery
1 (8 ounce) can water
chestnuts, chopped
2 teaspoons grated onion
1 1/2 cups mayonnaise

1 (14 ounce) can cream of
chicken soup
1/4 cup slivered onions
3/4 cup grated Cheddar
cheese
1 1/2 cups potato chips

Combine chicken, celery, water chestnuts, onion, mayonnaise, soup, and onions. Place in 8x8 inch casserole dish. Top casserole with mixed grated cheese and potato chips. Bake at 325° for 45 minutes.

Barbara Orr

WILD RICE CHICKEN SALAD

1 cup wild rice
2 cups chicken broth
3 cups cooked diced
chicken
1 cup diced celery
1/3 cup green onions (some
tops)

1 (8 ounce) can sliced water
chestnuts
1 cup salted cashews
1 can mandarin oranges
Salt and pepper

DRESSING:
1 cup Miracle Whip salad
dressing
2 tablespoons brown sugar

1 tablespoon lemon juice
1 tablespoon vinegar

Pour boiling water over rice and let stand 15 minutes. Pour off water and repeat a second time, pouring off second water. Cook rice in 2 cups of chicken broth. Set aside and cool. Mix rice, chicken, celery, onions, water chestnuts, cashews, and mandarin oranges in large bowl. Add salt and pepper to taste. Mix together ingredients for dressing and pour over salad mixture. Mix well. Serves 8.

Martha Mason

NOTES

Game

Game

BAKED QUAIL WITH MUSHROOMS

1/3 cup all-purpose flour
1 teaspoon salt
1/2 teaspoon pepper
6 quail, cleaned
2 tablespoons butter
1/4 cup plus 1 tablespoon
   all-purpose flour

2 cups chicken broth
1/2 cup sherry flavoring
1/2 pound fresh mushrooms,
   sliced
1/2 cup butter
Hot cooked rice

Combine 1/3 cup flour, salt, and pepper. Dredge quail in flour mixture and set aside. Melt 2 tablespoons butter in a large skillet; add mushrooms and sauté 4 minutes. Remove mushrooms from skillet; set aside. Melt 1/2 cup butter in skillet; brown quail on both sides. Remove quail to a 11/2 quart casserole. Add 1/4 cup plus 1 tablespoon flour to drippings in skillet, cook 1 minute, stirring constantly. Gradually add chicken broth and flavoring; cook over medium heat, stirring constantly until gravy is thickened and bubbly. Stir in mushrooms. Pour mushroom gravy over quail. Cover and bake at 350° for 1 hour. Serve over rice. Yield: 6 servings.

Jewell Kopp

DOVE BREASTS STROGANOFF

12 to 18 breasts
1 medium onion, chopped
2 tablespoons melted butter
1 can cream of celery soup
4 ounce can mushrooms
1/2 cup Sauterne flavoring or
   water

1/2 teaspoon oregano
1/2 teaspoon rosemary
Salt and pepper, to taste
1 teaspoon brown bouquet
   sauce
1 cup sour cream
Cooked wild rice

Arrange meat in a large baking dish. Sauté onion in butter. Add remaining ingredients, except sour cream and wild rice. Pour mixture over meat. Cover lightly with foil. Bake at 325° for 1 hour, turning meat occasionally. Add sour cream; stir into sauce. Bake, uncovered, an additional 20 minutes. Spoon over wild rice.

Betsy Clark

DOVE WITH WILD RICE

PREPARING THE DOVES:

8 doves
1/2 cup butter
2 cups sliced mushrooms
1/2 cup chopped green onion
1 cup water

2 tablespoons fresh lemon
 juice
Salt
Freshly ground pepper

In a heavy frying pan, brown the doves in butter. Remove and set aside. In the same pan, sauté the mushrooms and onions. Place the doves, mushrooms, and onions in a shallow baking dish and cover with foil. Combine water, lemon juice, salt, and pepper; set aside. Bake the doves at 350° for 1 hour. For the last 15 minutes, remove the foil and baste frequently with the lemon juice mixture.

WILD RICE:

1 1/2 cups wild rice (or long
 grain and wild rice
 combined)
4 cans undiluted bouillon (or
 beef broth)
1 cup chopped onion

1 cup chopped green pepper
1 cup sliced mushrooms
1/4 cup soft butter
1 cup heavy cream
Salt and pepper, to taste

Wash the raw rice and then cook with the bouillon until most of the liquid has been absorbed - about 20 to 30 minutes. (Packaged quick rice can also be used: substitute the bouillon for the water and follow package directions for cooking time.) Sauté the onion, peppers and mushrooms in butter. Add the cream and salt and pepper. Stir in the drained rice and place in a 9x13 inch baking dish. Bake at 350° for 20 minutes. To serve, place the doves on the wild rice. Garnish with parsley. Serves 8.

NOTE: This is an elegant dish.

Bunny Winge

DOVE (OR QUAIL) AND RICE

12 dove or quail	1 cup beef consomme
1 cup uncooked rice	1 can onion soup
1/4 cup chopped bell pepper	1/2 cup flour
1/4 cup chopped onion	Salt and pepper

Sauté sliced and floured birds in a small amount of butter or bacon drippings. Put rice in a buttered oblong casserole. Place birds on top of rice, sprinkling peppers and onions on top. Pour consomme and soup over all. Cover and bake at 350° for 45 minutes.

Betsy Clark

FRIED VENISON TENDERLOIN

Venison tenderloin	Self-rising flour
Milk	Peanut oil
Salt and pepper, to taste	

Very carefully remove the thin, skin-like membrane from venison tenderloin. (This preparation is very important because the membrane will be tough if not removed.) Then, cut across the grain of tenderloin in 1/2 inch slices. When meat is cut, marinate slices overnight in milk. When ready to cook, drain meat, salt and pepper to taste and dredge in self-rising flour. Deep fry in oil. Be careful not to overcook. When light brown and floating, remove and drain.

Cookbook Committee

VENISON BURGERS

2½ pounds ground venison
½ cup minced onion
1 clove garlic, minced

⅔ cup dry red wine
2 tablespoons soy sauce
Salt and pepper

Mix all ingredients and form into patties. Cook over coals.

Betsy Clark

VENISON CHILI

1 pound ground venison
½ pound sausage
1 clove garlic, crushed
1 large onion, chopped
2 to 3 tablespoons chili
    powder
32 ounces tomato sauce

½ teaspoon thyme
1 teaspoon oregano
1 bay leaf
32 ounces red kidney
    beans, drained
12 ounces beer
Salt and pepper

Brown venison and sausage. Drain meat, and add onions and garlic to grease and sauté. Mix meat, onions, garlic, chili powder, tomato sauce, thyme, oregano, bay leaf, kidney beans, and beer. Cover and simmer for at least one hour.

Betsy Clark

CROCKPOT VENISON
This is super with venison or beef.

1 venison roast
¼ cup water
1 envelope of dry onion soup

1 medium onion, sliced
1 (10½ ounce) can cream
    of mushroom soup

Place roast in crock pot. Sprinkle dry onion soup mix on meat. Add mushroom soup and onion slices. Place lid on crock pot, cook on high 6 to 8 hours. Gravy will be a little thin and will need thickening. We have used this with venison steaks also.

Dot Gibson

VENISON ROLL DELIGHT
Also great with ground beef.

2 eggs, beaten
1 cup soft bread crumbs
2/3 cup tomato sauce
2 tablespoons chopped parsley
1/2 teaspoon oregano
1/4 teaspoon salt
1/4 teaspoon pepper

1/4 teaspoon garlic powder
2 pounds ground venison
8 thin deli slices of ham
1 1/2 cups (6 ounces) shredded
   mozzarella cheese
3 slices mozzarella cheese,
   halved diagonally

Combine eggs, bread crumbs, tomato sauce, parsley, oregano, salt, pepper, and garlic. Stir in ground venison, mixing well. On waxed paper pat meat into a 12x10 inch rectangle. Arrange ham slices on top of meat, leaving a small margin around edges. Sprinkle shredded cheese over ham. Starting from short end, carefully roll up meat, using paper to lift as you roll. Seal edges and ends. Place roll, seam side down, in a 13x9x2 inch pan. Bake in a 350° oven for 55 to 60 minutes, or until done. Remove from oven and place cheese slices over top of roll; return to oven 3 to 5 minutes or until cheese melts. Yield: 8 to 10 slices.

Dot Gibson

SMOKED VENISON TENDERLOIN

1 tenderloin or backstrap of
   venison
Bacon
Slices of onion rings

Sliced bell pepper rings
Fresh mushrooms, sliced
   (optional)
Bottle of Italian dressing

Slice tenderloin in chunks about 1 to 1 1/2 inches thick, only 3/4 of the way through. (You want it to still be in a long piece.) Cut bacon in 2 inch strips and put between sections of tenderloin. Place onions, bell peppers and fresh mushrooms on top of tenderloin. Pour a bottle of Italian dressing over and marinate for about 2 to 3 hours. Using a pan that can be put on your smoker, place tenderloin in pan, uncovered, and smoke on smoker for 3 to 4 hours, or until tender.

NOTE: Pork tenderloin is delicious cooked this same way.

Dale James

VENISON STEW

3 or 4 pounds venison
1/4 cup flour
3 tablespoons of bacon
  drippings
1 1/2 to 2 cups hot water
1 1/2 cups red wine (optional)
1 teaspoon mixed dried
  herbs (thyme, marjoram,
  basil)

1 teaspoon dried parsley
1 large onion, diced
1 1/2 teaspoons salt
1/2 teaspoon pepper
4 carrots, scraped and
  quartered
4 potatoes, pared and
  quartered

Cut sinews and bones from venison. Cut meat into bite-size pieces; roll in flour. In a large deep kettle, heat bacon drippings; then brown floured venison. Add hot water, wine, herbs, parsley, onion, salt, and pepper. Cover kettle and bring mixture to a boil. Reduce heat and simmer about 2 hours. Add carrots and potatoes. Cover and simmer for 1 hour; add a little more water if needed. Serves 8.

Eddie Rimes

BAKED DUCK BREAST

4 to 6 Wood duck breasts
1 large onion, chopped
3 cups water

1 teaspoon herb seasoning
2 chicken bouillon cubes
Bacon strips

Salt and pepper birds, place in baking dish. Add bouillon cubes and herb seasoning to water - pour in baking dish. Add onion. Lay strips of bacon over each breast. Bake at 300° for 3 hours, basting every 30 minutes. Remove ducks, thicken drippings for gravy.

Dot Gibson

GINNY'S ROAST DUCK

5 to 6 Teal or Wood ducks	**Soda**
(or 3 Mallards), cleaned	**2 to 3 apples, sectioned**
1 slice bacon per duck	**2 to 3 onions, sectioned**
Salt	**Pepper**
Vinegar	**Juice of 3 oranges**

Soak ducks overnight in the following mixture: 2 cups water, 1 to 2 teaspoons salt, 2 to 3 teaspoons vinegar, 1 teaspoon soda PER DUCK. Pour water off and dry ducks thoroughly. Salt and pepper each duck inside and out. Stuff cavity of each duck with 1/2 apple (sectioned) and 1/2 onion (sectioned). Place a strip of bacon over each duck. Put in roaster, adding water to the level of the roaster rack. Cook, covered, in a 350° oven for 1 to 1 1/2 hours (for Wood or Teal) or 2 1/2 to 2 hours (for Mallard). Baste every 45 to 60 minutes with orange juice. Servings: Wood duck or Teal: 1 duck per person / Mallard: 1/2 duck per person.

Janet Herrin

NOTES

Desserts

Desserts

APPLE DUMPLING

1 stick margarine or butter	2 cups sifted all-purpose
1 cup sugar	flour
1½ cups water	2 teaspoons baking powder
¼ teaspoon cinnamon	1 teaspoon salt
6 medium, whole apples,	⅔ cup shortening
pared and cored	½ cup milk

Combine margarine, sugar, water, and cinnamon. Cook until margarine is melted and sugar dissolves. Remove from heat; set aside. Sift together flour, baking powder and salt; cut in shortening until mixture resembles coarse crumbs. Add milk all at one and stir until flour is moistened. On a lightly floured surface, roll about ¼ inch thick into 18x12 inch rectangle. Cut into 6 inch squares. Place whole apple in each square (or use ½ apple, sliced, in each square of pastry). Sprinkle each apple generously with sugar, and cinnamon. Moisten edges of squares. Fold in corners to center and pinch edges together. Place 1 inch apart in ungreased 11½x7½x1½ inch baking dish. Pour the syrup over the dumplings; sprinkle with sugar. Bake at 400° for 15 minutes and 300° for 45 minutes or until apples are done. Serve warm with cream. Serves 6.

Lylburn Booker

APPLE CRISP

6 to 8 tart apples	¾ cup flour
1 cup brown sugar	1 teaspoon cinnamon
½ cup butter	

Peel and slice apples. Place in bottom of baking dish. Mix sugar, butter, flour, and cinnamon. Sprinkle over top of apples. Bake at 350° for 1 hour.

Susan Peterman

BANANA PUDDING

1 (6 ounce) package instant
   vanilla pudding mix
3 cups cold milk
1 (8 ounce) package cream
   cheese
1 can sweetened condensed
   milk

1 (12 ounce) Cool Whip
6 or 8 bananas
1 teaspoon vanilla
1 box of vanilla wafers

In a deep, large bowl, mix vanilla pudding and milk according to package directions. Mix softened cream cheese and condensed milk. Add to pudding mixture. Fold in 1/3 of whipped topping. Layer sliced bananas and vanilla wafers alternately with pudding mixture. Top with remaining whipped topping. Refrigerate. Serves 12.

Wendy Brantley Good

BAKED CUSTARD

3 cups milk
6 tablespoons sugar
1/4 teaspoon salt
3 eggs, slightly beaten

1 teaspoon vanilla
1 tablespoon butter
Ground nutmeg or cinnamon

Scald milk with sugar and salt. Stir slowly into beaten eggs, and add vanilla. Pour into custard cups or large baking dish, dot with butter, and add a dash of nutmeg or cinnamon. Set cups or baking dish in a shallow pan of water. Set on center rack of oven and bake at 325° until done, about 30 minutes. To test for doneness, insert knife in center of custard. When knife comes out clean, custard is done.

Eunice Burns

OLD FASHIONED BOILED CUSTARD

1 cup sugar	1 teaspoon vanilla
1/4 teaspoon salt	4 cups of milk, scalded
3 eggs, beaten	

Mix sugar, salt, and eggs in heavy saucepan. Slowly add scalded milk, stirring constantly. Cook over medium heat until mixture coats wooden spoon. Remove from heat immediately and pour into bowl. Add vanilla. Cool. Double this recipe for ice cream. Simply freeze in gallon ice cream churn.

NOTE: Use Hot Fudge Sauce with this recipe.

Evelyn Steele

HOT FUDGE SAUCE

4 squares unsweetened chocolate	1 cup canned evaporated milk
2 tablespoons butter or margarine	1 (14 ounce) can sweetened condensed milk
2 cups sugar	

In double boiler, melt chocolate and butter. Add sugar and evaporated milk. Cook until slightly thickened. Add condensed milk and cook over medium-low heat for 20 minutes.

NOTE: Wonderful over pound cake or ice cream.

Jane Hart

SCUPPERNOG GRAPE ICE CREAM

4 to 6 cups grape juice*
1 quart whipping cream
2 to 2 1/2 cups sugar

3/4 cup to 4 cups whole milk
Dash of lemon juice

Combine all ingredients and freeze in hand or electric ice cream churn. While the 4 cups of juice produces a mild refreshing flavor, it is even better with additional juice. The variation in amount of sugar depends on the sweetness of the grapes, and needs to be done by tasting. Since homemade ice cream seems to lose some of its sweetness during the churning process, it is necessary to have it slightly sweeter than tastes good before freezing it. Add milk to within 2 inches to top of churn.

* About 3 to 4 pounds of grapes are necessary for this amount of juice. Grapes should be washed and may be mashed by hand in a flat container with high sides, such as a turkey roaster, then strained. Another way is to use a large cone shaped colander on a metal tripod, with a long, two-inch wide wooden pestle. Juice may be frozen, without any sugar or water and will keep indefinitely.

Sue Clark

FLORRIE PEDRICK'S RITZ CRACKER MERINGUE

30 Ritz crackers, crushed
3 egg whites
1 cup sugar

1 teaspoon vanilla
1/2 cup pecans, chopped

Beat egg whites until frothy, add sugar gradually. Beat until creamy and stiff. Fold in cracker crumbs, vanilla, and nuts. Bake in greased 9 inch pie pan for 20 minutes at 350°. (When using a pie pan, press down the center and up the sides of pan so that it forms a shell for filling. Individual meringue shells may be made. If so, place on a greased cookie sheet and bake accordingly.) Let cool. Fill with strawberries, peaches, or desired fruit. Top with whipped cream.

NOTE: This recipe was in my mother's recipe file. I have enjoyed it through the years. It is a good recipe.

Nancy Kellam Witherington

BISHOP'S COCKTAIL
(Scuppernong Slush)

Scuppernong juice, frozen

Thaw juice partially; stir in blender until icy like slush. Serve immediately.

Sue Clark

OREO ICE CREAM DESSERT

30 Oreo cookies
1/2 cup margarine

1/2 gallon vanilla ice cream

Put cookies in the blender to make crumbs. Add 1/2 cup of butter. Stir well and pack firmly in bottom of 9x13x2 inch pan. Place in freezer and allow to get very firm. Spread ice cream over this, cover and return to freezer.

CHOCOLATE SAUCE TOPPING:
4 squares of unsweetened
    chocolate
1 cup of sugar
2 tablespoons margarine

2 (5 1/3 ounce) cans
    evaporated milk
Chopped pecans (optional)

Mix all ingredients in double boiler and cook, stirring until thick. Cool and pour over ice cream. Sprinkle with chopped pecans, cover well and return to freezer until ready to serve. This is a nice do ahead dessert and makes 15 squares. For variety the chocolate layer may be spread with 1 (8 ounce) carton Cool Whip.

Bettie Mayo

KISS TARTS

4 egg whites
1¹/₃ cups sugar
1 teaspoon lemon juice

1 teaspoon vanilla
Lemon Filling (see below)

Grease cookie sheet or cover with waxed paper. Beat egg whites until mixture holds it shape when you lift a spoonful. Gradually add sugar a little at a time. Add lemon juice and vanilla. Drop large spoonfuls of meringue mixture on cookie sheet about 2 inches apart. (Meringues will double in size.) Bake at 225° for 1 hour or to bake overnight, heat oven to 400°, place tarts in oven and turn off heat. Let sit overnight. DO NOT OPEN OVEN DOOR until the next day. Top with fresh fruit or Lemon Filling and whipped cream. Serves 6 to 8.

NOTE: Egg whites beat best at room temperature. Always use ¹/₃ cup of sugar for each egg white.

LEMON FILLING:
4 egg yolks, beaten (lemon
    colored)
1 teaspoon grated lemon rind

2 tablespoons lemon juice
¹/₂ cup sugar, folded in

Cook in top of double boiler until thick. Cool.

Martha Mason

LEMON PUDDING

2 tablespoons butter
1 cup sugar
1 lemon, juice and rind

2 eggs, separated
2 tablespoons flour
1 cup milk

Cream butter and sugar; add lemon juice, rind, egg yolks, flour and milk. Mix well. Fold in two stiffly beaten egg whites. Pour into a 1-quart casserole dish. Place casserole (or 8 custard cups) in shallow pan; pour hot water around casserole, 1-inch deep. Bake at 375° for 30 to 45 minutes. Serves 6 to 8.

Melba Mayo

LEMON ANGEL TRIFLE

1 envelope unflavored
  gelatin
1/2 cup water
2 tablespoons grated lemon
  rind

3/4 cup lemon juice
11/4 cups sugar
6 eggs, separated
1 baked 10 inch angel food
  cake

Sprinkle gelatin over water to soften. Combine lemon rind and juice, 1/2 cup sugar, and egg yolks in top of double boiler. Beat with rotary beater until well mixed. Cook over hot water, stirring constantly, until mixture thickens. Stir in gelatin until dissolved. Pour mixture into large bowl; cool. Beat egg whites in a large bowl with electric mixer until foamy. Gradually beat in remaining 3/4 cup of sugar until meringue forms stiff peaks; fold into lemon mixture. Break angel cake into walnut-size pieces and fold into mixture. Spoon into a 9-inch springform pan. Refrigerate 4 hours or overnight. To serve, loosen cake around edges with a spatula. Remove side of pan. Decorate cake with lemon slices and strawberries, if desired. May be put in individual sherbet dishes and chilled if you do not have a springform pan. Serves 12.

Christine Shields

LEMON SPONGE CUPS

2 tablespoons butter
1 cup sugar
4 tablespoons flour
1/4 teaspoon salt
5 tablespoons fresh lemon juice

Grated rind of 1 lemon
3 eggs, separated
11/2 cups milk

Cream butter, add sugar, flour, salt, lemon juice, and lemon rind. Add the well beaten egg yolks which have been mixed with the milk. Lastly, add the stiffly beaten egg whites. Pour into buttered custard cups. Set cups in a pan of water and bake 45 minutes in 350° preheated oven. When done each cup will contain custard at bottom of cup and sponge cake on top. Cool. Unmold on serving plate. It makes its own sauce. Serves 4 to 5.

Jewell Kopp

SOUTHERN GINGERBREAD

2 eggs, beaten
3/4 cup light brown sugar
3/4 cup molasses
3/4 cup melted shortening
2 1/2 cups all-purpose flour
1/2 teaspoon baking powder

2 teaspoons soda
1 1/2 teaspoons cinnamon
1 1/2 teaspoons ginger
1/2 teaspoon salt
1 cup boiling water

Add beaten egg to sugar, molasses and melted shortening. Add dry ingredients which have been mixed and sifted. Stir smooth. Add hot water and stir quickly. Pour into a greased and floured 9x13 inch pan. Bake at 350° for 30 to 40 minutes. Serve warm with Lemon Butter.

Carol Everett

DEATH BY CHOCOLATE TRIFLE
Best served in a pedestal bowl.

1 box family size brownie
  mix
2 (3.4 ounce) packages
  instant chocolate pudding
2 cups milk

2 cups whipping cream
6 Skor bars or Heath bars
1 (12 ounce) container Cool
  Whip

Make brownies and cool. Mix pudding with 2 cups of milk and 2 cups of whipping cream. Cube brownies to cover bottom of bowl. Crumble 2 Skor bars over brownies. Add 1/2 of the pudding, then 1/2 of the Cool Whip. Repeat beginning with brownies, add Skor bars, pudding, and Cool Whip. Crumble 1 Skor bar over the top. This leaves 1 Skor bar for you to hide from yourself. Serves 12.

Martha Mason

CHOCOLATE PATÉ

PATÉ:

1½ cups half and half
4 ounces semi-sweet
  chocolate, coarsely
  chopped

4 ounces white chocolate,
  coarsely chopped
4 large eggs, slightly beaten
2 tablespoons brandy flavoring

GLAZE:

1 cup semi-sweet chocolate
  chips
¼ cup unsalted butter

2 tablespoons corn syrup
Sliced almonds for garnish

Preheat oven to 350°. Combine half and half, semi-sweet chocolate, and white chocolate over low heat and cook, stirring constantly, until chocolates are melted and mixture is smooth. Cool slightly and gradually stir in eggs and flavoring. Pour into 8½x4½x2½ inch loaf pan lined with foil with 2 inch overhang. Place loaf pan in second pan and add 1 inch of very hot water. Bake until knife inserted halfway between edge and center comes out clean, 45 to 50 minutes. When done, remove loaf pan from water. Cool 1 hour, then cover and refrigerate at least 8 hours but not longer than 24 hours. Prepare chocolate glaze by combining chocolate, butter, and syrup over low heat and stirring constantly until chocolate is melted. Cool. Remove paté from pan by inverting onto serving plate. Carefully remove foil and spread glaze evenly over sides and top of paté. Decorate with almond slices in flower design.

Kathy Hackel

LEMON BUTTER

½ cup lemon juice
  (3 medium lemons)
3 eggs

¼ cup butter
2 cups sugar
⅛ teaspoon salt

Grate peel of lemons. Squeeze lemons to get ½ cup of juice. To beaten eggs in top of double boiler, add lemon peel, juice, butter, sugar, and salt. Cook over boiling water until thick, about 15 minutes. Delicious served warm with gingerbread or cake. Makes 2½ cups.

Dale James

FRESH RASPBERRIES WITH CRÉME ANGLAIS

2 pints raspberries
1/2 cup milk
1/2 cup cream
4 egg yolks

1/4 cup sugar
1/8 teaspoon salt
1 tablespoon Framboise

Whisk together the yolks, salt, and sugar. Combine the milk and cream and whisk that into the yolks. Cook over a medium-high heat stirring constantly until it thickens quite suddenly. Remove from the heat, strain and then whisk until cool. Add the Framboise and spoon the Créme Anglais over the raspberries. Can be served hot or cold.

NOTE: Créme Anglais can be refrigerated after you've made it.

Dan and Cheryl Lott

BLUEBERRY STREUSEL

3 cups quick oats, uncooked
2 1/2 cups flour
1 cup brown sugar, packed
3 sticks butter or margarine,
   melted

2 teaspoons flour
2/3 cup raspberry preserves
2 1/2 cups blueberries
1 1/2 teaspoons grated lemon
   peel

Combine oatmeal, 2 1/2 cups flour and sugar. Stir in butter and mix well. Save 2 cups of mixture. Press remaining mixture into bottom of baking dish. Bake 15 minutes. Combine blueberries with 2 teaspoons of flour. Stir in lemon peel and preserves. Spread over baked oatmeal mixture. Top with remaining oatmeal mixture. Bake at 350° for 25 minutes.

NOTE: This is delicious served warm with a dollop of sour cream.

Georgianne McGee

VERMONT BLUEBERRY PUDDING

2 cups flour (fork stir well
   before measuring)
2 teaspoons baking powder
1/2 teaspoon salt
3/4 cup sugar

1/4 cup oleo or butter
1 egg
1/2 cup milk
3 cups blueberries

Stir together flour, baking powder, and salt. Cream butter and sugar; beat in egg. Add flour and milk. Stir just until dry ingredients are dampened; fold in blueberries. Turn into a 9 inch squares cake pan. Sprinkle with topping. Bake at 375° for 45 to 50 minutes.

TOPPING:
1/2 cup sugar
1/3 cup flour

1/2 teaspoon cinnamon
1/4 cup soft oleo or butter

Blend together sugar, flour, cinnamon, and oleo or butter.

Ruth Reese

FRESH FRUIT COBBLER

4 cups fresh fruit (peaches,
   blueberries or your
   choice)
2 cups sugar
1 stick margarine

1 cup flour
2 teaspoons baking powder
1/2 teaspoon salt
3/4 cup milk

Preheat oven to 325°. Combine fruit and 1 cup sugar and set aside. In a 9x13 inch glass dish, melt margarine. Combine remaining sugar, 1 cup flour, baking powder, salt, and milk. Mix until smooth. Pour over margarine and spoon fruit over batter. Bake at 325° for 1 hour. May be served warm with whipped topping, whipped cream, or ice cream. Serves 8.

Imogene Hatfield

279

PEACHAROON FROZEN TORTE

2 cups mashed peaches
1¼ cups sugar
1 tablespoon lemon juice
1 cup heavy cream, whipped

1 cup coarse macaroon
crumbs (crush coconut
macaroon cookies)

To peaches, add sugar and lemon juice. Fold in whipped cream. Place ½ of crumbs in bottom of 1 quart refrigerator tray. Pour in peach mixture. Top with remaining crumbs. Freeze until firm. Cut in wedges, slices or squares. Top with peach slice. Serves 6 to 8.

Ruth Groover

HUGUENOT TORTE

CAKE:

2 cups finely ground mixed
  nuts (1/3 pecans, 1/3
  English walnuts and 1/3
  black walnuts)
2 large apples, peeled and
  finely chopped

4 large eggs, room
  temperature
1 large egg yolk, room
  temperature
13/4 cups sugar
3/4 cup unbleached flour

Finely grind the nuts in blender or food processor. Chop apples very finely with knife. In a warmed mixer bowl, beat the eggs and egg yolk on high speed until doubled in volume (10 minutes or more). Slowly add the sugar and continue beating until the volume is tripled. The eggs should be very thick and light in color. Sift the flour over the egg mixture. Sprinkle the ground nuts and apples over all. With a spatula, fold the mixture together rapidly, but gently. Divide the batter and pour into two 9 inch greased and lined pie pans. Put a pan of water in the bottom of the oven and bake cake at 375° for 25 to 30 minutes until top of cake is golden brown. Cool cake completely before removing from pans.

TOPPING:

16 perfect pecan halves,
  roasted

Granulated sugar
2/3 cup whipping cream

Lightly toast pecan halves in 325° oven for 15 minutes. While pecans are hot, quickly dip them in water, and then roll them in granulated sugar until lightly coated. Let dry on rack. When cakes are perfectly cool, turn onto serving plates. Whip cream until stiff and pipe 8 rosettes or 8 dollops of cream evenly around each cake. Garnish each with a sugared pecan and serve immediately or chilled. Serves 16.

Jane Groover Holt

EUROPEAN APPLE PIE

¾ cup sugar	1½ tablespoons butter
1 teaspoon cinnamon	2 (9 inch) pastry crusts for pie
6 to 7 apples, peeled and sliced	

Peel apples, quarter and core; cut into ¼ inch slices. Mix sugar and cinnamon. Add sugar mixture to apples and toss to cover fruit. Fill pastry shell with apple mixture. Dot with butter.

TOPPING:

½ cup brown sugar, packed	½ cup butter
1 cup flour	½ cup heavy cream

Combine brown sugar and flour. Cut in butter until mixture resembles coarse crumbs. Sprinkle mixture over apples. Cover pie with second crust. Seal the edges. Make extra long slits in top crust. Bake at 375° for 40 minutes. Remove pie from oven and pour ½ cup heavy cream through the slits in top crust. Return to oven and bake 5 minutes, watching not to burn. Serves 6 to 8.

NOTE: My family loves this every Thanksgiving, Christmas, and Easter.

Cynthia Raynor

FRESH BLUEBERRY CREAM PIE

1 cup sour cream	2½ cups fresh blueberries
2 tablespoons flour	1 (9 inch) pastry shell, unbaked
¾ cup sugar	3 tablespoons flour
1 teaspoon vanilla	3 tablespoons butter, softened
¼ teaspoon salt	3 tablespoons pecans, chopped
1 egg, beaten	

Combine sour cream, 2 tablespoons flour, sugar, vanilla, salt, and egg. Beat 5 minutes at medium speed. Fold in blueberries. Pour into pastry shell; bake at 400° for 25 minutes. Combine 3 tablespoons flour, butter, and chopped nuts, stirring well. Sprinkle over top of pie. Bake 10 additional minutes. Chill before serving. Serves 6 to 8.

Margaret Park

BAKED CHERRY CHEESE PIE

9 inch unbaked pie shell
(deep dish)
1 (1 pound 5 ounce) can
cherry pie filling
12 ounces cream cheese,
softened

1/2 cup sugar
2 eggs
1/2 teaspoon vanilla
Some whipped topping

Preheat oven to 425° F. Prepare pie shell. Spread half of cherry pie filling in bottom; refrigerate rest of the filling. Bake shell 15 minutes, or until crust is golden. Remove from oven. Reduce oven temperature to 350° F. Meanwhile, in a small bowl, with electric mixer, beat cheese with sugar, eggs, and vanilla until smooth. Pour over hot cherry pie filling; bake 25 minutes. (Filling will be slightly soft in the center.) Cool completely on wire rack. Before serving, pipe a border of whipped topping around pie, fill center with the remaining pie filling. Serves 8.

Hildegard Amspacher

COCONUT PIE
This pie makes its own crust.

4 eggs
1 1/2 cups sugar
1/2 cup self-rising flour
2 cups milk
1/2 stick margarine

1 (7 ounce) can coconut
1/2 teaspoon vanilla
Topping - whipped cream or
Cool Whip

Beat eggs. Add sugar, flour, and milk. Add coconut and vanilla. Pour into greased 9 or 10 inch pie pan and bake at 325° for 50 minutes. Top with whipped cream or Cool Whip. Serves 8.

Grace Proctor

COCONUT CREAM PIE

1/3 cup flour
2/3 cup sugar
1/4 teaspoon salt
2 cups milk, scalded
3 egg yolks

2 tablespoons butter
1 teaspoon vanilla
1 cup fresh grated or frozen
   coconut
1 pie shell, baked

Combine flour, sugar, and salt in top of a double boiler. Gradually add scalded milk and cook until thick, stirring constantly. Add small amount of hot mixture to beaten egg yolks, then stir into hot mixture. Cook, covered, for 2 minutes. Cool. Add butter, vanilla, and coconut. Pour into baked pie shell and cover with meringue. Sprinkle with a little coconut for garnish and bake at 350° for 10 minutes or until lightly browned.

MERINGUE:
3 egg whites, stiffly beaten   Pinch of salt
1/4 cup sugar

Add salt to egg whites and beat until stiff. Gradually beat in sugar. Spread on top of pie, sealing edges. Sprinkle with coconut and bake. Serves 6 to 8.

Bunny Winge

CHOCOLATE CREAM PIE
This is the pie men like!

3 tablespoons butter
1/4 cup flour
11/4 cups milk
1 teaspoon vanilla
1 cup sugar

1 egg, well beaten
2 squares semi-sweet
   chocolate
Whipped cream
1 (8 inch) pastry shell, baked

Cream butter until soft. Gradually blend in sugar, then flour. Combine beaten egg and milk and stir into first mixture. Break chocolate into smaller pieces; add. Cook entire mixture in top of double boiler until thick and smooth, stirring frequently. Add vanilla. Pour into baked pastry shell and cool. Top with whipped cream. Yields one 8 inch pie.

Pauline Hopkins

AUNT BURNET'S EGG CUSTARD PIE

4 eggs, slightly beaten
2 cups sugar
2 teaspoons vanilla
1/2 teaspoon salt
2 1/2 cups milk, scalded and
   slightly cooled

1/2 teaspoon nutmeg
1 (9 inch) deep dish pie
   shell, uncooked

Beat together eggs, sugar, vanilla, and salt. Slowly stir in milk. Pour into pie shell and sprinkle with nutmeg. Bake at 350° for 35 to 40 minutes.

Landy Rimes

FUDGE PIE
"Make one - share one!"

2 (9 inch) pie shells,
   unbaked
1 cup semi-sweet chocolate
   chips
2 sticks margarine or butter

2 cups sugar
4 eggs
1 cup nuts, chopped
1 teaspoon vanilla
Pinch of salt

Melt margarine and chocolate chips together over low heat. Beat eggs, sugar and salt together. Add chocolate mixture, nuts, and vanilla. Beat together. Pour mixture into 2 unbaked pie shells. Bake at 350° for 35 minutes. Serves 6 to 8 per pie.

NOTE: This is delicious with a scoop of vanilla ice cream on top!

Mikell McKee

HOTEL HERSHEY DERBY PIE

1 cup sugar
4 tablespoons cornstarch
2 eggs, lightly beaten
1 stick butter or margarine,
   melted and cooled

3 tablespoons bourbon
   flavoring or 1 teaspoon vanilla
1 (6 ounce) package
   semi-sweet chocolate pieces
1 cup pecans, finely chopped
1 (9 inch) pastry shell, unbaked

Combine sugar and cornstarch in a medium size bowl. Beat in eggs; mix in butter, flavoring, chocolate bits, and pecans. Pour into pastry shell. Bake at 350° for 40 minutes or until puffy and lightly browned. Cut pie into slim wedges (it's very rich) and top each portion with a dollop of Derby Whipped Cream.

DERBY WHIPPED CREAM:
1/2 cup heavy cream
2 tablespoons confectioners
   sugar

1/2 teaspoon vanilla

Beat cream with confectioners sugar in a small bowl to soft peaks. Add flavoring and beat to stiff peaks. Serves 8 to 10.

NOTE: This pie freezes well. When ready to serve, set unwrapped, but frozen pie in a warm oven (300°) and warm gently for 35 to 40 minutes.

Georgine Smith

HUMMINGBIRD PIE

1 (14 ounce) can condensed
   milk
1 small can frozen lemon
   concentrate juice
1 (12 ounce) carton whipped
   topping

1 (20 ounce) can crushed
   pineapple, well drained
1/2 cup chopped pecans, if
   desired
2 graham cracker pie shells

Thoroughly mix condensed milk with lemon concentrate. Add drained pineapple and nuts. Fold in topping. Fill pie shells. Place in refrigerator overnight. Serves 16.

Imogene Hatfield

EDMUND PEDRICK'S CHOCOLATE PIE

1 cup butter
3 squares unsweetened
    chocolate
2 tablespoons plain flour
1 cup sugar
2 cups brown sugar

4 large eggs
1/4 cup milk
2 teaspoons vanilla
2 (9 inch) pie crusts or 1
    deep dish 9 inch pie
    crust, uncooked

Melt butter and chocolate in double boiler. Add to flour and sugars. Mix in eggs, one at a time. Slowly add milk, stirring constantly until well blended. Add vanilla. Pour into pie shell. For regular pie shells, bake at 325° for 45 minutes. For deep dish shell, bake for 55 minutes. Serve with ice cream.

Edmund Pedrick

LEMON CHIFFON PIE

4 egg yolks, beaten
1 cup sugar, divided
1/2 cup lemon juice
1/8 teaspoon salt

1 tablespoon plain gelatin
1/4 cup cold water
4 egg whites
1 baked pie shell

Mix egg yolks, 1/2 cup sugar, lemon juice, and salt together. Cook in double boiler, stirring constantly until consistency of custard. Soak glatin in water until dissolved. Add to hot custard. Beat egg whites until foamy. Gradually add 1/2 cup sugar, beating until stiff. Carefully fold hot custard into egg whites. Put into baked pie shell and chill 3 hours.

Clyde King

CLOISTER LEMON MERINGUE PIE
Recipe given to me by a long time baker for the Cloister Resort Hotel on St. Simons Island.

9 inch pie shell (baked)
1½ cups sugar
7 tablespoons cornstarch
Dash salt
1½ cups water
3 beaten egg yolks

1 teaspoon grated lemon peel
2 tablespoons butter or margarine
½ cup lemon juice

In saucepan, combine sugar, cornstarch, and salt. Stir in water. Bring to boiling over medium heat and cook, stirring constantly until thick, about 5 minutes. Remove from heat, stir small amount of hot mixture into egg yolks then return to remaining mixture in pan. Bring to a boil and cook 1 minute, stirring constantly. Remove from heat. Add lemon peel and butter. Slowly stir in lemon juice. Cool to lukewarm. Pour into cooled baked pastry shell.

MERINGUE:
3 egg whites
1 teaspoon lemon juice

6 tablespoons sugar

Beat egg whites with 1 teaspoon lemon juice until soft peaks form. Gradually add 6 tablespoons sugar, beating until stiff. Spread meringue over filling, seal to edges of pastry. Bake in moderate oven (350°) for 12 to 15 minutes or until meringue is golden brown. Cool thoroughly before serving. Serves 6 to 8.

Frankie Miles

LEMON SPONGE PIE

4 eggs, separated
Pinch of salt
1 teaspoon grated rind
1 pie crust, baked

1 cup sugar
1/2 cup lemon juice
3 tablespoons butter

Beat egg yolks until light. Add sugar, salt, lemon juice, and butter. Cook until thick - add rind and slightly beaten egg whites. Pour into crust and bake at 425° until slightly brown. Top with Cool Whip.

Madge Herrin

KEY LIME PIE
This recipe comes from Marathon Key, Florida. Best used with fresh key limes.

1 pie shell, baked (may use
   graham cracker)
3 eggs, separated
1 (14 ounce) can sweetened
   condensed milk

1/2 cup key lime juice (5
   limes)
1 cup sugar (approximately)

Preheat oven to 350°. In a medium bowl, combine beaten egg yolks and condensed milk; stir in lime juice. (Reserve 1 teaspoon for meringue.) Add 1/2 cup of sugar. Pour into baked pie crust.

MERINGUE:
3 egg whites
1/3 cup sugar

1 teaspoon lime juice
Pinch of salt

Beat egg whites until stiff, gradually adding 1/3 cup of sugar and a scant teaspoon of lime juice. Spread meringue on top of pie filling, sealing carefully to edge of crust. Bake 15 minutes in moderate oven (350°) or until meringue is golden. Chill thoroughly before serving. Serves 6 to 8.

NOTE: When beating egg whites, a pinch of salt makes eggs fluffier.

Lois Groszmann

MOTHER'S MACAROON PIE

12 saltine crackers, crushed
12 dates, chopped fine (or ½
   of 8 ounce box chopped
   dates)
½ cup chopped pecans
1 cup sugar (less if dates
   are sugared)

¼ teaspoon baking powder
¼ teaspoon almond extract
3 egg whites, beaten until
   stiff

Mix saltines, dates, sugar, and baking powder. Beat egg whites until stiff and add almond extract. Fold egg whites into dry ingredients. Bake in a greased pie pan for 30 minutes at 325° (there is no crust). Serve topped with whipped cream.

Julie Tomlinson

PECAN CHIFFON PIE

4 eggs, separated
1 cup milk, scalded
¼ teaspoon salt
1 cup sugar
¾ cup chopped toasted
   pecans

1 package unflavored gelatin
¼ cup water
1 (9 inch) pie shell, baked

Sprinkle gelatin on ¼ cup water to soften. Scald milk in heavy saucepan. (DO NOT BOIL.) Beat egg yolks, sugar, and salt together. Slowly add to hot milk, stirring constantly. Cook until custard coats wooden spoon. Remove from heat and stir in softened gelatin. Stir until dissolved. Add toasted pecans. Cool until mixture begins to thicken. Beat egg whites until stiff, adding the remaining ½ cup of sugar. Fold egg whites into custard mixture. Pour into baked pie shell and refrigerate to congeal. Garnish with whipped cream and finely chopped toasted pecans.

Lorena Miller

SOUTHERN PECAN PIE

2 tablespoons margarine or
   butter
1/2 cup sugar
2 eggs
2 tablespoons flour

1/2 teaspoon salt
1 cup white Karo syrup
1 teaspoon vanilla
11/2 cups pecans, chopped
1 (9 inch) pie shell, unbaked

Cream butter and sugar, add beaten eggs, flour, salt, syrup, and vanilla. Stir well. Add pecans. Pour into unbaked pie crust. Bake at 375° for 10 minutes. Reduce heat to 350° and bake an additional 35 minutes. Makes 6 to 8 slices.

Coolie Hughes

"SECOND TIME AROUND" PECAN PIE
This unique pecan pie is the result of a disasterous first time try.
The second time around brought about a blue ribbon winner.

1/2 cup sugar
1 cup dark Karo syrup
2 eggs, beaten
1 tablespoon butter or
   margarine

1 teaspoon vanilla
2 cups pecans, chopped
1 (8 or 9 inch) pie shell,
   uncooked

Cook syrup and sugar together in heavy saucepan over medium heat. Stir until sugar melts and blends into the syrup. Pour very slowly into beaten eggs, beating BRISKLY with wire whisk so eggs don't scramble from the heat of the syrup. Add butter, vanilla and chopped pecans. Pour into pie crust. Bake at 350° for 30 minutes. Serves 6 to 8.

NOTE: My first success with this pie was handed out to all the neighbors because my husband was so proud of it! I've made hundreds since, but am always sure I hide a slice for myself.

Jane Hart

291

TOFFEE BAR CRUNCH PIE

1/3 cup caramel dessert
   topping
1 1/2 cups cold milk
1 (3 ounce) package instant
   vanilla pudding

1 (8 ounce) Cool Whip
   whipped topping
6 Heath bars, chopped
1 graham cracker pie crust

Spread dessert topping over bottom of crust. Pour milk into large bowl. Add pudding mix and beat with wire whisk for 2 minutes. Let stand 5 minutes. Stir in Cool Whip and chopped toffee bars. Spoon into crust. Freeze for 4 hours or until set. When serving, let stand at room temperature for 15 minutes before cutting. Serves 8.

Alex Hood

ORANGE SWEET POTATO PIE

2 cups cooked sweet
   potatoes, mashed
1 cup brown sugar
1/3 cup white sugar
1/3 cup evaporated milk
1/3 cup orange juice
1/3 stick butter, melted
1/3 teaspoon salt
1 teaspoon vanilla

2 teaspoons grated orange
   rind
2 well beaten eggs
1 (9 inch) pie shell, unbaked
Toasted nuts, optional
   topping
Coconut, optional topping
Dollop of whipped cream,
   optional topping

Combine sweet potatoes, sugars, milk, orange juice, melted butter, salt, vanilla, grated orange rind, and eggs. Bake in 9 inch pie shell for 1 hour at 350°. Garnish with topping of your choice. Serves 6 to 8.

Virginia Holtzendorf

SPICED MAPLE PUMPKIN PIE

3/4 cup sugar
1/2 teaspoon cinnamon
1/4 to 1/2 teaspoon ginger
1/4 teaspoon salt
1/8 teaspoon ground cloves
1 (16 ounce) can (2 cups)
   pumpkin

1 can evaporated milk
1/2 cup maple-flavored syrup
2 eggs, slightly beaten
1 (9 inch) pie shell, unbaked

Mix together sugar, cinnamon, ginger, salt, cloves, pumpkin, milk, syrup, and eggs. Bake at 350° for 50 to 60 minutes. Cool.

TOPPING:
1 cup whipping cream
2 tablespoons confectioners
   sugar

1 tablespoon maple-flavored
   syrup
1/4 teaspoon cinnamon

Whip cream, sugar, sryup, and cinnamon together until stiff. Spread over cooled pie. Serves 6 to 8.

NOTE: Maple syrup adds a subtle, new flavor to a traditional pumpkin pie.

Nickie Carter

STRAWBERRY PIE

1 cup boiling water
1 cup sugar
2 tablespoons cornstarch
2 tablespoons strawberry
   flavored gelatin

1 cup whipping cream
2 to 3 drops red food coloring
1 quart strawberries
1/4 teaspoon salt
1 (9 inch) pie shell, baked

Mix sugar, cornstarch and salt. Add water; cook until thick. Add gelatin and coloring; let cool. Line baked pastry shell with berries. Pour glaze over berries. Put in refrigerator and let congeal. Serve with whipped cream. Serves 6 to 8.

Lucy Mason

293

MILE HIGH STRAWBERRY PIE

1 (10 ounce) package frozen
  strawberries, thawed
1 cup sugar
1 tablespoon lemon juice
2 egg whites

1/4 teaspoon salt
1 cup whipping cream
1 teaspoon vanilla
1 (9 inch) deep dish pie
  shell, baked

Mix strawberries, sugar, lemon juice, egg whites, and salt in a large mixing bowl. Beat at high speed for about 15 minutes (mixture will go nearly to the top of the bowl). Whip cream and vanilla until stiff. Fold into strawberry mixture. Pour into baked pie shell and freeze. Remove pie from freezer 10 minutes before serving. This pie does not freeze really hard. Serves 8 to 10.

Nancy Kellam Witherington

ANGEL LEMON PIE

MERINGUE CRUST:
4 egg whites
3 cups sugar
1/4 teaspoon cream of tartar

Pinch of salt
10 inch pie pan

Beat egg whites and salt until frothy. Add cream of tartar; then add sugar gradually and beat until stiff. Spread in 10 inch greased pie pan. Bake 1 hour in slow (275°) oven until slightly brown and dry.

FILLING:
4 egg yolks
1/2 cup sugar
2 tablespoons orange juice
2 1/2 table spoons lemon juice

1 teaspoon grated lemon rind
1 cup cream, whipped
2 tablespoons powdered sugar

In doubl boiler, mix eggs, yolks, sugar, juices, and lemon rind. Stir constan y and cook until mixture thickens. Cool. Whip cream and add powdered sugar. Fold into egg mixture (reserve some for garnish). Pour into Meringue Crust. Garnish edges with reserved whipped cream. Refrigerate. Will freeze. Serves 6 to 8.

Myrtle Sands

ZUPER! ZWELL! ZWIEBACK PIE

CRUST:
3/4 box Zwieback   4 tablespoons sugar
3/4 stick butter, melted

Grind zwieback to fine crumbs. Mix with melted butter and sugar. Line inside of prepared pie plate, saving a little bit of mixture to sprinkle on top of pie. Pack crust well. Place in slow oven (275°) and brown slightly, about 15 minutes.

FILLING:
4 eggs (save 3 egg whites   3 tablespoons flour
   for meringue)   1/2 teaspoon vanilla
1/2 cup sugar   2 cups milk

Beat eggs (3 yolks, 1 whole) slightly. Add sugar, flour, and milk. Mix well. Cook over medium heat, stirring constantly. As it thickens, lower heat and cook until thick. Remove from heat and add vanilla. Pour into crust. Top with meringue. Sprinkle with reserved crumbs. Bake at 350° for 10 minutes or until lightly browned. Chill for 6 hours before serving.

MERINGUE:
3 egg whites   Pinch of salt
1/4 cup sugar

Beat egg whites with pinch of salt. Add sugar gradually. Beat until stiff. Spread over pie. Seal edges. Serves 6 to 8.

Ruth Groover

THE ULTIMATE CARAMEL CHOCOLATE PECAN PIE

CRUST:

2 cups finely chopped
   pecans
1/4 cup sugar

1/4 cup (1/2 stick) Parkay
   margarine, melted

Bake at 350° until lightly browned.

FILLING:

1 (14 ounce) package Kraft
   caramels
1/4 cup milk
1 cup pecans, chopped

1 (8 ounce) package
   semi-sweet chocolate
1/3 cup milk
1/2 teaspoon vanilla

Melt caramels and milk in top of double boiler. Cool and pour into pie crust. Sprinkle with 1 cup chopped nuts. Melt chocolate in milk. Add 1/2 teaspoon vanilla. Cool and pour over nuts. Top with whipped cream.

Dale James

DATE NUT PIE

2 cups boiling water
3/4 cup sugar
1 tablespoon cornstarch
1/4 teaspoon salt
8 ounces pitted dates,
   chopped

1 cup pecans, chopped
1 baked (9 inch) pie shell
1 (8 ounce) carton whipping
   cream, whipped

Mix sugar, cornstarch, and salt. Stir this gradually into boiling water. When mixture begins to thicken, put in dates and cook to a pulp. Add chopped pecans and pour into baked pie shell. Top each serving with whipped cream. Serves 6 to 8.

Mary Cox

CREAM CHEESE POUND CAKE

1½ cups butter (3 sticks)
1 (8 ounce) package cream
   cheese
3 cups sugar

6 eggs
3 cups flour
2 teaspoons vanilla flavoring

Cream together softened butter and cream cheese and sugar. Beat until light and fluffy. Add eggs, one at a time, beating well after each addition. Gradually stir in flour, beating until smooth. Blend in the vanilla. Pour into prepared tube pan and bake at 325° for 1½ hours. Leave in pan 10 minutes, then turn cake out and cool on rack. Glaze with Caramel Glaze.

CARAMEL GLAZE:
1 cup light brown sugar,
   packed
1 stick butter

¼ cup evaporated milk
1 teaspoon vanilla flavoring

In a heavy saucepan, over medium heat, stir together sugar, butter, and milk until butter has melted and is bubbly. Cook for 2 minutes WITHOUT stirring. Remove from heat and let cool 15 minutes (DO NOT STIR). Then add vanilla and beat until mixture thickens. Pour over cake.

Cile Lott

NOTE: To prepare a tube pan for cake baking, grease pan with vegetable shortening and dust generously with flour. Or to make it oh! so easy, just spray pan with "Baker's Joy". This product is found at the grocery store next to Pam. It is indeed and joy to use.

The Cookbook Committee

WHIPPED CREAM POUND CAKE

1/2 pound pure butter (no
   substitute)
3 cups sugar
1 teaspoon vanilla flavoring

1/2 pint whipping cream
31/4 cups cake flour
6 large eggs
Pinch of salt (optional)

Cream butter and sugar thoroughly; add vanilla then whipping cream, beating on highest speed for 1 minute. Add flour and eggs alternately, mixing well after each addition. Bake in prepared tube pan at 350° for about 1 hour. Cool 25 minutes before removing from pan.

Marie Carroll

WHIPPED CREAM FROSTING

1 teaspoon unflavored
   gelatin
4 teaspoons cold water
3 cups whipping cream
   (well chilled)

1/4 cup granulated sugar
1/2 teaspoon vanilla
   flavoring (or almond
   flavoring)

In a small saucepan, soften gelatin in cold water and then place over very low heat until gelatin dissolves. Remove from heat and cool slightly. Place cold whipping cream into a chilled mixing bowl and beat until soft peaks form. Gradually add sugar, vanilla, and cooled gelatin. Beat until thick and smooth. Frost cake and keep refrigerated. This icing will keep for 2 days if refrigerated.

The Cookbook Committee

MRS. HARPER'S SPECIAL POUND CAKE

3 cups sugar
2 sticks butter
5 large eggs
3 cups sifted flour
1/4 teaspoon soda

1 (8 ounce) carton sour cream
1/2 cup (or more) pecans
   pieces
1/2 cup sugar
2 teaspoons cinnamon

Cream sugar and butter well. Add eggs, one at a time, beating well after each addition. Sift flour and soda together three times and stir into creamed mixture alternately with sour cream. Pour 1/2 of batter in prepared (line bottom with wax paper) tube pan. Cover batter with half pecan pieces and sprinkle cinnamon and sugar on pecans. Add remainder of batter and top with pecans and more cinnamon and sugar. Bake at 300° for 1 1/2 hours. Remove from pan and put cake into a plastic container with cover while hot. Let cake cool while covered.

Arlie Nall

VIOLETTE KELLAM'S POUND CAKE

2 1/3 sticks butter, softened
2 1/3 cups sugar
6 eggs
4 cups cake flour
2 scant teaspoons baking
   powder

1/2 teaspoon vanilla
   flavoring
1/2 teaspoon lemon flavoring
1 cup milk (scant)

Cream together softened butter and flour, adding just enough milk to make mixture workable. Beat together sugar and eggs. Combine flour and egg mixture, blending well. Add vanilla and lemon flavoring. Pour into prepared tube pan and bake at 300° for 1 1/2 hours. DO NOT OVERCOOK. Run knife around cake in pan while it is hot. Cool and invert pan to remove cake.

NOTE: Many members of First United Methodist Church were lucky enough to receive gifts of my late mother-in-law's delicious pound cake. She said she put in an ingredient that could not be measured ... LOVE!

Louise Kellam

BROWN SUGAR POUND CAKE

1 cup butter	1/2 teaspoon salt
1/2 cup vegetable shortening	1 teaspoon baking powder
1 pound light brown sugar	1 cup milk
1 cup white sugar	1 teaspoon vanilla flavoring
5 eggs	1 cup chopped pecans
3 cups sifted flour	

In a large mixing bowl, cream together the butter, shortening, brown, and white sugar, beating well until the mixture is light and fluffy. Add the eggs, one at a time, beating well after each addition. Sift flour before measuring and stir in the salt and baking powder and sift again. Add flour mixture alternately with the milk and vanilla to the creamed mixture. Stir in the pecans. Pour into prepared tube pan and bake at 350° for 1 1/4 hours, or until a toothpick inserted comes out clean. Cool for ten minutes in pan before turning cake from pan. Glaze while still warm.

PECAN GLAZE:

2 tablespoons butter	1/2 teaspoon vanilla
1 cup powdered sugar, sifted	flavoring
6 tablespoons cream	1/2 cup chopped pecans

Cream together the butter and powdered sugar. Gradually add cream and vanilla, beating well. Stir in the chopped pecans and spoon over warm cake.

Bunny Winge

SOUTHERN CHOCOLATE POUND CAKE

1 cup butter or margarine
1/2 cup shortening
3 cups sugar
6 large eggs
3 cups cake flour
5 to 6 tablespoons cocoa
    (heaping)

1/2 teaspoon baking powder
1/2 teaspoon salt
1 cup milk
1 or 2 teaspoons vanilla

Cream butter, shortening, and sugar. Add eggs, one at a time, beating one minute after each addition. Add dry ingredients (which have been sifted together) and milk alternately. Stir in vanilla. Pour into large prepared tube pan or 2 loaf pans. Bake at 300° for 1 1/2 hours or until done.

NEVER-FAIL CHOCOLATE ICING:
2 cups sugar
1/2 cup milk
1 stick butter
1/4 cup cocoa (heaping)

1/2 to 2 teaspoons vanilla
    (you decide)
1/2 teaspoon salt (optional)

Combine sugar, milk, butter, cocoa, vanilla and salt in a saucepan and bring to a boil. After reaching a "rolling boil", boil for EXACTLY 2 MINUTES. Cool thoroughly. Go read a book for 45 minutes to one hour. Don't start beating icing until you can place your hand on the bottom of the saucepan and find it barely warm. You should then probably beat for only 1 to 1 1/2 minutes. Spread on pound cake.

Georgine Smith

SWEET CHOCOLATE CAKE

2 cups flour
2 cups sugar
1/2 teaspoon salt
2 sticks margarine
1 cup water

2 eggs, beaten
3 tablespoons cocoa
1 teaspoon baking soda
1/2 cup buttermilk
1 teaspoon vanilla flavoring

Sift flour, measure and re-sift with sugar and salt. In a saucepan, mix margarine, water, and cocoa and bring to a boil. Stir into flour mixture. In a separate bowl, beat eggs, add baking soda and buttermilk. Mix with flour mixture. Add vanilla and mix well. Pour into a prepared 13x9 inch pan. Bake at 350° for 30 minutes.

ICING:
1 stick margarine
3 tablespoons cocoa
6 tablespoons evaporated
  milk

1 (16 ounce) box powdered
  sugar
1/2 cup pecans, chopped

In a saucepan, mix together margarine, cocoa, and milk. Heat, but DO NOT BOIL. Mix with powdered sugar and nuts. Spread on cake while cake is still hot. Cool before cutting into squares.

NOTE: This cake is best made one day before you serve it. It also freezes well.

Martha Mason

GERMAN CHOCOLATE CAKE

1 (4 ounce) package German
  sweet chocolate
1/2 cup water
2 cups flour
1 teaspoon baking soda
1/4 teaspoon salt

2 sticks butter (or
  margarine), softened
2 cups sugar
4 eggs, separated
1 teaspoon vanilla flavoring
1 cup buttermilk

Melt chocolate in water over low heat or in microwave. Stir until chocolate is completely melted. Sift together flour, baking soda, and salt. Set aside. Cream butter and sugar in large bowl with electric mixer on medium speed until light and fluffy. Add egg yolks, one at a time, beating well after each addition. Stir in chocolate and vanilla. Add flour mixture alternately with buttermilk, beating after each addition until smooth. Beat egg whites in another large bowl until stiff peaks form. Gently fold into batter. Pour into prepared 9 inch round pans. Bake at 350° for 30 minutes or until cake springs back when touched. Immediately run spatula between cake and sides of pans. Cool 15 minutes; remove from pans.

COCONUT-PECAN FROSTING:
1 (12 ounce) can evaporated
  milk
1 1/2 cups sugar
3/4 cup butter or margarine
4 egg yolks, slightly beaten

1 1/2 teaspoons vanilla
1 (7 ounce) can Angel Flake
  coconut
1 1/2 cups chopped pecans

Mix milk, sugar, margarine, egg yolks and vanilla in large saucepan. Cook and stir on medium heat about 12 minutes or until thickened and golden brown. Remove from heat and stir in coconut and pecans. Beat until cool and of spreading consistency.

Sandy Strickland

CHOCOLATE ORANGE ROULAGE

CHOCOLATE CAKE ROLL:

Vegetable cooking spray
4 large eggs
1/2 cup water

1 (18.25 ounce) package Swiss
   chocolate, devil's food or
   fudge cake mix
3 to 4 tablespoons cocoa

Coat two (15x10x1 inch) jelly-roll pans with cooking spray; line with wax paper, and coat with cooking spray. Set aside. Beat eggs in a large mixing bowl at medium-high speed with an electric mixer 5 minutes. Add 1/2 cup water, beating at low speed just until blended. Gradually add package of cake mix, beating at low speed just until moistened. Beat mixture at medium-high speed 2 minutes. Divide batter in half, and spread batter evenly into prepared pans. (Layers will be thin.) Bake each cake at 350° on the middle rack of oven for 13 minutes or until cake springs back when lightly touched in the center. Sift 1 to 2 tablespoons cocoa in a 15x10 inch rectangle on a cloth towel; repeat with second towel. When cakes are done, immediately loosen from sides of pans, and turn each out onto a prepared towel. Peel off wax paper. Starting at narrow end, roll up each cake and towel together; place, seam side down, on wire racks to cool completely. Use cake rolls for Chocolate-Orange Roulage. Yield: 2 cake rolls.

ORANGE ROULAGE:

2 cups whipping cream
5 to 6 tablespoons frozen
   orange juice concentrate,
   thawed and undiluted,
   divided

1 tablespoon finely grated
   orange rind
Chocolate Cake Roll
Cocoa

Beat whipping cream with an electric mixer until soft peaks form. Fold in 2 to 3 tablespoons orange juice and orange rind; set aside. Unroll cake rolls; brush each lightly with remaining 3 tablespoons orange juice. Spread each cake with half of whipped cream mixture. Reroll cakes without towel; place, seam side down, on a baking sheet. Cover and freeze at least 1 hour or up to 3 months. Dust cakes with cocoa. Slice and serve. Garnish, if desired. Yield: 2 filled cake rolls (5 to 6 servings each).

Pam Barnhill

ESTHER ZORN'S FRUIT CAKE

1 pound pecan halves
1/2 pound walnuts
3/4 pound whole candied
   cherries, halved
1/2 pound diced candied
   pineapple
1/2 cup white raisins
1 cup sifted flour

1 1/2 cups butter
1 1/2 cups sugar
3 eggs
2 tablespoons vanilla
   flavoring
2 cups flour, sifted
3/4 teaspoon baking powder

Mix pecans, walnuts, cherries, pineapple, raisins, and 1 cup flour together. Set aside. Cream butter and sugar together. Add eggs, one at a time, beating well after each addition. Add vanilla. Sift together flour and baking powder and add to mixture. Fold in fruit and nut mixture. Bake in a prepared tube pan or two loaf pans. Bake at 300° for 2 1/2 hours. Leave for 5 minutes before removing from pan. Brush top with light corn syrup.

Bonnie Storey

CHRISTMAS NUT CAKE

1 pound butter
2 cups sugar
6 eggs, separated
4 cups flour
1 (1 1/2 ounce) bottle lemon
   flavoring
1 tablespoon vanilla
   flavoring

1/2 pound candied red
   cherries, chopped
1/2 pound candied green
   pineapple, chopped
1/2 pound white raisins,
   chopped
1 quart pecans, chopped

Cream butter and sugar well. Add egg yolks, one at a time, beating well after each addition. Add 3 cups flour, blending well. Add lemon and vanilla. Mix fruit and nuts and dredge with one cup flour. Fold into batter. Fold in stiffly beaten egg whites. Pour into prepared tube pan and bake at 325° for 30 minutes; reduce heat to 300° and bake one hour longer. Store as fruit cake. This will last several weeks.

Imogene Hatfield

FRUIT CAKE

2 pounds pitted dates, chopped	1 pound candied citrus peel, chopped
1 pound pecans, chopped	2 cups self-rising flour
1/2 pound candied cherries, chopped	2 cups sugar
1/2 pound candied pineapple, chopped	8 eggs
	4 tablespoons vanilla flavoring

Reserve some cherries and/or pineapple to decorate top of cake. Place chopped dates, pecans, cherries, pineapple, and citrus peel in a large mixing bowl. Mix together flour and sugar; then slowly pour over fruit and nuts until all fruit is well coated. Beat eggs and vanilla together in a separate bowl. Slowly pour over fruit mixture, stirring until all dry ingredients are moist. Pour fruit into desired pan, pressing down firmly. Decorate top as desired with reserved fruit pieces. Bake at 300° for appropriate time. Place a pan of water in oven to produce a moist cake. Watch closely. Do not overcook. The cake is done when a toothpick inserted comes out clean. This cake may be baked in 2 tube pans, 4 loaf pans, 4 layer cake pans, or baked as cupcakes (48 yield). Baking time: tube pan, 1 1/2 hours; loaf pan, 1 hour; layer cake pan, 1 hour and cupcakes, 20 to 30 minutes.

Elizabeth Copeland

POUND CAKE

1 cup Crisco	2 cups flour
1 3/4 cups sugar	1/8 teaspoon salt
5 eggs	5 tablespoons orange juice

Cream sugar and Crisco for 2 minutes on medium speed. Add eggs, one at a time, beating each egg one minute. After second egg has been added, alternate the flour with remaining eggs until all have been added. Add orange juice and beat for about a minute. Bake in a prepared tube pan at 325° for 1 hour.

Sue Brown

AUNT O'DINE'S GOLDEN FRUIT CUPCAKES

1½ cups candied pineapple
2 cups candied cherries
1 (15 ounce) package raisins
4 cups pecans, chopped
½ cup flour
1 (18 ounce) package yellow
   cake mix

4 eggs
½ cup orange juice
2 teaspoons lemon flavoring
2 teaspoons salt
1 scant tablespoon
   vegetable oil (for bottom
   of muffin cups)

Combine pineapple, cherries, raisins, and nuts in a bowl and dredge with flour. Set aside. Empty cake mix into another bowl and add 1 egg, orange juice, lemon flavoring, and salt. Beat 2 minutes on medium speed. Blend in remaining eggs, one at a time and beat 2 more minutes on medium speed. Blend batter into fruit mixture. Spoon batter into paper cup lined muffin tins and bake at 325° for 30 to 40 minutes until lightly browned. Place a pan of water in oven underneath muffin tins while baking. Adjust cooking time if using petit muffin tins. These muffins freeze well. Best if made ahead and allowed to "mellow".

Susan Sweat

SOUR CREAM POUND CAKE

1 cup butter, softened
2¾ cups sugar
6 eggs
2¾ cups cake flour, sifted

¼ teaspoon baking soda
1 (8 ounce) container sour
   cream
2 teaspoons vanilla

Cream butter well, gradually add sugar. Blend well. Add eggs, one at a time, beating well after each addition. Sift together flour and baking soda. Add alternately to mixture with sour cream. Blend well after each addition. Add vanilla. Pour into prepared tube pan. Place in COLD oven. Bake at 325° for 1¼ hours, or until done when tested. Let cool in pan for 10 to 15 minutes.

Ruth Reese

JAPANESE FRUIT CAKE

1/2 pound butter	**1 cup milk (or milk and**
2 cups sugar	**water)**
3 cups flour	**1/2 teaspoon lemon flavoring**
3 teaspoons baking powder	**1/2 teaspoon vanilla**
4 eggs	**flavoring**

Cream butter and sugar. Add eggs, one at a time. Sift together flour and baking powder. Add flour alternately with milk to egg mixture. Stir in lemon and vanilla. Pour one half of the batter into 2 prepared 8 or 9 inch round cake pans. To the other half of the batter, add:

1 teaspoon cinnamon	**1 teaspoon ground cloves**
1 teaspoon allspice	**1 1/2 cups chopped raisins**

Pour this mixture into third round pan. Bake three layers at 375° for 20 minutes. Remove from pan and cool.

FILLING:

1 1/2 cups sugar	**1 cup hot water**
2 lemons, rind and juice	**2 tablespoons cornstarch**
1 (7 ounce) can of coconut	
(or 1 grated fresh	
coconut)	

In a saucepan, combine sugar, lemon juice, grated rind, coconut, and hot water. Bring to a boil. Add cornstarch and cook until mixture is thick enough to drop from a spoon in big lumps. Ice cooled cake.

Eva Lott

BASIC LAYER CAKE

3 cups cake flour
4 teaspoons baking powder
1/2 teaspoon salt
2 sticks butter (1 stick butter
   and 1/2 cup Crisco)

2 cups sugar
4 large eggs
1 cup milk
1 teaspoon vanilla flavoring
1 teaspoon butter flavoring

Grease, flour and line three 9 inch round pans or four 8 inch round pans. Set aside. Sift together flour, baking powder, and salt. Cream butter and sugar. Add eggs, one at a time, beating well after each addition. Stir in flour mixture alternately with the milk, beginning and ending with the dry ingredients. Gently stir in vanilla and butter flavoring. Divide the batter evenly among the prepared pans. Bake at 325° for 25 to 30 minutes or until cake springs back from center when gently touched. Remove from pans and cool on cake racks. Ice with your favorite frosting!

NOTE: When baking a cake, always work with ingredients at room temperature. When adding flour and a liquid, start and end with flour. Before icing a layer cake, brush away crust and crumbs on side of each layer.

Cookbook Committee

MRS. AUSTRIA'S WHITE FLUFFY ICING

1 1/2 cups sugar
2 large egg whites
2 tablespoons white corn
   syrup

5 teaspoons water
1 teaspoon vanilla flavoring

Combine sugar, egg whites, syrup, and water in top of double boiler. Beat one minute to blend ingredients. Place over boiling water and beat for 7 minutes. Remove from heat and beat in vanilla. Continue to beat until icing is smooth and of spreading consistency. This is marvelous on pound cake, angel food cake, or chocolate cake.

Genie Fesperman

MRS. AUSTRIA'S LEMON CHEESE FILLING

1 cup sugar
1 stick butter, melted

2 lemons, juice and find
2 eggs, well beaten

Combine sugar, butter, lemon juice and rind in top of double boiler. Cook until sugar is dissolved. Stir in beaten eggs and cook slowly until mixture thickens and coats wooden spoon. Use on layer cakes.

NOTE: Mrs. Austria was one of Waycross' best cake bakers. She would bake from early morning until noon and was loved and appreciated by all.

Genie Fesperman

CHOCOLATE ICING

2 (2 ounce) squares
    semi-sweet chocolate
1 stick butter
1 small can evaporated milk
1 tablespoon white corn
    syrup

2 cups sugar
Pinch salt
1/2 teaspoon vanilla

In a heavy saucepan, mix together chocolate, butter, milk, syrup, sugar and salt. Cook over moderate heat, stirring constantly until mixture begins a rolling boil. Let boil for 2 minutes without stirring. Remove from heat, add vanilla and beat until spreading consistency. Will cover a 2 or 3 layer cake.

Edwina Foster

COCONUT FLUFF CAKE

2½ cups sifted cake flour
4½ teaspoons baking
   powder
1 teaspoon salt (optional)
1¾ cups sugar

¾ cup vegetable shortening
   (Crisco)
1⅛ cups milk
5 egg whites
1 teaspoon almond flavoring

All ingredients must be at room temperature. Sift together flour, baking powder, and salt. Add shortening and milk. Beat for 2 minutes until batter is well blended and glossy; then add egg whites and almond flavoring. Beat 2 minutes more. Pour into 2 prepared 9 inch cake pans. Bake at 350° for 35 to 40 minutes or until cake springs back when touched. Frost with Fluffy White Frosting.

FLUFFY WHITE FROSTING:
1⅓ cups sugar
⅓ cup white corn syrup
4 egg whites
3 tablespoons water
¼ teaspoon cream of tartar

1 teaspoon almond flavoring
1 freshly grated coconut (12
   or 18 ounces frozen
   coconut)

Combine sugar, corn syrup, egg whites, water, and cream of tartar in top of double boiler over rapidly boiling water. Beat with mixer for 4 to 5 minutes until mixture stands in soft mounds. Remove pan from boiling water and cool. Add almond flavoring and continue beating until frosting stands in peaks. Spread on cooled layers and sprinkle with freshly grated or frozen coconut.

Pauline Hopkins

CREAMY COCONUT CAKE

1/2 cup Crisco	1 teaspoon baking soda
1/2 cup butter or margarine, softened	1/4 teaspoon salt
2 cups sugar	1 cup buttermilk
5 eggs, separated	1 teaspoon vanilla flavoring
2 cups flour	1/3 cup flaked coconut
	Pinch cream of tartar

Cream shortening, butter and sugar until light and fluffy. Add egg yolks, one at a time, beating well after each addition. Combine flour, soda and salt after sifting flour. Add to creamed mixture alternately with buttermilk, beginning and ending with flour. Mix well. Stir in vanilla and coconut. Beat egg whites until frothy. Add pinch of cream of tartar. Continue beating until egg whites are stiff. Fold into cake batter. Spoon cake batter into three prepared round cake pans. Bake at 350° for 25 minutes or until cake tests done. Cool on wire racks. Spread with Coconut-Pecan Frosting. Store in refrigerator.

COCONUT PECAN FROSTING:

1 (8 ounce) package cream cheese, softened	1 tablespoon vanilla flavoring
1/2 cup butter or margarine, softened	Dash of salt
	1/2 cup flaked coconut
1 (16 ounce) package powdered sugar, sifted	1/2 cup chopped pecans

Beat cream cheese and butter until light and fluffy. Gradually add sugar, beating until smooth. Add vanilla and salt. Stir in coconut and pecans. Spread on cake layers and top. Refrigerate.

Marian Park

HOLIDAY COCONUT CAKE

HOT MILK CAKE:

4 eggs
2 cups sugar
1 cup milk

2 cups flour
2 teaspoons baking powder
1 stick real butter

Beat eggs and sugar until thick and lemon colored. Add 2 cups flour sifted with baking powder. Mix well. In a saucepan, melt butter in hot milk. Stir this into first mixture. Mixture will be thin. Pour into two 9 inch round cake pans (or three 8 inch round cake pans). Bake at 350° for 25 minutes or until cake springs back when touched. (If using 9 inch pans, slice each layer in half to make four layers.)

COCONUT FILLING:

2 cups sugar
1 (16 ounce) carton sour
   cream
2 (6 ounce) packages frozen
   coconut, thawed

1½ cups frozen whipped
   topping, thawed

Mix together sugar, sour cream, coconut, and whipped topping. Remove 1 cup of mixture. Spread remainder of filling between cake layers. Mix reserved cup of mixture with whipped topping and spread on top and sides of cake. Sprinkle additional coconut on top of cake. Place cake in an airtight container and refrigerate for two days before serving. This cake tastes better every day.

NOTE: The hot milk cake was my grandmother Edenfield's recipe and it is a good cake for any filling!

Bonnie Storey

313

ITALIAN CREAM CAKE

1/2 cup margarine
1/2 cup shortening
2 cups sugar
5 eggs, separated
2 cups flour

1 teaspoon baking soda
1 cup buttermilk
1 teaspoon vanilla flavoring
3/4 cup coconut, grated
1 cup nuts, chopped

Cream margarine, shortening and sugar until light and fluffy. Add egg yolks, one at a time, beating well after each addition. Sift flour and soda together. Add to creamed mixture alternately with buttermilk. Add vanilla, coconut, and nuts. Fold in stiffly beaten egg whites. Pour into three 9 inch prepared round cake pans. Bake at 350° for 30 to 35 minutes or until done. Remove from pans and cool. Ice with Cream Cheese Frosting. Sprinkle a little coconut over the top after icing.

Sara Stewart Cotton

RED VELVET CAKE

1 1/2 cups sugar
2 eggs, beaten
2 1/2 cups cake flour
1 1/2 cups cooking oil
1 cup buttermilk
1 teaspoon vanilla flavoring

1 teaspoon soda
1 teaspoon vinegar
2 tablespoons cocoa
1 (5/8 ounce) bottle red food
    coloring

Stir together sugar, beaten eggs, oil, and vinegar. Sift flour, cocoa, and soda together; add to first mixture. Slowly add milk, cake coloring and vanilla, pour into three 8 inch round cake pans and bake at 350° for 25 minutes. Ice with Cream Cheese Frosting.

Bonnie Storey

AUNT JO'S CARAMEL CAKE

1 cup butter, softened
2 cups sugar
4 eggs
3 cups flour

4 teaspoons baking powder
1/2 teaspoon salt
1 teaspoon vanilla flavoring
1 cup milk

Cream butter and sugar together. Add eggs, one at a time, beating well after each addition. Sift together the flour, baking powder, and salt. Add flour mixture alternately with the milk. Add vanilla. Pour into prepared cake pans and bake at 350° for 25 to 30 minutes.

CARAMEL ICING:
31/2 cups sugar
1 cup milk
1 teaspoon vanilla

2/3 cup butter
1/8 teaspoon baking soda
1/4 teaspoon salt

Combine 3 cups sugar, milk, vanilla, butter, soda, and salt in a double boiler. Heat over boiling water. Meanwhile, in a small saucepan, heat 1/2 cup sugar until it melts. To this, add 1/2 cup hot water and continue to cook until sugar is dissolved again. Add to other mixture. Don't stir much. Cook until mixture bubbles up and turns browner (or until it forms a soft ball). Remove from heat, pour into mixing bowl and beat hard. When icing reaches a spreading consistency, ice cake layers, sides and top.

Josephine Lott Webb, Submitted by Sue Clark

CARROT CAKE

3 1/2 cups flour
1/2 cup sugar
1 tablespoon baking powder
2 teaspoons baking soda
2 teaspoons cinnamon
1 teaspoon ginger
3/4 teaspoon salt

1 cup brown sugar, packed
1 cup non-fat plain yogurt
1/3 cup vegetable oil
2 large eggs
2 egg whites
2 teaspoons vanilla flavoring
1 pound carrots, grated

Sift together flour, sugar, baking powder, soda, cinnamon, and salt. Set aside. Mix together yogurt, oil, eggs and egg whites. Gradually add brown sugar, and flour mixture. Blend in vanilla and carrots. Pour into prepared tube pan and bake at 350° for 50 minutes. Frost with Cream Cheese Frosting.

CREAM CHEESE FROSTING:
1 (8 ounce) package cream
   cheese, softened
1 (16 ounce) box powdered sugar

1/2 stick butter, softened
1 teaspoon vanilla

Mix cream cheese and butter together. Gradually beat in sugar and vanilla.

Julie Stewart

HUMMINGBIRD CAKE

3 cups flour
1 teaspoon salt
1 teaspoon cinnamon
1 teaspoon soda
1 (8 ounce) can crushed
   pineapple, undrained

2 cups sugar
1 1/2 cups vegetable oil
3 eggs
1 1/2 teaspoons vanilla flavoring
2 cups mashed ripe bananas
1/2 cup chopped pecans

Mix together flour, salt, cinnamon, soda, pineapple, sugar, oil, eggs, vanilla, bananas, and pecans in a large mixing bowl with a spoon. Pour batter into a greased and floured Bundt or tube pan. Bake at 325° for 1 1/2 hours. Cool in pan for one hour before removing. Allow cake to cool completely. Ice with Cream Cheese Frosting. This cake can be frozen.

Virginia Sims

APPLE NUT CAKE

1½ cups vegetable oil
1½ cups sugar
½ cup light brown sugar,
    firmly packed
3 eggs
3 cups flour
2 teaspoons cinnamon

½ teaspoon nutmeg
1 teaspoon soda
½ teaspoon salt
3½ to 4 cups Granny Smith
    apples, peeled and diced
1½ cups nuts, chopped
2 teaspoons vanilla flavoring

Combine oil and sugar in large bowl and blend well. Add eggs, one at a time, beating well after each. Sift together 3 times the flour, cinnamon, nutmeg, soda, and salt. Add dry ingredients to egg mixture and blend thoroughly. Stir in apples, nuts, and vanilla. Pour into prepared 10 inch tube pan and bake at 325° for 1 hour and 45 minutes. Let cool in pan 20 minutes. Turn out and continue cooling while preparing glaze.

NOTE: Keep the apples from browning by placing them in a large bowl of lightly salted water. They need not be drained; just lift them out of the water with your hands and add to batter.

GLAZE:
3 tablespoons butter
3 tablespoons light brown
    sugar
3 tablespoons sugar

3 tablespoons whipping
    cream
¼ teaspoon vanilla flavoring

Combine butter, sugar, cream and vanilla in heavy saucepan. Bring to a boil over medium heat. Let boil 1 minute. Spoon over warm cake.

Carol Everett

APPLESAUCE CAKE

3¹/₂ cups flour, sifted
1 teaspoon baking soda
¹/₂ teaspoon salt
2 teaspoons cinnamon
1 teaspoon ground cloves
1 cup shortening (or 2 sticks
    butter)

2 cups sugar
2 eggs, well beaten
2 cups pecans, chopped
2 cups raisins
2 cups hot thick applesauce

Sift flour once, remeasure and add soda, salt, cinnamon, cloves, and sift together three times. Add pecans and raisins to dry ingredients. Set aside. Cream butter, gradually adding sugar. Add beaten eggs, one at a time and beat after each addition until light and fluffy. Fold in flour mixture alternately with hot applesauce. (Applesauce my be heated in microwave or in pan on top of stove.) Pour into prepared tube pan. Bake at 300° for 2 hours.

NOTE: This cake can be used at holidays as a fruitcake. Bake several weeks ahead of time and store in airtight container surrounded by sliced apples. (Apples may mold, be careful that they do not touch cake.) Or, season and store this cake as you would any fruit cake.

Jane Crawley

DEVIL'S FOOD CAKE

1³/₄ cups cake flour, sifted
1 teaspoon cinnamon
1 teaspoon soda
1 teaspoon baking powder
1 teaspoon salt (optional)

¹/₂ cup cocoa
1¹/₂ cups sugar
1 cup Crisco
²/₃ cup buttermilk
¹/₂ cup coffee

BEAT 2 MINUTES, THEN ADD:
2 eggs
¹/₃ cup buttermilk

1 teaspoon vanilla

Beat until well blended. Pour into two 9 inch prepared round cake pans. Bake at 350° for 30 minutes or until cake springs back when touched. Ice with chocolate icing or fluffy white frosting.

Pauline Hopkins

AUNT LOUISE'S APRICOT NECTAR CAKE

1 (18 ounce) box lemon
   supreme cake mix
3/4 cup vegetable oil

3/4 cup apricot nectar
2 1/2 tablespoons lemon juice
4 eggs, separated

Mix together cake mix, oil, apricot nectar, lemon juice, and egg yolks for 1 minute; beat for 4 minutes. Fold in stiffly beaten egg whites. Bake in prepared 10 inch tube pan at 325° for 40 minutes until done. Let cake stand in pan 5 minutes then glaze warm cake while still in pan. Allow cake to remain in pan one hour before removing.

GLAZE:
Juice of 2 lemons

2 cups powdered sugar

Mix juice and sugar together.

Anna Fesperman

BANANA SPLIT CAKE

1/2 cup butter or margarine,
   melted
2 cups graham cracker
   crumbs
2 eggs
2 cups sifted powdered
   sugar
3/4 cup butter, softened
1 teaspoon vanilla flavoring

1 (20 ounce) can crushed
   pineapple, drained
4 medium bananas, sliced
1 (9 ounce) carton whipped
   topping
1/2 cup chopped pecans
1 (4 ounce) jar maraschino
   cherries, drained

Combine melted butter and cracker crumbs. Pat into bottom of a 9x13 inch pan. Beat eggs on high speed until light (about 4 minutes). Add powdered sugar, softened butter and vanilla and beat for 5 more minutes. Spread this mixture over crumbs and chill 30 minutes in freezer. Then remove from freezer and spread pineapple over. Arrange bananas over pineapple, cover with whipped topping, sprinkle with nuts and maraschino cherries. Refrigerate 6 hours before serving. Serves 10.

Hazel Cook

BLUEBERRY CAKE

1 cup butter, softened
2 cups sugar
3 eggs
3 cups flour
1 1/2 teaspoons baking
  powder

1/8 teaspoon salt
1/4 teaspoon mace
1/2 cup milk
2 cups blueberries
2 teaspoons sugar
2 teaspoons flour

Cream butter and 2 cups sugar until light and fluffy. Add eggs, one at a time, beating well after each addition. Sift together flour, baking powder, salt, and mace; add to creamed mixture alternately with the milk, beating well after each addition. Coat blueberries with remaining sugar and flour; fold into batter. Pour into prepared 10 inch tube pan or Bundt pan. Bake at 350° for 70 to 80 minutes.

NOTE: This cake can be baked in 2 ring mold pans and when cool, sifted with powdered sugar. It is a nice cake to give to friends to enjoy as a coffee cake when they have house guests.

Christine Shields

PINEAPPLE UPSIDE DOWN CAKE

1/2 cup brown sugar, packed
1/4 cup butter
3 tablespoons water
1 (20 ounce) can sliced
  pineapple, drained
6 maraschino cherries
1/4 cup nuts, chopped or whole
1/2 cup shortening

1 cup sugar
2 eggs, well beaten
1 3/4 cups flour
2 1/2 teaspoons baking
  powder
1/2 cup milk
1/8 teaspoon salt
1 teaspoon vanilla flavoring

In a heavy cake pan, heat together the brown sugar, butter, and water until dissolved. Arrange in this mixture a layer of sliced pineapple. Decorate with cherries and nuts. Cream shortening and sugar. Beat in eggs. Sift together flour and baking powder. Add dry ingredients alternately with milk. Stir in vanilla. Turn batter over fruit in pan. Bake at 375° for 45 minutes.

NOTE: This is Jim Clark's favorite dessert!

Penn Clark

KATHY'S ORANGE DATE NUT CAKE

2 cups sugar
4 eggs, separated
4 cups plain flour
2 tablespoons grated orange
   peel
1 cup pecans, chopped

1 cup shortening
1⅓ cups buttermilk
1 teaspoon baking soda
1 package chopped dates
Pinch of salt

Set aside 1 cup of flour to dredge chopped dates and pecans. Cream shortening, sugar, adding egg yolks one at a time. Mix flour with soda and add alternating with buttermilk. Fold in stiffly beaten egg whites. Fold in dredged nuts and dates and salt. Pour into greased tube pan and bake at 325° for 1½ hours (approximately). Remove from oven and while cake is hot, punch holes with pick. Dribble icing and let soak. Turn out and punch holes from bottom, using rest of icing in same manner.

ICING:
2 cups sugar
2 tablespoons grated orange
   rind

1 cup orange juice

Mix well.

NOTE: This was my very first cake. I won the girl scout bake off in my hometown with this recipe at the age of 10.

Kathy Hackel

PRUNELLA CAKE

1 cup salad oil
1 1/2 to 2 cups sugar
3 eggs
2 cups flour
1 teaspoon soda
1 teaspoon cinnamon
1 teaspoon nutmeg

1 teaspoon allspice
1 teaspoon salt
1 cup buttermilk
1 teaspoon vanilla
1 cup cooked prunes,
    chopped
1 cup chopped nuts

Blend sugar, oil, and eggs. Add sifted dry ingredients alternately with buttermilk. Add vanilla; fold in nuts and prunes. Pour into greased 11x14 inch pan. Bake at 325° for 1 hour. (Cake my be baked in a well-greased tube pan at 350° for 1 hour and 15 minutes.) Cool completely and ice. Serves 10 to 20.

ICING:

1 pound powdered sugar
1/4 cup shortening

2 teaspoons cinnamon
Prune juice to soften

Sift sugar and cinnamon. Blend with shortening. Add prune juice slowly until desired consistency.

Danita Cannon

OLD FASHION SOUTHERN GINGERBREAD

1/2 cup butter and lard mixed
1/2 cup sugar
1 egg, beaten
1 cup cane syrup or
    molasses
2 1/2 cups flour, sifted

1 1/2 teaspoon baking soda
1 teaspoon cinnamon
1 teaspoon ginger
1/2 teaspoon ground cloves
1/2 teaspoon salt
1 cup hot water

Cream shortening and sugar. Add beaten egg and syrup. Sift together flour, soda, cinnamon, ginger, cloves, and salt. Add to sugar mixture. Add hot water last and beat until smooth. The batter is soft, but it makes a fine cake. Pour into a prepared 9x13 inch pan. Bake at 350° for 35 minutes or until done. Yield: 15 servings.

NOTE: This recipe is said to be well over 100 years old.

Missouri Talley

PINEAPPLE CAKE WITH COCONUT FROSTING

CAKE:

2 cups flour, sifted
1 1/2 cups sugar
2 teaspoons baking soda
2 eggs, beaten

1/2 cup vegetable oil
1 (20 ounce) can crushed
    pineapple, undrained

Combine flour, 1 1/4 cups sugar, and baking soda in a large mixing bowl. Add eggs, oil, and pineapple. Mix thoroughly. Turn batter into a lightly greased 9x13 inch baking pan and bake at 350° for 30 to 35 minutes. Test with a straw for doneness.

FROSTING:

1/2 cup butter
1 1/4 cups sugar
1 (5 ounce) can evaporated
    milk

1 cup shredded coconut
1 cup chopped pecans
1/2 teaspoon vanilla

Combine butter, sugar, and evaporated milk in a large saucepan. Bring to a boil over medium heat and continue to boil without stirring for 3 to 4 minutes. Cool slightly. Stir in coconut, pecans, and vanilla. Spread evenly over hot cake in pan. Refrigerate, if you have any left, after first serving.

NOTE: This is a new twist on an old favorite recipe, "Fruit Cocktail Sheet Cake". It is wonderful to take to a "covered dish" affair or for bridge club. It can be made ahead and gets better as it mellows.

Jeanette Darden

MANDARIN ORANGE CAKE

1 (18.25 ounce) box butter
   cake mix
1 (11 ounce) can mandarin
   oranges, undrained

4 eggs
1/2 cup vegetable oil

Stir together cake mix, undrained oranges, eggs and oil. Beat until oranges become pulp. Pour into 2 prepared 9 inch cake pans (or one 9x13 inch pan). Bake at 325° for 25 to 30 minutes. Cool.

ICING:
1 (5 1/4 ounce) box instant
   vanilla pudding

1 (20 ounce) can crushed
   pineapple, undrained
1 (9 ounce) carton Cool Whip

Mix instant pudding and pineapple. Fold in Cool Whip. Frost cake. Keep refrigerated. This is a moist and refreshing cake!

Lois Groszmann

STRAWBERRY CAKE

1 (18.25 ounce) package
   white cake mix
4 eggs
1 cup vegetable oil

1 (3 ounce) package
   strawberry gelatin
1/2 cup hot water
1/2 cup juice from small package
   frozen strawberries

Soften gelatin in hot water. Combine with strawberry juice. Set aside. Prepare cake according to package directions. Stir in strawberry mixture. Bake in three 8 inch round cake pans at 350° for about 30 minutes.

ICING:
1/2 stick butter, softened
1 small package frozen strawberries, thawed and drained

1 (16 ounce) box powdered
   sugar

Cream butter and sugar. Add as much of the drained strawberries as the mixture will take. Ice cake. Refrigerate until icing is firm.

NOTE: Children love this cake made as cupcakes!

Lucille Murray

FROZEN MOCHA CHEESECAKE

1½ cups chocolate wafer
  cookie crumbs (24
  cookies)
¼ cup sugar
¼ cup butter or margarine,
  melted
1 (8 ounce) package cream
  cheese, softened
1 (14 ounce) can sweetened
  condensed milk

⅔ cup chocolate flavored
  syrup
2 tablespoons strong coffee
1 (8 ounce) whipped
  topping, thawed
Whipped cream or
  raspberries for garnish

In a small bowl, combine crumbs, sugar and butter. In buttered 9 inch springform pan or 9x13 inch baking dish, pat crumbs firmly on bottom and up sides of pan. Chill. (A store bought chocolate crumb crust will be just as good, if you cannot find chocolate cookies.) In a large mixer bowl, beat cheese until soft. Add sweetened condensed milk, syrup, coffee, and whipped topping. Pour into prepared pan. Cover. Freeze 6 hours or until firm. Garnish with chocolate crumbs, whipped cream, or raspberries. Return leftovers to freezer. Serves 10 to 12.

Coralyn Gaston

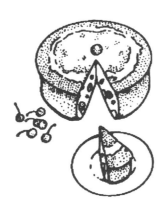

WHITE CHOCOLATE AND RASPBERRY CHEESECAKE

CRUST:

18 vanilla wafer cookies
1 cup almonds, toasted

4½ tablespoons unsalted
  butter, melted

Preheat oven to 350°. Use 8 inch springform pan, butter pan. Finely grind cookies and almonds in processor. Add butter and blend until mixture forms very moist crumbs. Using plastic wrap as aid, press crumbs firmly onto bottom and 2 inches up sides of pan. Bake until golden, about 10 minutes. Cool. Maintain oven temperature.

FILLING:

4 ounces imported white
  chocolate (such as
  Lindt), chopped
2 (8 ounce) packages cream
  cheese, room temperature
2/3 cup sugar

2 teaspoons vanilla extract
3/4 teaspoon grated lemon peel
2 large eggs
3/4 cup fresh raspberries or
  frozen, unsweetened,
  thawed, drained

Melt white chocolate in top of double boiler over simmering water until smooth, stirring often. Remove from over water. Using electric mixer, beat cream cheese, sugar, vanilla, and peel in large bowl until smooth. Add eggs, one at a time, beating just until combined. Beat in white chocolate. Spoon half of batter into crust. Top with 3/4 cup berries. Spoon remaining batter over. Bake until edges of cake are set but center 3 inches still moves when cake is shaken, about 45 minutes. Cool 20 minutes. Maintain oven temperature. Using fingertips, press down gently on edges of cheesecake to flatten slightly.

TOPPING:

1 (8 ounce) container sour
  cream
3 tablespoons sugar
1/2 teaspoon vanilla extract

2 (1/2 pint) baskets raspberries
  or 1 (1 pint) basket strawberries
1/2 cup seedless raspberry jam

Whisk sour cream, sugar, and vanilla in bowl. Spoon over cake, spreading to edge of pan. Bake 5 minutes. Transfer cake in pan to rack. Run small knife around sides of cake. Cool completely. Chill cake

(continued on next page)

overnight. Lift cake pan off cheesecake. Transfer cheesecake to platter. Cover cake with berries. Bring jam to simmer in small saucepan, stirring often. Gently brush jam over berries. (Can be prepared 3 hours ahead; chill.) 8 servings.

Kathy D. Hackel

PUMPKIN CHEESECAKE

CRUST:
1 cup graham cracker crumbs
1 tablespoon sugar

4 tablespoons butter or margarine, melted

Combine cracker crumbs, sugar, and melted butter. Press into bottom of a 9 inch springform pan; chill.

FILLING:
2 (8 ounce) packages cream cheese, softened
3/4 cup sugar
1 (16 ounce) can pumpkin
1 1/2 teaspoons ground cinnamon

1/2 teaspoon ground ginger
1/2 teaspoon ground nutmeg
1/4 teaspoon salt
2 eggs

Beat cream cheese and sugar in a large mixing bowl until well blended. Beat in pumpkin, spices and salt. Add eggs, one at a time, beating well after each. Pour into crust. Bake at 350° for 50 minutes.

TOPPING:
2 cups sour cream
2 tablespoons sugar

1 teaspoon vanilla flavoring
12 to 16 pecans halves

Combine sour cream, sugar, and vanilla. Spread over filling and bake 5 minutes more. Cool on rack; chill overnight. Garnish each slice with a pecan half. This is delicious!

Margaret Park

GRAHAM CRACKER BRITTLE

10 honey graham crackers
   (40 broken)
1 stick butter

1 stick margarine
1/2 cup sugar
1 cup nuts, finely chopped

Grease or spray 9x13 inch baking pan. Line pan with graham crackers. Boil butter, margarine and sugar together for 3 minutes, stirring often. Quickly pour over crackers and sprinkle with chopped nuts. Bake at 350° for 10 minutes. Take up while still warm and cool on wax paper.

Melba Mayo

DATE CRUNCH BARS

1 pound whole pitted dates
2/3 cup brown sugar

2/3 cup orange juice
3 tablespoons vanilla

In a saucepan over medium heat, stir together dates, sugar, and orange juice and simmer for three minutes or until mixture is syrupy. Cool; then add vanilla.

CRUST:
11/2 cups old fashioned oats
11/2 cups flour
1 cup brown sugar
1 teaspoon cinnamon

1/2 teaspoon baking soda
2 sticks unsalted butter
3/4 cup walnuts, chopped

Mix together oats, flour, sugar, cinnamon and baking soda. Cut in butter until mixture resembles coarse meal. Press crumbs into greased 13x9x2 inch baking dish and sprinkle with 1/2 cup chopped nuts. Spread filling over crust, topping with remaining 1/4 cup chopped nuts. Bake at 350° for 40 minutes. Cool in pan. Cut in squares to serve.

Bonelle Memory

MACAROONS

1 (14 ounce) package of
  coconut
1 (14 ounce) can sweetened
  condensed milk

2 teaspoons vanilla

Combine coconut, milk, and vanilla. Drop by spoonfuls and bake at 350° for 10 to 12 minutes (until lightly browned) on well greased pan. Remove at once from pan after baking. Yields 5 dozen.

Susan Sweat

CHOCOLATE-CARAMEL BARS

1 (14 ounce) package
  caramels
2/3 cup evaporated milk
  (divided)
1 (18.5 ounce) package
  German chocolate cake
  mix

2/3 cup butter or margarine
1 (6 ounce) package
  chocolate chips
1 1/2 cups walnuts, chopped

Melt caramels in double boiler or microwave. Stir in 1/3 cup milk; set aside. In mixing bowl, combine cake mix, butter and remaining milk. Press half of mixture into a greased 13x9x2 inch baking pan. Bake at 350° for 6 minutes. Remove from oven and sprinkle with chocolate chips and walnuts. Pour caramel mixture over; spoon remaining cake mixture on top. Return to oven and bake for 20 minutes. Cut into squares and enjoy!

Jane Gillis

NANA'S FIG BARS

1 (18.25 ounce) box cake
   mix (orange or lemon
   supreme)
1/2 cup vegetable oil

1 egg
1 cup fig preserves
1 1/2 cups nuts, chopped

In a large mixing bowl, combine cake mix, oil, egg, and fig preserves. Beat with electric mixer until well blended. Stir in nuts. Pour into greased 13x9x2 inch pan. Bake at 350° for 30 to 35 minutes. Cool in pan. Cut into squares.

Coolie Hughes

CHOCOLATE BUTTER SWEET COOKIES

COOKIE:
1/2 cup butter
1/4 teaspoon salt

1 teaspoon vanilla
1 cup flour

CREAMY NUT FILLING:
1 (3 ounce) package cream
   cheese, softened
1 cup confectioners sugar
2 tablespoons flour

1 teaspoon vanilla
1/2 cup flaked coconut
1/2 cup nuts, chopped

CHOCOLATE TOPPING:
1/2 cup chocolate chips
2 tablespoons butter

2 tablespoons water
1/2 cup confectioners sugar

Cream butter, salt, sugar, and vanilla. Gradually add flour. Take 1 teaspoonful of dough and roll into ball. Place on ungreased cookie sheet and punch a hole in the center (with finger) of each cookie. Bake at 350° for 12 to 15 minutes until light brown. After the cookie is cool, fill hole with filling, which has been stirred together. Melt chocolate chips, butter, and water over low heat. Add sugar, cool and drizzle over cookies.

Lylburn Booker

FROSTED APRICOT JEWELS

1¼ cups flour
¼ cup sugar
¼ teaspoon salt
1½ teaspoons baking
   powder

1 (3 ounce) package cream
   cheese, softened
½ cup flaked coconut
½ cup apricot preserves
Pecan halves

Combine flour, sugar, baking powder, and salt. Cut in butter and cream cheese until mixture resembles coarse meal. Add coconut and preserves, mixing well. Drop dough by teaspoonfuls onto cookie sheet. Bake at 350° for 15 to 18 minutes or until lightly browned.

FROSTING:
1 cup confectioners sugar,
   sifted

1 tablespoon butter, softened
¼ cup apricot preserves

Combine sugar, butter, and apricot preserves and beat until smooth. Spread each cookie with frosting and top with a pecan half.

Myrtle Sands

CHEWIES

1 stick oleo
1 (16 ounce) box light brown
   sugar
3 eggs
2 cups self-rising flour (do
   not sift)

2 teaspoons vanilla
1 cup chopped nuts
1 (6 ounce) package
   chocolate chips

Cream oleo and sugar. Then, add eggs, one at a time. Add vanilla and blend in flour, nuts and chocolate chips. Put in greased oblong pan and bake at 350° for 25 to 30 minutes until light brown. Let cool and cut in small squares.

Laney Hopkins

331

NUT SQUARES

1 cup (heaping) pecans,
   chopped
1 cup dark brown sugar
1 egg

5 rounded tablespoons flour
1/4 teaspoon salt
1/4 teaspoon soda

Beat egg and add sugar, mixing well. Sift together flour, salt, and soda. Stir mixtures together and add nuts. Place in medium size pan and bake at 375° for 25 minutes. Do not cut until cold.

Betty Hopkins

CHOCOLATE PILLOWS

2 1/2 cups flour, sifted
1/2 teaspoon salt
1 cup butter or margarine,
   softened
1 egg, unbeaten

3/4 cup sugar
2 teaspoons vanilla
6 Hershey milk chocolate
   candy bars

Stir together the flour and salt. Set aside. Cream butter and sugar well. Add unbeaten egg and vanilla; beat well. Stir in dry ingredients. Press dough through a cookie press, using sawtooth (spritz) plate, in stips on ungreased cookie sheet. Break candy bars along indentations on bars and place pieces approximately 1/4 inch apart on strips of dough. Press another strip of dough over candy, covering completely. Mark bars between chocolate pieces. Bake at 375° for 12 to 15 minutes until light golden brown. Cut immediately into pieces.

Frankie Miles

QUICK CHOCOLATE CHIP COOKIES

1 (18.5 ounce) box white
  cake mix
1/4 cup light brown sugar
1 (6 ounce) package
  semi-sweet chocolate
  chips

1/2 cup nuts, chopped
  (optional)
3/4 cup vegetable oil
1 egg

Blend cake mix, sugar, chocolate chips, nuts, oil, and egg together. Drop by spoonfuls onto cookie sheet. Bake at 350° for 12 minutes. Remove from pan and cool on wire rack.

Cheryl Monroe

AUNT SALLY'S PEANUT BUTTER COOKIES

1 cup peanut butter (smooth
  or crunchy)
1 cup light brown sugar
1 cup granulated sugar

1 cup shortening (Crisco)
3 (or 3 1/2) cups flour
1 teaspoon baking soda
2 eggs

Mix peanut butter, both sugars, shortening, and eggs in a large bowl with hands. Stir soda into 3 cups of flour. Work flour into mixture. Add additional flour until dough does not stick to hand. Shape dough into small balls (1 inch diameter) and place 2 inches apart on an ungreased cookie sheet. Press dough with fork. Bake at 350° for 10 minutes. These cookies are suppose to have a good keeping quality, but they never last very long around my house.

Ida Rodocker

PECAN SANDY BUTTER COOKIES

2 sticks butter
3/4 cup sugar
2 cups flour

1 cup pecans, chopped
1 teaspoon vanilla

Cream butter and sugar. Work in flour, nuts and vanilla. Roll into finger shape or 1 inch balls. Bake at 325° for 20 minutes. Roll in powdered sugar while hot.

Frances Gray

NEIMAN'S $250 COOKIE RECIPE

1 cup butter
1 cup sugar
1 cup light brown sugar
2½ cups blended oatmeal
1 teaspoon baking soda
1 (12 ounce) package
   chocolate chips
2 cups pecans, chopped

2 eggs
1 teaspoon vanilla extract
2 cups flour
½ teaspoon salt
1 teaspoon baking powder
4 ounces grated Hershey
   bars

Cream butter and both sugars. Add eggs and vanilla extract. Mix flour, oatmeal, salt, baking powder, and soda. Add to mixture. Add nuts and chocolates. Roll into balls and place 2 inches apart on a lightly greased cookie sheet. Bake 6 to 8 minutes at 375°. Makes 60 to 70 cookies. Recipe is easily doubled.

Eddie Mae Spear

FRUIT CAKE COOKIES

1 cup butter
1 cup light brown sugar,
    packed
3 cups flour
1 teaspoon cinnamon
1 teaspoon soda
1/2 cup milk
3 eggs

3 teaspoons vanilla
1 pound candied dates,
    chopped
1 pound candied cherries,
    chopped
1 pound candied pineapple,
    chopped
7 cups nuts, chopped

Cream butter and sugar. Sift together flour, cinnamon, and soda. Add eggs to butter/sugar mixture. Then, add milk and vanilla. Fold in chopped fruit and nuts. Drop from spoon on greased cookie sheet. (About the size of a walnut.) Bake at 300° for 30 minutes.

Harriette Woodard

COOKIES WHILE YOU SLEEP

2 egg whites
Pinch of salt
1/2 teaspoon cream of tartar
2/3 cup sugar

1/4 teaspoon almond extract
1 teaspoon vanilla
1 cup chopped nuts
1 cup chocolate morsels

Preheat oven to 350° while mixing the cookie batter. Beat egg whites until foamy. Add salt, cream of tartar, and sugar; continue beating until stiff. Add almond and vanilla extract. Fold in nuts and chocolate morsels. Drop by teaspoonfuls on a greased cookie sheet. Place in oven and turn off the heat. Leave overnight. Yield: Approximately 4 dozen.

Genie Fesperman

PECAN DELIGHT COOKIES

1 cup butter	1 teaspoon vanilla
2 cups flour, sifted	3 tablespoons water
2/3 cup sugar	2 cups nuts, chopped

Cream butter and sugar, then add vanilla and water. Fold in flour and nuts. Drop by spoonfuls and bake at 300° about 25 minutes. DO NOT let cookies get too brown.

Marian Park

LEMON-ALMOND COOKIES

1 cup butter	2 cups cake flour
1 cup granulated sugar	1½ tablespoons fresh
1 large egg	grated lemon peel
1 teaspoon vanilla	1 package sliced almonds

Heat oven to 350°. Beat butter and sugar until fluffy. Beat in egg, then vanilla. Stir in flour and lemon peel. Drop by teaspoonful 2 inches apart on ungreased cookie sheet. Press 1 to 2 almonds into center of each cookie. Bake 8 to 10 minutes. Cool 1 minute. Remove from cookie sheet. Makes 80 cookies.

TIP: Put cookie dough in a zip lock bag and cut one end, then press out cookies - it's quicker.

Mary Winn Pruet

POTATO CHIP COOKIES

4 sticks butter, softened
1 cup sugar
3 cups flour

2 teaspoons vanilla
1 cup nuts, chopped
1 cup crushed potato chips

Cream together butter and sugar. Stir in flour, vanilla, and potato chips. Drop 1/2 teaspoonful on ungreased baking sheet. Bake at 350° for 10 to 15 minutes.

Lois Groszmann

MORAVIAN COOKIES

3/4 cup butter and Crisco,
  mixed
3/4 cup dark brown sugar,
  packed
2 cups black molasses
7 1/2 cups flour
4 tablespoons ground cloves

4 tablespoons ground
  cinnamon
4 tablespoons ground ginger
1 teaspoon salt
1 tablespoon baking soda
1/4 cup boiling water

Mix butter and Crisco with sugar. Add molasses. Sift together flour, cloves, cinnamon, ginger, and salt. Add soda to boiling water. Mix together butter/sugar mixture, flour mixture and soda water. Work dough until smooth with hands. Cover and store in refrigerator overnight (preferably longer). Roll as thin as paper. Cut in desired shape with cookie cutter. (Round browns evenly.) Bake on greased cookie sheet at 350° for 8 to 10 minutes or just until cookies begin to brown. DO NOT OVER-COOK. REMOVE FROM PAN IMMEDIATELY. This cookie will store well in a tin. These melt in your mouth cookies are traditionally served at Christmas.

TIP: For best results, roll dough to the desired thinness by using a pastry cloth, and cover the rolling pin with a white stockenette or sock.

Lisa Fesperman

OATMEAL COOKIES

1 cup Wesson oil	4 tablespoons milk
1 cup sugar	1 teaspoon soda
2 eggs	1 teaspoon cinnamon
2 cups flour	1/2 teaspoon cloves
2 cups old-fashioned Quaker oats	11/2 cups nuts

Cream oil and sugar. Add eggs. Beat hard. Put soda in milk. Add milk. Add flour, spices, oatmeal, and nuts. Drop on cookie sheet and bake at 350° about 10 minutes or until lightly browned.

Clyde King

TEA CAKES
Granma Lillie's Recipe

1 quart (4 cups) flour	2 eggs
1 teaspoon soda	2 teaspoons vanilla
A little salt	A little grated nutmeg
2/3 cup shortening	1/2 cup of milk (scant)
11/2 cups sugar	

Sift together flour, soda and salt. Cream together shortening and sugar. Add eggs, one at a time, to creamed shortening and sugar; add flavoring. Stir in flour mixture alternately with milk. Chill dough. Roll out on floured surface and cut into desired shapes with cookie cutter. Place cookies on cookie sheet and bake at 350° for 10 to 12 minutes, or until lightly browned.

Missouri Talley

JO'S BEST COOKIE

2 sticks margarine or butter
1 cup granulated sugar
1 cup light brown sugar
1 egg
1 cup vegetable oil
1 cup quick oats (not
  instant)

1 cup crushed corn flakes
1/2 cup flaked coconut
1/2 cup pecans, chopped
31/2 cups flour
1 teaspoon salt
1 teaspoon soda
2 teaspoons vanilla

Cream margarine and sugar. Add egg and salad oil. Sift flour, salt, and soda together and add to mixture. Add corn flakes and vanilla; then stir in coconut, oats, and pecans. Form into small ball (walnut size) in palm of hand. Place on cookie sheet and press down with fork. Bake at 350° for 15 to 20 minutes.

Georgianne McGee

ICE BOX COOKIES

2 sticks margarine
1 cup Crisco
2 cups sugar
1 egg

6 cups flour
1/2 teaspoon salt
2 teaspoons vanilla

Cream margarine, Crisco, and sugar with hands in a large mixing bowl. Add egg and flour, salt and vanilla. Mix thoroughly. This makes a very stiff dough. Divide into four or five sections. Roll each section in wax paper which has been floured. Let stand in refrigerator overnight. Slice and bake at 350° for about 10 minutes or until slightly brown.

Sue Brown

CINNAMON STICKS

1½ sticks butter or oleo	**2 cups flour**
1 cup sugar	**2 teaspoons cinnamon**
1 egg, separated	**1 cup nuts, finely chopped**

Cream together butter and sugar. Add egg yolk. Combine flour and cinnamon and add to mixture. Knead mixture until well blended. Pat on 15x10x1 inch cookie sheet. Brush top with unbeaten egg white. Spread with finely chopped nuts. Bake in slow oven (325°), until brown. Cut into sticks while warm.

Georgia McDonald

GINGERBREAD MEN

CREAM:

1 cup sugar	**¾ cup shortening**

BEAT IN:

1 egg	**2 tablespoons molasses**

SIFT AND ADD:

2½ cups flour	**½ teaspoon ground cloves**
1 teaspoon ground ginger	**Pinch of salt**

Make into small balls about one inch in diameter. Allow four balls for each man - one for the head, one for the body, divide one for the arms, and divide the other one for the legs. Features and buttons may be raisins, chocolate chips, or scraps of cookie dough. Bake 8 to 10 minutes at 375° F. This recipe makes 10 to 15 people.

NOTE: This recipe is great to have children make and bake.

Mary Dillard

BECKY'S SHORTBREAD

1 cup butter, softened
2 cups flour
1/2 cup confectioners sugar

1/4 teaspoon salt
Granulated sugar, optional

Cream butter. Sift together flour, sugar and salt. Add to butter, mixing well. Pat stiff dough into an ungreased 9x9 inch pan. Pierce dough with a fork every 1/2 inch. Sprinkle top with granulated sugar, if desired. Bake at 325° for 25 to 30 minutes or until very lightly browned. Do not overcook or shortbread will be hard. Cut into squares while hot.

Becky Rivenbark

CHILDREN'S CHRISTMAS NUT BALLS

1 pound box graham
   crackers
1 large bag marshmallows

1 jar of cherries
1 stick oleo
2 cups nuts, chopped

Melt marshmallows and oleo. While this is melting on slow heat, have the children crush the graham crackers. (Put crackers in plastic bags and give each a rolling pin.) The children can also cut the cherries up with scissors, and the nuts. When the marshmallows and oleo have melted, stir and add the cracker crumbs, cherries and nuts. When cool enough (should be just warm), let the children roll into balls. (If you like they may be rolled in confectioners sugar.) Two or three of these cookies can be placed in a sandwich plastic bag, tied with ribbon - makes a nice gift for parents and friends.

NOTE: This recipe is great to have children make and bake.

Mary Dillard

DISNEY DELIGHTS

String 2 marshmallows on a popsicle stick. Roll in sweetened condensed milk, then in chopped nuts, if desired. Allow to harden in a standing position. Eat and enjoy!

NOTE: This recipe is great to have children make and bake.

Mary Dillard

MARY DILLARD'S KINDERGARTEN COOKIES

CREAM TOGETHER:
1 cup margarine (2 sticks)   **1 cup sugar**

ADD:
2 eggs   **1 teaspoon vanilla flavoring**
3 cups plain flour

Mix well; roll out portions on floured waxed paper; cut with cookie cutters; use various decorations. Bake at 350° approximately 10 minutes.

NOTE: This recipe is great to have children make and bake.

Mary Dillard

DIVINITY

3 cups granulated sugar
1/8 teaspoon salt
1/2 cup of light corn syrup
1/2 cup water

2 egg whites
1 teaspoon vanilla
1/2 teaspoon almond
  flavoring

Boil sugar, salt, corn syrup, and water together until syrup will form a firm ball when put in cold water (250° F. on candy thermometer). Pour gradually over egg whites which have been beaten stiff. Continue beating until mixture will hold shape. Add flavorings. Drop quickly with teaspoons on waxed paper. If desired a nut half may be pressed in the center of each piece.

Myrrl Young

BEST BROWNIES YOU'VE EVER EATEN

1 cup Crisco
6 tablespoons cocoa
2 cups sugar
4 tablespoons Karo syrup

4 eggs
2 cups nuts, chopped
1 1/2 cups self-rising flour

Melt Crisco and cocoa in a boiler. Mix with sugar, Karo syrup, and eggs. Fold in flour and nuts. Pour into 9x13 inch prepared pan and bake at 325° for 30 minutes. Cool.

FROSTING:
2 cups sugar
1 cup evaporated milk
1/2 cup cocoa

1 stick butter
1 teaspoon vanilla

Cook sugar, evaporated milk, cocoa and butter in heavy saucepan (or in top of double boiler) until mixture reaches soft ball stage. Remove from heat and add vanilla. Let cool and beat until spreading consistency. Frost brownies.

Kaye Pendley

343

CARNATION FIVE MINUTE FUDGE

2/3 cup evaporated milk
12/3 cups sugar
2 cups miniature
   marshmallows

1/2 cup nuts, chopped
11/2 cups semi-sweet
   chocolate bits
1 teaspoon vanilla

Combine milk and sugar in a heavy saucepan. Heat just to boiling. Cook 5 minutes, stirring constantly. Remove from heat. Stir in marshmallows, nuts, chocolate, and vanilla. Continue stirring until all the marshmallows are melted. Pour into 8x9 inch greased pan. Cool. Garnish with nut halves, if desired. Cut into squares.

Arlie Nall

MICROWAVE FUDGE

2 (16 ounce) boxes
   confectioners sugar
1 cup cocoa
1/2 cup milk

2 sticks butter or margarine
1 cup nuts, chopped
   (optional)
2 tablespoons vanilla

In a large microwave bowl, combine sugar and cocoa. Add milk, but DO NOT STIR. Place butter on top of mixture. Cover loosely. Microwave on high for 41/2 to 6 minutes or until butter has melted. Remove from microwave. Add vanilla and stir mixture until fairly smooth. Stir in nuts and pour into a large greased Pyrex dish. Refrigerate until cool. Cut into squares and serve.

Claire Smith

ONE BOWL CHOCOLATE FUDGE

2 packages (8 squares
    each) Baker's
    semi-sweet chocolate
1 (14 ounce) can sweetened
    condensed milk

2 teaspoons vanilla
1½ cups nuts, chopped

Microwave chocolate and condensed milk in large microwavable bowl on high 2 to 3 minutes (or until chocolate is almost melted), stirring halfway through heating time. After removing from microwave, stir again until chocolate is completely melted. Stir in vanilla and nuts. Spread in greased 8-inch square pan. Refrigerate until firm. Cut into squares. Yield: 4 dozen.

Mildred Bell

SECRET FUDGE

1 package fudge brownie
    mix
1 stick margarine or butter
4 tablespoons cocoa

⅓ cup buttermilk
1 (16 ounce) box
    confectioners sugar
1 cup nuts, chopped

Prepare brownies according to directions on box. To make icing, boil margarine, cocoa and buttermilk until well blended. Remove from heat and beat in sugar. Add nuts. Frost brownies while hot and still in pan.

Laura Strickland

LILLIAN RIVENBARK'S PEANUT BRITTLE

1½ cups sugar
½ cup white Karo syrup
½ cup water
2 cups raw peanuts

1 lump paraffin (size of a
   pea)
1 tablespoon soda

Cook sugar, syrup, water, and peanuts in saucepan over medium heat until peanuts pop (about 20 minutes after mixture boils). Remove from heat. Stir in lump of paraffin until it melts. Stir in soda (it will bubble up). Quickly spread on greased cookie sheet. When cool, break into pieces.

Lylburn Booker

LOUISIANA PECAN PRALINES

1 cup light brown sugar (not
   packed)
1 cup white sugar
½ cup evaporated milk
2 tablespoons butter

2 tablespoons white Karo
   syrup
⅛ teaspoon salt
1 teaspoon vanilla
2 cups pecan halves

In a 2-quart saucepan, using a wooden spoon, mix both sugars, milk, butter, corn syrup, and salt. Over a medium heat, cook to a soft ball stage, about 10 minutes. (Test by dropping a drop of mixture into a cup of cold water. Drop should be soft when picked up with fingers.) Remove from heat, add vanilla and nuts. Beat until mixture begins to thicken - about 1 minute. Drop by teaspoonfuls onto waxed paper. Makes about 2 dozen creamy pralines. Allow to harden, then store in airtight container or wrap individually. Yield: 24.

Georgine Smith

MICROWAVE PRALINES

1 (16 ounce) box light brown
　sugar
1 cup heavy cream
1 tablespoon white Karo
　syrup

1 tablespoon margarine or
　butter
3/4 to 1 cup pecans, chopped

Microwave sugar, cream, and Karo syrup on high for 12 to 13 minutes (stir every 4 minutes). Remove from microwave and let cool until the bubbling ceases. Stir in margarine and nuts. Beat until the glaze goes away (about 2 minutes). After beating, drop quickly by spoonful on waxed paper or foil. Easy and so delicious!

Jeanette Darden

MARTHA WASHINGTON CANDY

1 stick butter, melted
2 (16 ounce) boxes
　confectioners sugar
2 cups nuts, chopped

1 teaspoon vanilla
1 (14 ounce) can sweetened
　condensed milk

Cream together butter, sugar, and milk; work until smooth with hand. Add nuts and vanilla. Roll into small balls (any size you like) and place on waxed paper. Chill overnight in the refrigerator.

COATING:

1/2 pound bittersweet
　chocolate

1 block paraffin

Melt chocolate and paraffin together in top of double boiler. Cool until warm. Dip candy balls into mixture. Warm chocolate mixture again if it thickens.

Nancy Lee

PEANUT BUTTER BALLS

1½ cups crunchy peanut
   butter
2 cups margarine
1 teaspoon vanilla extract
2½ (16 ounce) boxes
   powdered sugar

1 (12 ounce) package
   semi-sweet chocolate
   chips
1 (4 ounce) cake paraffin

Melt peanut butter and margarine in saucepan over low heat. Stir in vanilla and remove from heat. Add powdered sugar, mix well and shape into 1 inch balls. Melt chocolate morsels and paraffin in a saucepan over very low heat. Dip each ball into chocolate, and cool on waxed paper. Reheat chocolate it it thickens. Yield: 9 dozen.

Nancy Lee

Potpourri

Potpourri

APPLE BAKE CASSEROLE

2 (16 ounce) cans sliced apples
1 (8 ounce) package
   Velveeta cheese

1 stick margarine
1 cup sugar
1/2 cup flour

Place apples in medium casserole dish. Melt cheese and margarine together, then add sugar and flour. Pour over apples. Bake at 350° for about 30 minutes.

Gloria Murray

MIXED FRUIT

1 cantaloupe, cubed
1 can peaches, drained and
   cubed
1 can pears, drained and
   cubed

1 pint whole strawberries
2 or 3 bananas, sliced
6 ounces frozen orange
   juice, undiluted
2 or 3 apples, cubed

Mix, chill and serve.

Hazel Shipes

CRANBERRY APPLE BAKE

2 cups fresh cranberries
3 cups chopped apples,
   unpeeled (about 3)
3/4 cup sugar
1 stick margarine, melted

1 cup oatmeal
1/3 cup flour
1/2 cup brown sugar
1/2 cup chopped nuts

Combine cranberries and apples. Place in a greased 2 or 3 quart casserole. Combine margarine, oatmeal, flour, sugar and nuts. Sprinkle over cranberry-apple mixture. Bake at 350° for 45 minutes.

NOTE: This is a marvelous holiday buffet dish. It is good with turkey or chicken.

Kalista Morton

BRANDIED FRUIT

STARTER:

1 cup sugar

1 package dry yeast

1 cup of well drained fruit,
cut up

Mix sugar and yeast with fruit. Stir and let ferment about 2 weeks before feeding or using in a recipe.

FEEDER:

1 cup sugar

1 cup well drained fruit

Every 2 weeks, add a cup of sugar and a cup of fruit. Stir to dissolve sugar. Always use a glass jar to keep fruit in. Cover should not be air tight. Never refrigerate and keep in a warm, not hot place. Always keep 1½ cups of mixture in jar.

Jean Hancock

HOT CURRIED FRUIT

½ cup margarine, melted

¾ cup light brown sugar,
packed

2 tablespoons curry powder

2 tablespoons pineapple
juice

1 (15¼ ounce) can
pineapple chunks

1 (20 ounce) can pear halves

1 (29 ounce) can peach
halves

1 (16 ounce) can apricot
halves

10 maraschino cherries

Drain fruit well. Reserve 2 tablespoons pineapple juice. In a 3 quart baking dish, place peaches, pears, hollow side up. Place apricots on top. Sprinkle pineapple and cherries over fruit. Combine margarine, sugar, curry powder, and pineapple juice. Sprinkle over fruit. Bake at 325° for 1 hour, basting 3 or 4 times.

NOTE: This is great served with ham or pork.

Genie Fesperman

PINEAPPLE SOUFFLÉ

3 eggs
1¾ cups sugar
1 (20 ounce) can crushed
   pineapple, undrained

6 slices white bread (regular
   thickness, trimmed and
   cubed)
1 stick butter or margarine

Spray 2 quart casserole with vegetable spray. Melt butter and toss bread cubes in it. Beat eggs until frothy and dissolve sugar in this. Add pineapple and mix well. Pour mixture over buttered cubes in casserole. Bake at 350° for about an hour. If desired, this can be refrigerated before baking. Serve with baked ham. 6 to 8 servings.

NOTE: 1 teaspoon of almond or vanilla flavoring may be added, if you prefer.

Jewell Kopp

HOT PINEAPPLE

2 (20 ounce) cans pineapple
   tidbits, drained
1 cup grated Cheddar
   cheese
½ cup sugar

3 tablespoons flour
1 stack Ritz crackers,
   crushed
½ stick butter, melted

Pour drained pineapple in baking dish. Mix cheese, sugar, and flour together. Sprinkle over pineapple. Cover casserole with Ritz cracker crumbs. Drizzle melted butter over top of crumbs. Bake at 350° for 20 to 30 minutes.

NOTE: This is delicious served with any meal. Any "leftovers" can be refrigerated, and reheated later.

Ellen Council

STRAWBERRY-FIG PRESERVES

5 cups ripe figs, mashed	**1 (6 ounce) package**
3 cups sugar	**strawberry gelatin**

Combine all ingredients in heavy saucepan. Stir over low heat until sugar starts to dissolve. Bring to rolling boil and cook for seventeen minutes over medium heat.

Dale James

MINT JELLY

1½ cups washed, packed,	**1 (1¾ ounce) box Sure Jell**
fresh mint	**4 cups sugar**
3¼ cups water	**Green food coloring**
1 tablespoon fresh lemon	
juice	

Crush mint. Add water. Bring to a boil. Remove from heat and let stand until cool. Strain and measure 3 cups liquid. Add food coloring and lemon juice. Add Sure Jell. Dissolve and bring to a boil. Add sugar. Cook fast until it comes to a boil that cannot be stirred down. Cook one minute more. Pour into sterilized half pint jars and seal. Very nice with lamb or pork. Yield: 6 half pints.

Anne Fesperman

NO-COOK STRAWBERRY FREEZER JAM

2 cups crushed strawberries   3/4 cup water
  (1 quart ripe fruit)   1 box Sure Jell fruit pectin
4 cups sugar

Thoroughly mix fruit and sugar in large bowl. Mix Sure Jell and water in small saucepan. Boil one minute, stirring constantly. Remove from heat and stir into fruit. Continue stirring three minutes. Ladle quickly into six one-cup jars. Cover at once with tight lids. Let stand overnight. Then, store in freezer. Yield: 6 cups.

Lisa Fesperman

PEPPER JELLY

3/4 cup ground green pepper   1 (16 ounce) bottle fruit
1/4 cup ground hot pepper   pectin or 2 packets pectin
6 cups sugar   Green food coloring,
1 1/2 cups white vinegar   optional

Combine peppers, sugar, and vinegar in saucepan. Bring to a hard boil. Stir constantly one minute. Remove from heat and stir in pectin. Let stand five minutes. Strain. Add food coloring. Skim off foam if any has formed. Pour into hot, sterile jars at once. Yield: 6 half pints.

NOTE: Delicious as appetizer on cream cheese with Triscuits.

Genie Fesperman

"BORN AGAIN" PICKLES

1 (42 ounce) jar kosher dill
   pickles
3 cups sugar
1 teaspoon mustard seed

18 to 20 cloves
1 teaspoon celery seed
1 cup cider vinegar

NOTE: Can use 3 tablespoons pickling spice placed in a cheesecloth bag in place of mustard seed, cloves and celery seed.

Drain and rinse kosher dills. Slice pickles crossways. Mix together sugar, spices and vinegar in medium saucepan. Bring to a boil. Pack pickles into jars. Pour hot mixture over sliced pickles. These pickles must be kept refrigerated. The longer you keep them, the crispier they get.

Ida Rodocker

MICROWAVE BREAD-AND-BUTTER PICKLES

1 large cucumber, sliced in
   1/4 inch thick rounds (2
   cups)
1 medium onion, sliced in
   thin rounds (3/4 cup)
1 cup granulated sugar

1/2 cup white vinegar
1 teaspoon salt
1/2 teaspoon mustard seeds
1/4 teaspoon celery seeds
1/4 teaspoon turmeric

Mix all ingredients in a 2 quart microwave-safe bowl. Microwave on High 7 to 8 minutes, stirring twice, until cucumber is crisp-tender and onion translucent. Ladle into a glass jar (rinsed with hot water to prevent cracking). Cover, cool slightly and refrigerate. Makes about 2 1/2 cups.

Fran Lormand

PICKLED OKRA

1 clove garlic for each jar
1 hot pepper for each jar
Fresh, young okra
1 teaspoon dill seed per jar

1 quart white vinegar
1 cup water
1/4 cup salt
A little sugar, optional

Use young okra and trim stem end just enough so that stem end is open. Clean well and pack in hot pint jars. Place one hot pepper and one clove garlic into each jar. Add one teaspoon dill seed to each jar. Bring to a boil the vinegar, water, and salt. Simmer about five minutes and pour while hot into jars over okra. Seal immediately. (The above pickling solution will fill five to seven pint jars.)

Genie Fesperman

PICKLED OLIVES

2 (5³/4 ounce) cans pitted
    ripe olives, drained
2 teaspoons mixed pickling
    spice
1 large clove garlic,
    chopped or crushed

1 teaspoon crushed dried
    red pepper flakes
1/4 cup vegetable oil (or olive
    oil, or combination)
1/4 cup red wine vinegar

Combine all ingredients in a large jar with a screw top. Shake gently. Refrigerate several days, shaking jar occasionally.

Fran Lormand

PICKLED PINEAPPLE

1 (20 ounce) can and 1 (8
    ounce) can pineapple
    chunks, drain and save
    juice
3/4 cup cup vinegar

1¼ cups sugar
Pinch of salt
1 (3 inch) stick cinnamon
6 to 8 whole cloves
Juice from pineapple

Combine all ingredients except pineapple in large saucepan. Bring to a boil and simmer 10 minutes. Pour over pineapple. Refrigerate when cool. Keeps well and improves after several days in refrigerator.

Fran Lormand

QUICK AS A WINK PICKLED MUSHROOMS

8 ounces fresh mushrooms
1 (8 ounce) bottle light Italian
    dressing

Wash and clean mushrooms. Place in a glass bowl or sealable plastic container. Add Italian dressing. Refrigerate overnight. Stir twice.

Ida Rodocker

ARTICHOKE PICKLE

2 to 3 quarts artichokes
(more or less as supply
indicates)
2 quarts bell peppers (mix
red and green for esthetic
effect)*
1¹/₂ to 2 quarts chopped
cabbage

1¹/₂ quarts celery
5 cups sugar
¹/₂ cup dry mustard
1¹/₂ to 2 cups salt
2 quarts onions
2 quarts vinegar
³/₄ cup plain flour
3 tablespoons turmeric

* Cut canned pepper can be used or peppers might be stripped and frozen in plastic bags, without blanching, during season.

Mix flour, mustard, turmeric and 1 cup of sugar with some of the vinegar and then stir mixture into the rest of the vinegar and other 4 cups of sugar that has been put on to boil. Bring to a boil. and let boil slowly for five minutes or more. Then, put in chopped ingredients, except artichokes, and bring back to a boil. After vegetables have come to a good boil, put in artichokes and bring back to boil. Allow to boil only a few minutes and put in jars and seal. Peppers, cabbage, onions and celery are prepared by dicing, putting in large container and adding enough salt to bring out water. Vegetables should be squeezed well before being added to vinegar mixture. Artichokes are prepared by washing, cutting (after trimming), and storing in refrigerator until 15 or 30 minutes before use, when they are taken out and covered with ice or put in iced water where they remain until they are to be drained and put with other ingredients for final act of preparation of pickle. Prepare artichokes first. Cut vegetables and either store in refrigerator or put directly into baker or whatever is to be used for drawing the water by salting. Allow salt to cover vegetables for approximately 2 hours. Prepare vinegar, etc. and proceed. GOOD LUCK!

NOTE: This was my mother's treasured recipe.

Genie Fesperman

HOLIDAY RELISH

1 pound raw cranberries,
   ground
2 apples, chopped
1 (8 ounce) can crushed
   pineapple

1 cup small pecan pieces
Juice of 2 oranges
2 3/4 cups sugar

Combine all ingredients and refrigerate. Serves 6 to 8.

NOTE: Good with turkey and chicken.

Carol B. Garbutt (Sunnyland Farms)

ELISE'S SPICY PEAR AND PEPPER RELISH

1 gallon peeled, cored, and
   diced, ripe, firm pears
   (about 14 medium sized
   pears)
8 medium sized red bell
   peppers, halved, seeded
   and chopped (use the
   food processor)
6 green bell peppers,
   prepared as above
6 medium onions, peeled
   and chopped in food
   processor

1/2 cup pickling salt
4 cups sugar
2 teaspoons celery seeds
2 teaspoons ground
   cinnamon
2 teaspoons dry mustard
1 teaspoon white pepper
1/2 teaspoon ground mace
1 quart white vinegar

Combine pears, peppers and onions. Sprinkle with salt. Toss lightly and let stand, uncovered, at room temperature for 3 hours. Drain well, rinse and drain again pressing out as much liquid as possible. Mix sugar with celery seeds, cinnamon, mustard, pepper, and mace in a very large heavy enamel or stainless steel pot. Stir in vinegar and bring to a boil. Add pears and boil for 4 minutes. Leave in boiling liquid for 10 minute and dip into jars.

Landy Rimes

SHRIMP RELISH

1¹/2 pounds cleaned and
   cooked shrimp
1 cup sliced Vidalia onion
1 cup snipped parsley
2/3 cup salad oil

1/3 cup vinegar
1 clove garlic, minced
1¹/2 teaspoons salt
Pinch pepper

Combine shrimp, onion, and parsley in large bowl. In a small bowl, combine salad oil, garlic, vinegar, salt, and pepper. Whisk together and pour over shrimp; refrigerate.

Georgianne McGee

CRANBERRY-ORANGE CHUTNEY

1 cup fresh orange sections
1/4 cup orange juice
4 cups cranberries, washed
2 cups sugar
1 cup chopped, unpeeled
   tart apple

1/2 cup raisins
1/4 cup chopped walnuts
1 tablespoon vinegar
1/2 teaspoon ground ginger
1/2 teaspoon ground
   cinnamon

Combine all ingredients in a large saucepan, and bring to a boil. Reduce heat and simmer 5 minutes or until berries begin to burst. Chill until serving time. Yield: 5¹/2 cups.

Jewell Kopp

NOTES

EQUIVALENT CHART

A pinch ....1/8 teaspoon or less	1/4 lb. crumbled Bleu cheese ....1 c.
3 tsp. ....1 tbsp.	1 lemon ....3 tbsp. juice
2 tbsp. ....1/8 c.	1 orange ....1/3 c. juice
4 tbsp. ....1/4 c.	1 lb. unshelled
8 tbsp. ....1/2 c.	walnuts................1-1/2 to 1-3/4 c. shelled
16 tbsp. ....1 c.	2 c. fat...1 lb.
5 tbsp. + 1 tsp. ....1/3 c.	1 lb. butter ....2 c. or 4 sticks
12 tbsp. ....3/4 c.	2 c. granulated sugar..............................1 lb.
4 oz. ....1/2 c.	3-1/2 to 4 c. unsifted powdered sugar ....1 lb.
8 oz. ....1 c.	2-1/4 c. packed brown sugar ....1 lb.
16 oz. ....1 lb.	4 c. sifted flour ....1 lb.
1 oz.............................2 tbsp. fat or liquid	4-1/2 c. cake flour ....1 lb.
2 c. ....1 pt.	3-1/2 c. unsifted whole wheat flour.........1 lb.
2 pt. ....1 qt.	4 oz. (1 to 1-1/4 c.) uncooked
1 qt. ....4 c.	macaroni ....2-1/4 c. cooked
5/8 c. ....1/2 c. + 2 tbsp.	7 oz. spaghetti.............................4 c. cooked
7/8 c. ....3/4 c. + 2 tbsp.	4 oz. (1-1/2 to 2 c.) uncooked
1 jigger ....1-1/2 fl. oz. (3 tbsp.)	noodles ....2 c. cooked
8 to 10 egg whites................................1 c.	28 saltine crackers......................1 c. crumbs
12 to 14 egg yolks................................1 c.	4 slices bread.............................1 c. crumbs
1 c. unwhipped cream ....2 c. whipped	14 square graham crackers........1 c. crumbs
1 lb. shredded American cheese ....4 c.	22 vanilla wafers........................1 c. crumbs

SUBSTITUTIONS FOR A MISSING INGREDIENT

1 square **chocolate** (1 ounce) = 3 or 4 tablespoons cocoa plus 1/2 tablespoon fat.

1 tablespoon **cornstarch** (for thickening) = 2 tablespoons flour.

1 cup sifted **all-purpose flour** = 1 cup plus 2 tablespoons sifted cake flour.

1 cup sifted **cake flour** = 1 cup minus 2 tablespoons sifted all-purpose flour.

1 teaspoon **baking powder** = 1/4 teaspoon baking soda plus 1/2 teaspoon cream of tartar.

1 cup **sour milk** = 1 cup sweet milk into which 1 tablespoon vinegar or lemon juice has been stirred; or 1 cup buttermilk (let stand for 5 minutes).

1 cup **sweet milk** = 1 cup sour milk or buttermilk plus 1/2 teaspoon baking soda.

3/4 cup **cracker crumbs** = 1 cup bread crumbs.

1 cup **cream, sour, heavy** = 1/3 cup butter and 2/3 cup milk in any sour milk recipe.

1 teaspoon **dried herbs** = 1 tablespoon fresh herbs.

1 cup **whole milk** = 1/2 cup evaporated milk and 1/2 cup water or 1 cup reconstituted nonfat dry milk and 1 tablespoon butter.

1 package **active dry yeast** = 1 cake compressed yeast.

1 tablespoon **instant minced onion, rehydrated** = 1 small fresh onion.

1 tablespoon **prepared mustard** = 1 teaspoon dry mustard.

1/8 teaspoon **garlic powder** = 1 small pressed clove of garlic.

3 c. dry **corn flakes** = 1 cup crushed.

3 medium **bananas** = 1 cup mashed.

1 lb. **whole dates** = 1-1/2 cups pitted and cut.

10 **miniature marshmallows** = 1 large marshmallow.

MICROWAVE HINTS

Place an open box of hardened brown sugar in the microwave oven with 1 cup hot water. Microwave at high for 1-1/2 to 2 minutes for 1/2 pound or 2 to 3 minutes for 1 pound.

Soften hard ice cream by microwaving at 30% power. One pint will take 15 to 30 seconds; one quart, 30 to 45 seconds; and one-half gallon 45 seconds to one minute.

One stick of butter or margarine will soften in 1 minute when microwaved at 20% power.

Thaw frozen orange juice right in the container. Remove the top metal lid. Place the opened container in the microwave and heat on high power 30 seconds for 6 ounces and 45 seconds for 12 ounces.

Soften Jello that has set up too hard — perhaps you were to chill it until slightly thickened and forgot it. Heat on a low power setting for a very short time.

Heat hot packs in a microwave oven. A wet finger tip towel will take about 25 seconds. It depends on the temperature of the water used to wet the towel.

To scald milk, cook 1 cup milk for 2 to 2-1/2 minutes, stirring once each minute.

To make dry bread crumbs, cut 6 slices bread into 1/2-inch cubes. Microwave in 3-quart casserole 6 to 7 minutes, or until dry, stirring after 3 minutes. Crush in blender.

Refresh stale potato chips, crackers or other snacks of such type by putting a plateful in the microwave oven for about 30 to 45 seconds. Let stand for 1 minute to crisp. Cereals can also be crisped.

Nuts will be easier to shell if you place 2 cups of nuts in a 1-quart casserole with 1 cup of water. Cook for 4 to 5 minutes and the nutmeats will slip out whole after cracking the shell.

For stamp collectors: place a few drops of water on stamp to be removed from envelope. Heat in the microwave for 20 seconds and the stamp will come right off.

Using a round dish instead of a square one eliminates overcooked corners in baking cakes.

When preparing chicken in a dish, place meaty pieces around the edges and the boney pieces in the center of the dish.

Shaping meatloaf into a ring eliminates undercooked center. A glass set in the center of a dish can serve as the mold.

Treat fresh meat cuts for 15 to 20 seconds on high in the microwave oven. This cuts down meat-spoiling types of bacteria.

A crusty coating of chopped walnuts surrounding many microwave-cooked cakes and quick breads enhances the looks and eating quality. Sprinkle a layer of medium, finely-chopped walnuts evenly onto the bottom and sides of a ring pan or bundt cake pan. Pour in batter and microwave as recipe directs.

Do not salt foods on the surface as it causes dehydration (meats and vegetables) and toughens the food. Salt the meat after you remove it from the oven unless the recipe calls for using salt in the mixture.

HANDY HERB GUIDE

Allspice – (Whole) pickles, meats, boiled fish, gravies. (Ground) Puddings, relishes, fruit preserves, baking

Basil – Potatoes, cheese, eggs, fish, lamb, tomatoes, peas, squash, duck

Bay Leaf – Soups, meat stews, tomato sauces and juice, pickling

Caraway – Breads, sauerkraut, noodles, cheese spreads, fried potatoes, liver, canned asparagus

Chives – Eggs, potatoes, salads, garnish for meats and fish

Curry Powder – Lamb, chicken, rice, eggs, vegetables, curry puffs

Dill – Fish, potatoes, pickles, tomatoes, cream and cottage cheese, fish and vegetable salads

Garlic – Meats, vegetables, salads, egg, cheese

Marjoram – Vegetable soups, eggs, cheese dishes, beef, lamb, stuffings

Mint – Beverages, cakes, pies, ice cream, candies, jellies, potatoes

Oregano – Tomato sauces, pizza, vegetable salads, chili, pork and veal

Parsley – Meat, vegetables, eggs, cheese, soup

Rosemary – Potatoes, cauliflower, fish, duck, veal, poultry stuffing

Sage – Sausages, poultry, hamburgers, pork, stuffings

Tarragon – Vinegar, pickles, chicken, tomatoes, sauces for vegetables and meats, egg and cheese dishes, fish, salads

Thyme – Soups, beef, lamb, veal, pork, oysters, fish, eggs, cheese, stuffings

Turmeric – A flavoring and coloring in prepared mustard and in combination with mustard as a flavoring for meats, dressings, salads

Index

Index

Index

Index

Index

377

Southern Manna

P. O. Box 935
Waycross, GA 31502

Please send me _____ copies of Southern Manna, $16.95 per copy. GA residents add $1.19 sales tax.

Add $2.50 postage and handling for first book, $1.00 postage and handling for each additional book.

Enclosed is my check or money order in the amount of $_____ Visa/Mastercard accepted. Call 1-800-336-8095

Name _____

Address _____

City_____State_____Zip _____

Phone ( ) _____

Southern Manna

P. O. Box 935
Waycross, GA 31502

Please send me _____ copies of Southern Manna, $16.95 per copy. GA residents add $1.19 sales tax.

Add $2.50 postage and handling for first book, $1.00 postage and handling for each additional book.

Enclosed is my check or money order in the amount of $_____ Visa/Mastercard accepted. Call 1-800-336-8095

Name _____

Address _____

City_____State_____Zip _____

Phone ( ) _____

Southern Manna

P. O. Box 935
Waycross, GA 31502

Please send me _____ copies of Southern Manna, $16.95 per copy.
GA residents add $1.19 sales tax.

Add $2.50 postage and handling for first book, $1.00 postage and
handling for each additional book.

Enclosed is my check or money order in the amount of $_____
Visa/Mastercard accepted. Call 1-800-336-8095

Name _____

Address _____

City_____State_____Zip _____

Phone (   ) _____

Southern Manna

P. O. Box 935
Waycross, GA 31502

Please send me _____ copies of Southern Manna, $16.95 per copy.
GA residents add $1.19 sales tax.

Add $2.50 postage and handling for first book, $1.00 postage and
handling for each additional book.

Enclosed is my check or money order in the amount of $_____
Visa/Mastercard accepted. Call 1-800-336-8095

Name _____

Address _____

City_____State_____Zip _____

Phone (   ) _____